I hope I may be pardoned if these discoveries incline me a little to abate of that profound veneration which I am naturally apt to pay to persons of high rank, who ought to be treated with the utmost respect due to their sublime dignity, by us their inferiors.

— Jonathan Swift

CONTENTS

FOREWORD

Thirty-three years ago as an impressionable young neophyte working in the State Department, I developed the impression that the U.S. Senate, and in particular the Senate Foreign Relations Committee, was a thoughtful, mature and generally admirable institution. (I had developed no such impression of the House, where I had worked for a total of six months.) Only later did I learn that I had been misled. It just happened that I had stumbled across a particularly thoughtful, admirable and invariably humorous person named Jeff Bergner, who was the committee staff director at the time. Two years later he had moved on, and I presume the Senate returned to normal.

Here are the things I did not know at the time. I did not know that this streetwise, amiable, scotch-drinking fellow had already been a professor of political philosophy at the University of Pennsylvania, and thus brought to his job an unusually deep knowledge of American political and constitutional history. Jeff knew more about the actions and intentions of the American founders and those who followed them than just about anyone. I did not know that in a short time he had acquired the most in-depth understanding not only of how the Senate and the rest of the government worked but also personal knowledge of the men and women who served in that body, their foibles and fears, their public face and their hidden motives, the "inner" story of the Senate. I did not know, in short, that he was the truest student of politics in the broadest and deepest sense of the word—a Senate staff Socrates.

This book is the fruit of Jeff's long and extraordinary experience dealing with the Congress, from the inside as a trusted and respected staffer, from the outside as a high-ranking State Department official and influential lobbyist, and from above, as it were, as a teacher and political philosopher. This book takes us on a most enjoyable tour of the Congress and its colorful cast of remarkable characters. It is written with humor and the insights that sometimes only humor reveals—like the Senator who accidentally walked into a closet and would not leave it for fear of revealing his mistake, or the Senator who wanted to offer an amendment to a bill but did not know or, apparently, care what the amendment proposed. For the average reader unfamiliar with the ways of Washington, it is a primer on the nuts and bolts of the legislative process, explaining clearly and pithily how ideas become bills and bills become laws, and all the madness that occurs in between. For those impressionable youths making their first foray to the nation's capital in search of a job, it offers invaluable insiders' advice. For savvy, cynical veterans it offers both wisdom and delightful entertainment.

For me it brings back memories of late afternoons, scotch-filled or not, listening to Jeff's tales of the Senate, of men and women both pompous and sincere, heroic and comic, trying to do good, usually for themselves, occasionally for their constituents, and sometimes even for the nation. I will not say it makes one nostalgic for better times. It is not clear to me how much better they were, though Jeff makes the case that things have certainly gotten worse. But reading Jeff's book does remind me why I once had the idea, however briefly, that the Senate was a remarkable place to be.

Robert Kagan
Senior Fellow, the Brookings Institution

PROLOGUE

Out of the Closet

There is a story which circulates in Washington, D. C. which is often thought to be apocryphal, an urban legend as we say today. It is just too perfect to be true. But I saw it with my own eyes.

I was sitting on the dais at a Senate committee hearing. As a staff member, I sat in a small hardback chair behind the plush leather chairs in which Senators hold forth.

I no longer recall the subject of the hearing, but it unfolded like any other; witnesses testified and Senators alternated between political parties to question the witnesses. One Senator—whom the reader will hopefully forgive me for allowing to remain nameless—completed his questions, gathered up his papers, stood and turned to go.

As he did, he hesitated. There were two doors, one leading to an anteroom to depart (without having to encounter the querulous public) and the other to a small supply closet whose dimensions were perhaps four by six feet. I sensed he was uncertain which door led to the anteroom. He hesitated. I watched, drawn more to this unfolding drama than to the monotony of the hearing.

Unfortunately, he chose the wrong door. He opened the door to the supply closet. Apparently unwilling to acknowledge his mistake publicly, he entered the closet and closed the door behind him. Now I was hooked. Fifteen seconds, thirty seconds elapsed. I could not contain myself. I explained to a fellow staff member that there was a United States Senator in the unlit supply closet. "No way," he said. "Yes," I assured him emphatically, "Really." We both watched.

Another fifteen seconds, thirty seconds. My credibility was quickly eroding.

At once, the door opened and the Senator backed out. As he did, he said audibly "Thanks a lot. Good to talk with you." He departed through the door to the anteroom.

What a recovery!

I have often thought of that event and what it signifies about Washington. I suppose it is possible to make too much of small, seemingly meaningless events. But as the poet Goethe observed, wherever there is a joke a problem lies hidden. I have wondered what problem lies hidden in this tale. What does this story tell us about Washington and the men and women who govern us?

****

The framers of our new government thought long and hard about how to construct its institutions. They debated especially carefully how the legislative branch, the Congress, should be organized. They put much weight on the notion that a small number of elected representatives would govern us better than we could govern ourselves directly. After all, *Federalist Paper* # 55 says that if "every Athenian citizen had been a Socrates, every Athenian assembly would still have been a mob." So much for direct democracy.

But good government was not just a matter of electing representatives, dividing the legislature in two, and hemming it in with numerous restrictions. The framers of our government thought the representatives we elected would, on the whole, be better and more qualified than the general mass of citizens. They thought the passions of the public would be "refined and enlarged" by passing through elected representatives who would possess a degree of wisdom beyond that of the citizenry.

These framers favored only a few formal restrictions like age and residency on who could be elected. They argued that in a truly representative democracy "the door ought to be equally open to all." But they were under no illusion that everyone had an equal chance to walk through that door. They believed that citizens would elect those whose "acquired endowments" would make them better guardians of the public good. In short, we would be governed by our betters. Freely chosen, but still our betters.

Is this actually true? If it was ever true, is it still true today? I will have more to say about this in later chapters, but for now perhaps two points of orientation will suffice. First, whoever has witnessed the American government up close will understand immediately and viscerally that our leaders are not possessed of either innate or acquired wisdom or virtue that much surpasses that of the broad American citizenry. Our legislators and executives put on their pants— or today their pantsuits—one leg at a time. They are moved by all of the human passions, vanities, peculiarities, foibles, enthusiasms and limitations that move us all.

That said, I would not doubt for a moment that they are also far more skilled than ordinary citizens—whether by nature or attainment I am not sure—at presenting themselves in a favorable light. As we will have occasion to see in succeeding chapters, our elected leaders have devised nearly endless ways to minimize or deny shortcomings and failures, muddy up and disguise mediocrity, and maximize the credit which they take for anything good which happens.

> **Our elected leaders have devised nearly endless ways to minimize or deny shortcomings and failures, muddy up and disguise mediocrity, and maximize the credit which they take for anything good which happens.**

Our Senator in the closet displays all of this to perfection.

Much that is amusing happens in Washington each and every day. One doesn't have to wait long to find it; one simply has to open one's eyes and take in the show. In a way it could not possibly be otherwise; both virtues and vices tend to be magnified on a large stage and no stage in governance today is larger than Washington, D. C.

The framers of the Constitution believed that Congress would be the strongest branch of government, tending to draw all into its vortex. No prediction of the framers seems more wide of the mark today than this one. Why is today's Congress so infirm? To what can we attribute Congress' current weakness and the many powers that have—often by default—gravitated to the president and the executive branch, to the independent agencies and to the judiciary (which lately seems to have acquired its own legislative power by promulgating national-level policy injunctions)?

This outcome is doubtless partially a result of America's leading role in the world today, a role which inevitably strengthens the president's hand. But much of Congress' infirmity is the result of complex, labyrinthine procedures which Congress has imposed on itself. In short, many of Congress' current limitations are self-created.

We will look at today's members of Congress and their penchant for making simple matters more complicated than they need be. We will recommend ways in which Congress—if it wishes to—can re-gain some of the role which the Constitution's authors envisioned for it.

I. WORKING IN CONGRESS

Coming to Washington

The Princeton Connection

As I sat waiting to be interviewed for a job on Capitol Hill, I reflected on the path that had brought me there. I had driven down from Philadelphia the previous evening, stopping at a friend's house to borrow a suit. As a young academic, I didn't own a suit and I was grateful my friend was not only generous but also roughly my size. I'm not sure I would choose the olive green at this point, but at the time I was happy to have it.

I had never intended to "use" Princeton to provide a Washington connection. In fact, I had not intended to use Princeton for any reason at all. In what I suppose is an admission against interest, it just never occurred to me. Nowadays I counsel young people to follow up with fellow alums when looking for jobs, but my attendance at Princeton never struck me at the time as a source of any such benefit in the so-called real world.

To the contrary, I attended graduate school at Princeton for purely intellectual reasons. I had been strongly attracted to political philosophy and wanted to study it, write about it and perhaps teach it.

Which is what I did. I enjoyed my years at Princeton, but soon enough it came time to look for a job. I landed a teaching position at Penn, which was wonderful in principle but less wonderful in practice. Penn was clearly a demotion from the Eden of Princeton. The Penn faculty all thought they should be teaching at Harvard, Yale or Princeton; Penn students all thought they should have been accepted there as well; the neighborhood was sketchy; and my department was run by an assortment of characters who comprised an academic version of the Star Wars airport bar.

After six years it was clear to me there was no future there; during my first five years all 14 assistant professors who had come up for tenure were denied. I knew I would have to move on and, to be honest, the prospect of leaving was not at all troubling. The pressing question for a young married professor with two children and a dog was where to go next.

Years earlier my then-girl friend (now wife) and I had spent spring semester of our junior year on a Washington Semester program. Spring of 1968 was a tempestuous, edgy but very exciting time in Washington. The Vietnam War was in full swing, sparking protests throughout the country; Martin Luther King and Bobby Kennedy were assassinated; sand bags and armed soldiers surrounded the Capitol and other buildings; and Resurrection City was under construction on the Mall. My program took me to meetings with senior U. S. government officials, members of Congress and Supreme Court justices. We met in a small group with the most reviled man on 1960's American campuses, General Lewis Hershey, who ran the military draft. When spring weather finally arrived and the trees and flowers blossomed, the city exuded a lush beauty that was brand new to our spare Midwestern sensibilities. All of this was, as my southern friends say, tall cotton. We vowed to return one day.

This was what brought me to the interview I awaited. I had applied to several places including the office of Senator Richard Lugar from Indiana. I confess I did not know too much about him at the time, but my Hoosier in-laws thought highly of him so I did what one did in those pre-internet days: I sent him a letter and a resume. I received a friendly response inviting me to meet with his chief of staff, a position which went by the unassuming clerical title of "administrative assistant."

It turned out that Senator Lugar's administrative assistant was a young guy by the name of Mitch Daniels. To this day I've never met anyone whose sheer political instincts and skill are better than his. He began the interview in his usual droll manner, suggesting that he wanted to see if I actually existed. Apparently conservative Senators were not getting many job applications from Ivy League professors in those days. Or now, for that matter.

Long story short, I learned that Mitch had also attended Princeton. He was apparently accustomed to being in an academic and political minority. He offered me a job, which I accepted. This by the way was an unexpected boon for family relations. I had always sensed that my parents-in-law wondered why their daughter had married a lowly professor who moved her halfway across the country. Now, however, their son-in-law worked for their United States Senator.

Altogether inadvertently, my Princeton connection had paid off. It would not be the last time.

****

Today's college students seem savvier than I was. They are no smarter than my generation, and on the whole they are less well-educated, but they are more worldly wise. They are wide open to using their academic degrees to help them in the "real world." Indeed, some students now evaluate the quality of colleges and universities by their record in placing their graduates in the work force.

Since I teach public policy at a university these days, I regard it as part of my job to counsel students and to help them advance their post-college plans. If students express an interest in working in Washington I dig down to see if they have a more specific interest. If they do not, but express only a generalized interest in working in Washington, I invariably recommend Capitol Hill as the place to begin.

It strikes me that working on Capitol Hill offers a great laboratory in which to explore further interests. Entry level work is often broad-gauged and one is not pigeon-holed too quickly into one or another specialty. In the course of their work, Capitol Hill staff meet the full panoply of people who care about Washington: they meet and interact with fellow staffers from their own and other offices; they meet with committee staff; they meet with executive branch employees; they meet with the media; they meet with business and labor leaders; they meet with constituents from their state or district; they meet with lobbyists and cause activists; and they meet with foreign visitors and dignitaries. In short, they meet with a full cross-section of people whose interests bring them to Washington. These days that is pretty much everybody.

It is true that there is very little job security on Capitol Hill. One's Senator or congressman can be defeated in a primary or general election. He or she can decide to take a job in the private sector or to retire. He or she can be killed in a plane crash, like Senator Paul Wellstone form Minnesota. In each of these cases there are no guarantees of future employment. Sometimes staff members are taken on by their member's successor if they are of the same political party, but there is no assurance of that.

Nor is there any guarantee of permanent employment even if the member remains in place. Members might change committee assignments and decide to hire new staff with more experience in their new committee area of jurisdiction. Or, if a member or chief of staff decides for any reason that they do not wish to continue a staff member's service, there is no recourse. One works entirely at the pleasure of one's member of Congress.

This is very different from the civil service which has layers of protection for every employee, no matter how ill-equipped or inept. I had one employee at the State Department who I dearly wished to terminate. Upon reflection, however, I decided that the effort would be simply too great to justify the end, and it might not succeed in any event. All civil service employees have a file full of semi-annual written reviews. Other things equal, these reviews tend to be favorable, highlighting at least one good quality the employee has demonstrated during the previous six months. In the face of this, terminating such a person is an uphill battle, to put it mildly.

I regret to say that in this instance I took the easy way out. When my employee mentioned that she was looking at a new State Department job which paid slightly more, my heart leapt. When asked for a recommendation from the potential new employer, I praised her virtues to the skies. I said that I was not sure how I could do without her. I felt a little bad being so misleading (a polite word for outright lying), but I knew that this practice worked the other way around as well.

There are no required semi-annual reviews, or any other kind of required reviews on Capitol Hill. Jobs on Capitol Hill are patronage jobs, pure and simple. Nor are there many rules and requirements for staff salaries, which are set—up to a cap—at the pleasure of the member of Congress. On the other hand, there are no step-level promotions or step-level salary increases to hold one back either. If one is talented, one can rise quickly through the ranks and ascend to a perch with enormous oversight responsibilities over executive branch programs. In a handful of years, one can benefit from salary increases which come far more quickly than in the executive branch. What Capitol Hill staff lack in job security, they gain in opportunities for advancement.

> **What Capitol Hill staff lack in job security, they gain in opportunities for advancement.**

It is occasionally said that Congress should pay its staff more in order to attract the best possible talent. This is an argument made in many fields of life, and as a general rule I suppose there is some truth to the idea that one gets what one pays for. However, in the case of congressional staff this seems to me neither warranted nor necessary. In the first place, salaries are not low when measured against comparable private sector jobs. Moreover, if one looks at the market, there is an enormous surplus of job seekers versus available positions, which surely suggests that salaries are not too low. Finally, Capitol Hill staff jobs often lead to employment in corporate or government representation jobs (aka lobbying) which are compensated very handsomely.

Working on Capitol Hill is a young person's job. Young people coming out of college these days are usually not married. Given today's demographic trends, they are certainly not parents. Working on Capitol Hill offers an interesting, fast-moving experience, long and irregular hours, and no job security. This is the time in one's life to work in this kind of job.

What are Capitol Hill staffs like and who is hired to work there? Most offices are structured in the same way. There is a chief of staff, usually called the administrative assistant (AA). This AA hires and fires the rest of the staff. Members of Congress offload this responsibility to their AAs for a very good reason: for every constituent a member would please by hiring a friend or relative, 100 others will be disappointed. As a rule, it is the job of the AA to be the bearer of bad news. AAs are often brought to Washington from the campaign staff of winning candidates. Sometimes they are promoted from within. And sometimes they are hired from the staff of departing members.

In addition to an AA, there is a staff of legislative assistants whose work is coordinated by a legislative director. Legislative assistants divide up the policy work of members of Congress, each specializing in an area or two of interest to the member. There is also a press secretary and perhaps an assistant press secretary as well as a scheduler. Schedulers are surprisingly important people, as they are often the gatekeepers for meetings with their boss. When I later became a Washington lobbyist, I made certain to know as many schedulers as possible.

There are also legislative correspondents who help to craft replies to constituents or others who correspond with their office. This work has changed considerably since the development of email, and even more since the events 9/11. Congressional offices used to receive huge amounts of mail each day and responses were sent under the frank, the privilege of sending free mail. Americans' correspondence pretty much occurs through email these days, a fact which has reduced the Post Office's workload as well as its profitability.

Each Capitol Hill office also employs one or two receptionists, who are the front line of defense for a congressional office. They welcome visitors from the state or district and individuals with appointments with their congressman or staff. I always made it a point to hire our receptionists from the state we represented. When a Hoosier walked in and asked our receptionist where he or she was from, I wanted the answer to be Fort Wayne and not Los Angeles.

Committee staff tend to be older, possess more specialized expertise, and are paid better. They come from the executive branch, Washington think tanks, corporations or lobbying firms, academia or the staff of members' personal offices. Staff from members' personal offices who work with committee staff are a rich source of new committee hires; they are known commodities.

How does one secure an entry level job on the Hill? Most applicants today are college graduates. This is not unique to the Hill, reflecting as it does the current American notion that a college degree is a passport to employment. I always found that those applicants who expressed a focused desire to work in our office, and who had done a little research to buttress their arguments, were preferable to applicants who obviously were prepared to work anywhere they might be offered a job. Capitol Hill is about the only place in America where it is not only permissible, but almost a requirement to have definite political views. An applicant who is indifferent about working for Senator Elizabeth Warren or Senator Ted Cruz would be out of place in either office. Recommendations, connections or advanced degrees might help an applicant's case, but are by no means necessary.

One job hunting strategy I regularly recommend to my students is to do an internship. If they cannot find Capitol Hill employment immediately, I recommend interning, even if only several days a week. One can easily fit an internship around part-time work. There is no substitute for being present in a Hill office. If one works diligently at an internship—paid or unpaid—and solves more problems each day than one creates, it is only natural that an intern would be high on the list when a full-time job comes open.

When I had occasion to take European parliamentarians around Capitol Hill, they were uniformly amazed. All that staff. All that help. All that expertise. Back home they were accustomed to a staff of one or two, mainly to answer the phone and coordinate constituent work. This reality reflects the vast difference between European parliamentary systems and our government's unique separation of powers. European parliamentarians are members of a party list. Their votes are determined in advance by their party leaders; they have no need for independent policy analysts. European parliamentarians who are awed by the size of American congressional offices experience viscerally the sheer independence and power of the American Congress. This power, as we will discuss in following chapters, has not been very much in evidence lately; but if and when Congress decides to act in a unified way, there is no stronger force in American politics.

Congressional Staff

The Biggest Mistake of My Young Life?

Newly hired, I prepared for my first day of work on Capitol Hill. I wore a new suit which I had purchased for the occasion. A bus trip to the Pentagon and two Metro rides later, I arrived at the appointed hour of nine a.m., a bit nervous but ready to go. I was prepared to tackle the world of politics.

I was escorted to the Capitol building by a staff member and sworn in to my new job. This was a new experience for me, which I thought then—and still do—added to the dignity of my new assignment.

When we returned to the office, however, I learned the first of many hard truths to come: no one was really expecting me. In the cramped, limited space of a Senator's office suite (more to be said about this in the next chapter) there was simply no place for me to sit. No office, no desk, no chair, nothing at all.

After some brief confusion, I was set up at a typing table pushed against the side of a legislative assistant's desk. For my younger readers—if there are any—perhaps I should explain that a typing table is a small 18" by 24" table on which to rest a typewriter. As to the latter, one can look it up on Google.

I was given a stack of folders and asked to familiarize myself with some of the issues on which the office was engaged. I sat on my swivel secretarial chair in front of my typing table and went to work.

As I did, I noticed that the young legislative assistant whose desk I abutted was crying. This seemed odd to me. Even more oddly, it continued off and on throughout the day. She would answer the phone and speak professionally to a constituent or a fellow staff member, hang up the phone, and begin sobbing again. As the day wore on, she produced an ever larger pyramid of wet Kleenex which grew to a quite impressive height.

I began to reflect. Though I had not cared much for Penn, I began to realize what I had given up: my own office. There I had a desk and comfortable chair; a phone; several small chairs for visitors; an area rug; a plush leather corner chair in which to think big thoughts; a wall of bookshelves; a window; and that most prized possession of all, a door that closed.

It turned out the young legislative assistant had been unceremoniously dumped by her boy friend the evening before I arrived. This was obviously a momentous and painful matter, from which it took many days to recover. I began to wonder what I had done.

When I returned home that evening, my wife asked expectantly how my first day had gone. I am not sure what answer she was expecting, but probably not the one I offered: "I think I may have just made the biggest mistake of my young life."

****

We used to joke as congressional staff that the Labor Department's Office of Occupational Health and Safety Administration (OSHA) would never certify Congress as a safe place to work. This was a joke, of course, because Congress had exempted itself from OSHA regulations (more about this in the following chapter). In Senate offices as many as 30 staffers or more are crowded into four or five medium-sized offices. The situation in House offices is no better.

Congressional Staff: 2015

House

Committee staff   1,164
Personal staff   6,030
Leadership staff   201
Officers of the House 308

Senate

Committee staff   951
Personal staff   3,917
Leadership staff   173
Officers of the Senate 846

Joint committee staff 99

Total 13,689

Source: Brookings, Vital Statistics on Congress

Today there are roughly 10,000 staff members who work directly for House and Senate members. This does not include House and Senate committee staff—which comprise another 2,000— leadership staff, or other congressional employees. Nor does it count the substantial number of staff who work at legislative branch organizations like the Congressional Budget Office (CBO), the Government Accountability Office (GAO) and the Library of Congress. The many thousands of personal and committee staff are crowded into six House and Senate office buildings. This raises the question whether there are too many staff members or too few office buildings.

Why are there so many congressional staff? It was not always so. Prior to the Civil War no members of the House or Senate employed personal staff members to support them. Even as late as the 1940's members of Congress had only a handful of staff. Committee staff members were even scarcer. In the midst of World War II in 1943, for example, total House committee staff numbered 114 and Senate committee staff numbered 190. Given the large number of committees that existed at the time, this meant that each committee functioned with an average of only 3-5 staff members.

Significant changes occurred in the Legislative Reorganization Act of 1946, one of many sweeping post-war changes. This Act—mercifully—reduced Senate committees from 33 to 15 and House committees from 48 to 19. At the same time, however, the Act provided for a large increase in the number of both personal and committee staff. This trend was magnified in the 1960s and early 1970s; between 1960 and 1974 legislative branch staff doubled. Some of this increase occurred because of the creation of the CBO and the now defunct Office of Technology Assessment (OTA) but personal and committee staffs expanded rapidly as well.

Why so many staff? Several arguments have been advanced to explain, if not to justify, the growth of congressional staff. The first is that the issues which the country faces are now more complex than ever. I would note, however, that in the 1940s and early 1950s the Senate Foreign Relations Committee employed only three or four committee staff. Somehow the Committee managed to function throughout World War II, the creation of the United Nations and the creation of NATO. In the immediate post-war period Congress also authorized the creation of the Department of Defense, the Central Intelligence Agency, the National Security Council and the General Agreement on Tariffs and Trade. These were not minor events in the history of the nation.

I will return to this argument in a moment, but here I would also note that the growth of congressional staff occurred at precisely the same time Congress was busy offloading its responsibilities to independent regulatory agencies. Much congressional legislation these days consists in the wholesale authorization of enormous power and responsibility to the alphabet soup of independent agencies it has created: the Securities and Exchange Commission, the Federal Aviation Commission, the Federal Communications Commission, the Food and Drug Administration and scores of additional agencies.

It might be more accurate to say that there are more congressional staff in the modern period because Congress involves itself in many more issues. There is almost no area of life that is untouched by the federal government, including the Congress. For example, once upon a time the federal government played no role at all in providing health care for Americans. Today the federal government is up to its eyebrows trying to direct a health care system that comprises more than 16% of the nation's Gross Domestic Product. It is less clear to me that Congress is required to process more information than ever before than that it is interested in intervening in more of the nation's life than ever before.

The second argument for the growth of congressional staff conforms more closely to the facts. This argument suggests that Congress decided to employ more staff in order to defend itself against the executive branch. The executive branch is of course the far larger enterprise. Throughout the 1950s there were 1.8 million executive branch civilian employees. This number grew to roughly 2.1 million civilian employees during the mid-to-late 1960s and has remained relatively flat ever since. However, this number excludes postal employees who number roughly 508,000, active duty military personnel who number 1.3 million, and more than 800,000 members of the military reserves and National Guard. This totals more than four million executive branch employees. Moreover, this number does not reflect the vastly expanded—and growing—number of government contractors who are paid by the federal government as well.

A loss of confidence in executive branch leadership occurred beginning in the mid-to-late 1960s. A principal cause of this loss of confidence was the Vietnam War. The Korean War was not exactly a triumphal victory in the manner of Germany's and Japan's unconditional surrenders in 1945, but at least it was relatively brief. The Vietnam War played out on American television screens for over a decade. There was a sense—correct, as it turned out—the the executive branch under both Lyndon Johnson and Richard Nixon was neither conducting a successful war policy nor being very honest about it either. Congress put in place the War Powers Resolution in 1973, the same year the U. S. withdrew its forces from Vietnam.

An intense dislike on the part of congressional Democrats for President Nixon played a role as well. In particular, congressional Democrats were deeply opposed to President Nixon's decision to "impound," that is, fail to spend funds which Congress had appropriated. By the early 1970s congressional Democrats were distrustful of virtually every action of the Nixon administration, including the economic forecasts on which it based many of its economic proposals. In response, Congress created the CBO to provide its own, in-house economic projections. And it also created the OTA to provide an in-house ability to understand technological questions which were increasingly coming before it.

I have a certain sympathy, up to a point, with Congress's notion that it needs its own, independent sources of economic information. Whether these sources have always been an actual improvement over executive branch projections is another matter, particularly when it comes to estimating the out-year costs of legislation which has not yet passed. The framers, and especially Alexander Hamilton, were worried that the president should have the means to protect himself against a powerful legislature. Fair enough. But given the enormous growth of executive power since World War II, a bit of protection for Congress against the executive branch is not entirely far-fetched.

I have always been suspicious, however, of the argument that the increasingly complex nature of today's issues requires Congress to employ more staff. I have already noted the critical decisions Congress was able to make with very few staff in the post-World War II years. More generally, the solution to complexity is not to create more complexity. Nor is the solution to specialization to create even more specialization. More congressional staff is not a proper response to complexity; my experience has been that congressional staff help to create that very complexity. Members of Congress provided with a stable of experts will invariably accede to their desire to craft legislation on minute topics which would otherwise never occur to them. Congressional staff are behind the enormous rise in bills which are introduced but which never pass. Congress would be better advised to introduce fewer bills, pass more of them, and spend a bit of time ensuring that those bills they do pass are being properly implemented.

> **More congressional staff is not a proper response to complexity; congressional staff help to create that very complexity.**

I would also have more sympathy for the argument about complexity if Congress were passing ever more complex bills rather than handing over their law-making power to the executive branch and to independent agencies. The Affordable Care Act offers a good example. Here, one might think, Congress has with its 906 page bill done a deep dive into the specifics of health insurance. What one finds, however, is that on many pages of the bill Congress has transferred to "the Secretary" (of Health and Human Services) such decisions as the Secretary thinks fit.

For this reason, it has always seemed to me that Congress would function better with fewer, not more, staff. I would have been willing at any point to agree to mutual staff disarmament with my partisan counterparts. As counter-intuitive as it may seem, a Congress with 20% fewer staff would probably function 20% more effectively.

Congressional Perks and Privileges

Space is at a Premium

Given the enormous number of Congressional staff who must be housed in only a handful of office buildings, space is at a premium. One is always on the lookout for more. Desperate times call for desperate measures, not all of which always make one proud.

My colleague and I were crammed together in a small area in the back of the office furthest from our Senator. One day we noticed that a legislative assistant on the other side of a moveable partition had more than her share of square footage, and certainly more than we did. We hit on a plan. Each night after she left we moved the partition an inch or so in her direction, giving us an inch or so more space. We never moved the partition enough on any given night to be obvious.

This went on for several weeks, and we were more than pleased with ourselves. We added an additional chair to our more spacious quarters. We noticed, much to our amusement, that as time went by the legislative assistant would have to turn her shoulders slightly just to enter her cubicle.

At last she sensed something was amiss. She discovered quickly enough what had been occurring; there was a telltale indentation in the carpet where the partition had originally rested. We were busted and we agreed to return our newly acquired territory. Our days of empire were over.

This young legislative assistant was a perfectly good and decent person who surely did not deserve such grasping imperialists as neighbors. But it was worth a try.

I never did give up trying to obtain more space on Capitol Hill, even after I no longer worked there. While at the State Department I thought it would be useful for the Department to have a Senate outpost to mirror the office we used in one of the House office buildings. Though a far cry from the well-stocked row of offices the military services maintain on each side of Capitol Hill, a modest office would provide a foothold from which to handle visa, passport and other State Department business for members of Congress.

I thought I had staged a coup. I discovered a beautiful Dirksen Senate Office Building corner suite overlooking the Capitol. It was assigned to the Vice President, though neither he nor any of his staff ever used it. They preferred to work out of the ornate vice presidential office just off the Senate floor in the Capitol. Who wouldn't? I snooped around and discovered the Dirksen office hadn't been used in years. I made a stealthy approach to the Senate Rules Committee to have its jurisdiction transferred to the State Department. I was almost home free when one of Vice President Cheney's staff uncovered the plot and threatened to involve the Vice President personally if I did not cease my plotting immediately. Once again my imperial dreams were dashed.

****

It is one thing for Congress to staff up to defend itself and to maintain its independence from the executive branch. It is another thing entirely for Congress to give itself special treatment, especially by exempting itself from the laws it passes. No provision which exempts Congress from its own laws has as its purpose to strengthen Congress as an institution. Such provisions exist solely to provide members of Congress with special privileges.

It is hard to overstate the importance of Congress living by its own laws. In discussing the House of Representatives, Madison said in *Federalist #57* that this would provide a powerful restraint against oppression. He said that Congress:

...can make no law which will not have its full operation on themselves and their friends, as well as the great mass of society. This has always been deemed one of the strongest bonds by which human policy can connect the rulers and the people together. It creates between them that communion of interests and sympathy of sentiments of which few governments have furnished examples; but without which every government degenerates into tyranny.

Does Congress exempt itself from its own laws? Does Congress grant itself special privileges unavailable to the populace as a whole? Much has been written on this topic, some impassioned and wildly mistaken. What is the truth? We might begin by dividing the question, as it is somewhat different for Congress to exempt itself from its own laws than to grant itself special privileges.

One might fairly say that over the years Congress has gradually moved away from straightforward exemptions from the laws it passes. It has done so slowly and grudgingly and often in the wake of scandals that have shamed Congress into changing its ways. When Congress passed the Fair Labor Standards Act of 1938 it exempted itself from all workplace standards including the minimum wage, the 40-hour work week and overtime pay. Congress also exempted itself from numerous provisions of the Civil Rights Act of 1964 including practices relating to racial and sexual discrimination. Congress also exempted itself from federal securities laws against insider trading. These are but three of ten statutes in which Congress exempted itself from the provisions of the law.

Over the past several decades this practice began to change. In 1995 Congress ended its unique exemption from many workplace laws when it passed the Congressional Accountability Act. In 2012 Congress moved to tighten insider trading laws against members of Congress when it passed the Stop Trading on Congressional

Knowledge Act (STOCK Act). Congress also abolished the practice of accepting speaking honoraria, or payments from groups with an interest in legislation before the Congress, a practice which in the private sector would be considered somewhat akin to bribery.

Yet a variety of exemptions remain. One such exemption concerns cases of discrimination and sexual harassment. Cases of this sort are handled in a special way. As part of the 1995 accountability act, staff members who raise allegations of harassment must go through a period of counseling followed by a mandatory mediation process. Only if this process fails to resolve the matter is a complainant able to file a lawsuit. If a complainant accepts cash recompense this is usually paid not from members' personal funds but by a special congressional fund managed by the Orwellian-sounding Office of Compliance. This office has paid out roughly $17 million to settle 246 cases of various types over the past 20 years. The entire process is managed through what is Congress' clearly preferred form of oversight: self-regulation.

In the wake of the sexual harassment scandals that arose in 2017, Congress took an additional step to require mandatory sexual training for members and staff. It did not, however, fundamentally alter the fact that Congress continues to regulate itself in this area.

Members of Congress who are defeated or who choose not to run for re-election often control large campaign contribution war chests. Elsewhere in American society it is not possible for money raised for one stated purpose to be magically transformed into another purpose altogether. Under certain circumstances this is known as fraud. However, members of Congress can retain these campaign funds and direct them to charitable proposes of their own choosing, purposes which often benefit the members themselves.

Members of Congress and their staffs are required to participate in the health insurance exchanges set up under the Affordable Care Act (ACA, also known as Obamacare). However, they are able to do so under a special set of circumstances. The salary for members of

Congress is currently $174,000. Senior staff aides can earn nearly as much as members of Congress. These salaries put members and many congressional staff well beyond the income level to qualify for a subsidy under the ACA. A special arrangement was worked out to allow for a roughly 70% employer subsidy for all members of Congress and staff under the ACA, an arrangement which is not available to other individuals who buy health insurance on the exchanges.

Until passage of the 2017 tax bill, members of Congress also had a unique tax deduction written into law. They were able to take a $3,000 deduction for expenses of living in Washington, on the premise that Washington is more expensive than most congressional districts. This was not a wildly generous perk (it was written into law in the 1950s and was never updated), nor is it different from a number of business expense deductions that other citizens can take. In the case of other citizens, however, these deductions have to be itemized and justified, as opposed to being written into law.

There are a host of other perks which members of Congress enjoy. It would not be fair, however, to regard these as benefits which accrue from exempting themselves from laws which Congress passes. For example, members of Congress participate in what is by all odds a very generous retirement system. Members of Congress vest in their retirement program after five years, which is somewhat rare in the private sector. But private sector enterprises are free to establish a variety of retirement programs, some of which are also very generous. Congress is a happy beneficiary of a generous retirement program, but this program is not carved out as an exemption from law. So too with many other congressional benefits including a death benefit of one year's salary for members' families, the use of congressional gyms, free parking at Washington airports, on-site barbershops (though members must now pay for haircuts), on-site free emergency medical attention, a free travel agency, free pharmacy delivery service and the like. These are all very generous and very convenient, but many private sector businesses offer a menu of similar benefits and these do not benefit Congress as the result of an exemption from public laws.

One of the larger perks for members of Congress is their personal and office expense account, called the Members' Representational Allowance (MRA) on the House side. These funds are provided to all members for the purpose of hiring staff, for office expenses and for mailings. We have also learned recently that these funds can be and have been used to pay private settlements related to allegations of sexual harassment. House members' allowances are currently about $1.2 million annually. For Senators the comparable figure ranges between $3 – $4.8 million, depending on the population of a Senator's state. Strictly speaking, these funds are not to be used for members' personal expenses, but only for official work. However, given the availability of these representational funds, campaign funds which can be used for campaign-related travel and expenses, and government funds for foreign travel, members of Congress have the financial flexibility to cast out a very wide financial net indeed.

Salaries for members of Congress are a very controversial topic, not least for members themselves. For much of our history congressional salaries were established by Congress through direct provisions of law in appropriations bills. In the past several decades, however, members have struggled over this issue. Voting for a salary increase, even if contained within a large appropriation bill to fund the government, is not politically popular. To ease the necessity of affirmative votes in favor of salary increases, Congress adopted a different approach: salary increases permanently linked to increases in the cost of living. The notion behind this stratagem was to obviate the need for politically difficult affirmative congressional votes to increase salaries. However, each year since 2009 Congress has included in its annual appropriation bill a provision to prevent a cost of living increase from taking effect. Thus, Congressional salaries have been frozen since 2009 at $174,000.

Though the automatic cost of living salary increase has not taken effect over the past nine years, the concept was one by which Congress creatively sought to resolve a difficult issue by avoiding difficult votes. There are other examples of this practice, perhaps the best one being the military Base Closing and Realignment (BRAC) process. Voting to close military bases in members' states or districts is not easy. Congress hit upon a plan where it could offload some of the responsibility for base closures onto an outside commission. A base closure process was established whereby a commission of outside experts recommends which bases to close, and unless Congress votes to override the commission the bases are closed. This process is certainly not a profile in congressional courage, but at least it seems to work.

> **Whatever obligations Congress chooses to put on Americans it should put upon itself as well.**

The reader should not take me to be enthusiastic about every requirement Congress regularly puts on the American people. One alternative would be to reduce and/or eliminate many of these congressional requirements altogether. Indeed, compelling Congress to live under its own laws was understood by the framers as a way to moderate Congress' appetite to control the American people. But the main point is that whatever obligations Congress chooses to put on Americans it should put upon itself as well.

Congress has been slow to adopt this principle across the board and there are still areas where it has not fully done so. A government which lives under its own laws is vital to a free nation. Madison asks in *Federalist #57* what is to restrain the legislature from exempting itself from its own laws:

I answer: the genius of the whole system; the nature of just and constitutional laws; and, above all, the vigilant and manly spirit which actuates the people of America – a spirit which nourishes freedom, and which in return is nourished by it. If this spirit shall ever be so far debased as to tolerate a law not obligatory on the legislature, as well as on the people, the people will be prepared to tolerate anything but liberty.

Amen.

Are Members of Congress Different Today?

The Gift that Keeps on Giving

"Does Senator Pell have a problem with you?" the Chairman of the Foreign Relations Committee asked me. "Not to my knowledge, Mr. Chairman," I answered honestly. "Well, he asked to see me about you this afternoon, so I guess we will find out."

I had become staff director of the Foreign Relations Committee about six weeks earlier (more about this later). I chose to err on the side of fresh blood rather than institutional memory and had terminated a number of the then-current staff members. I was determined to create a committee staff which was the best of the best and which would rival any other foreign policy team in Washington. I also shook up a number of protocols which had been standard operating procedure for years. I kept the Chairman carefully informed along the way and he seemed generally to approve of my actions.

Apparently not everyone else did. The minority staff had complained about the new order to Senator Pell, who was then the ranking minority member of the Committee.

The Chairman said he would let me know what occurred at his meeting with Senator Pell. I have to admit I was more than curious. After the meeting ended, it seemed the Chairman was in no hurry to fill me in. When he finally called me into his office, he seemed to be enjoying the situation way too much.

He said that Senator Pell complained that bipartisan collegiality on the Committee staff had eroded. Since he knew Senator Lugar was too much of a gentleman to be responsible for this, he assumed that I must be the problem. He said it seemed that I had "sharp elbows."

Though by that time I had spent nearly six years working with the Committee, Senator Pell asked where I had come from. Senator Lugar said he was at a loss as to what Senator Pell wanted to know, but explained that I had been his administrative assistant before becoming Committee staff director. Prior to that, he said that I had been a professor. Then he said he mentioned, for no particular reason, that I had attended Princeton.

"Princeton?" Senator Pell asked. "Princeton? Really? Well, that changes everything. I attended Princeton. I will have to get to know him better." Chairman Lugar was clearly amused by this, and quite pleased that a random thought had defused a potentially tense situation.

From that day forward Senator Pell was unfailingly gracious and kind to me. When we passed in the hallway he would greet me cordially and often ask if there was any way he might be helpful to me. He was a gentleman of the old school. Once again—through no plan or cleverness on my part—Princeton had come to my rescue.

****

Senator Pell was indeed a gentleman of the "old school." Refined in his manner and not overly excitable, he was one of a dying breed of Senators. This raises the question as to whether today's Congress is the same as ever. Has Congress changed? Are there new and different types of members? Is Congress today better than ever? Worse than ever?

In writing history there are two common approaches, neither of which is honest. Each begins with a preconception and aims to marshal facts and information to prove that preconception. The one approach, common to many biographies (and worse yet, many autobiographies), aims to demonstrate the virtue, the foresight, and the genuine greatness of its subject. The other approach—especially frequent when dealing with politics—is to prove that things today are worse than ever. The country has gone to hell in a hand basket, and if we do not act quickly there is no saving it.

I will aim to avoid these extremes and have a fair look at the question. We might begin by noting that since 1789 there have been a number of constitutional changes that touch on Congress but only one that directly affects its membership. This is the XVII amendment, ratified in 1913, which establishes direct election of Senators. The Constitution had put in place a very different system, whereby Senators were "chosen by the Legislature" of each state. Why the original mode and why the change?

The framers of the Constitution adopted the mode of choosing Senators by state legislatures because they really had no choice. *Federalist #62* presents some advantages for this approach, saying that it will favor a "select appointment" and that it will form a "convenient link" between the state governments and the new federal government. But never is an argument made that this is the only sensible way to choose Senators, much less that it is most consistent with republican government. Indeed, a motion to provide for direct election of Senators was offered during debates in the Constitutional Convention, but was defeated by a vote of 10-1—of the state delegations. The author of *Federalist #62* is quite clear that there is no reason to make a strong theoretical defense of this mode of choosing senators (any more than regarding the compromise between small and large states which created the Senate itself). This mode is the result of a compromise, a practice currently out of favor but which is often necessary in shaping human affairs. *Federalist #62* goes on to add with ironic understatement, that this mode is "probably the most congenial with the public opinion." Elsewhere the *Federalist Papers* hint that as the nation becomes more homogenous and more unified, there will be less reason for the states to be represented qua states in the Senate.

Efforts to establish direct election of Senators began as early as 1826. In the 1890s the House—in a rare act of interference in the other chamber's business—passed several resolutions to adopt an amendment to require direct election of Senators. Unsurprisingly, the Senate was slow to see the wisdom of this. It was not until the states threatened to call another constitutional convention that the Senate agreed to send a constitutional amendment to the states. This by the way also suggests why there will never be another constitutional convention. Congress will be slow to act on any potential amendment which restricts its powers (such as a requirement to balance the federal budget). It will resist until it sees that the only alternative is a second constitutional convention, at which there is likely to be no more restraint than was shown at the first one.

What has been the effect of the constitutional amendment establishing direct election of Senators? The amendment was propelled by self-named progressives who argued that this would make the Senate more democratic. Has it changed the quality or orientation of Senators? Some observers have argued that directly elected Senators are less closely tied to the interests of their states and that direct election has facilitated the erosion of states' rights. This strikes me as a difficult case to prove, as there are numerous other factors which seem to have eroded states' rights including the commercial realities of a large and growing nation.

Senators today still aim to protect what they take to be the interests of their states. The recent debate over eliminating the deduction of state and local taxes from federal taxes is a good example. In any event it is less clear that Senators chosen by their legislatures were doing the bidding of their states than the bidding of party leaders of the majority faction in their state legislatures. One could make an argument that this resulted in more care to protect the rights and privileges of the state legislatures, but I have never seen strong evidence to suggest that this is so. The process of selection by state legislatures also produced some occasionally murky results, especially when the nation was deeply divided in the 1850s.

Though it may be a minority view, it has always struck me that another project of progressives has had a far more noticeable impact on members of Congress than direct election of Senators. That is the adoption of the primary election process for selecting party candidates. This too was a project whose origins are found at the turn of the twentieth century. Minnesota established the first statewide primary election process in 1899. It is a process which is now all but universal in federal elections.

The purpose of this reform was to take the selection of party nominees out of the hands of party leaders and place them in the hands of the people, either the party electorate (in closed primaries) or the electorate generally (in open primaries). This had the effect of creating a two-tier electoral process, in which voters get two bites at the apple. This could reasonably be argued to have democratized American elections, though this would be a tough case to make about the South for most of the first half of the twentieth century. There the primary process was used to disenfranchise black voters through a series of party rules outside the purview of general election laws. This process more or less guaranteed the continuation of the South as a bastion of the Democratic Party until well into the second half of the twentieth century.

What have been the effects of the adoption of the primary process? It would be difficult to make a compelling case that members of Congress elected through the two-tier primary and general election process are less well-qualified than those chosen before the adoption of the primary system. Legislators today are every bit as intelligent as those who came before. For reasons the framers predicted, elites—that is, those who are better connected and richer—still govern America. The extent to which they are not as well-steeped in history, philosophy, theology and the classics owes more to the decline of American education than to the primary election process.

What then has changed? First, campaigns are now far longer. The United States is virtually unique in its two-step election process. Other democracies, which are mainly parliamentary democracies, choose their party candidate slates through internal party processes, and voters have only one bite at the electoral apple. Though there are undoubtedly ways to shorten what seem to be interminable American election campaigns, a good portion of our current and very lengthy campaigns is baked into the primary election process.

Second, it has been argued that the primary process polarizes the nominees of the parties, who tend to play to their ideological or political bases to secure their nominations. This may be partially true, though there are other factors which have contributed to party polarization as well. One is the number of relatively "safe seats" that exist in today's Congress, a matter to which partisan gerrymandering has contributed. I will have more to say about this in following chapters. In all of this it is important to remember one overarching reality: the federal government is involved in far more of the American peoples' lives than ever before. The stakes regarding federal policies are far higher now than ever. Though it is unlikely to happen, one way to dial back partisanship in Washington would be for Washington to reduce its role in peoples' lives.

Third, an argument has been made that primaries are more democratic because they supplement electoral choices in states and districts where one political party is dominant. That is to say, where the outcome of a general election is a foregone conclusion, primary elections will bring at least some level of competition to the process. This has been much studied by academics. At the risk of oversimplifying, academic studies more or less confirm conventional wisdom on this score. Where there is an open seat in a state or district controlled by one political party, the dominant party is more likely to have a competitive primary; wining the primary is tantamount to being elected. However, once an open seat is filled, the incumbent usually runs for re-election without significant party opposition. The minority party in a state or district may attract a number of primary competitors, but none is likely to have a strong chance of winning the general election.

The power of incumbency is vast and the primary election process has done little to change that. This is true at both the state and federal levels. It is not that incumbents cannot be challenged in a primary, or even occasionally defeated, but it is rare. Perhaps there is no better example than Senator Ted Kennedy's challenge to President Carter in the 1980 Democratic primary. Kennedy was an icon of the party, and although he made mistakes in his campaign, he ought to have had a decent chance against a weak president with an extremely anemic economy. Carter, however, easily brushed aside the challenge from Kennedy.

Perhaps it would be appropriate to say a word here about ranked-choice voting. This is an idea which seems to have found favor in some quarters lately. Under this system, voters rank candidates according to their preferences. If no candidate receives 50% of the vote, the bottom candidate is eliminated and his or her votes go to the candidate who was ranked second by these voters. This process continues until one candidate has secured 50% or more of the vote.

For example, suppose a Senate race featured a Republican, a Democrat and a Libertarian candidate. Suppose further that after the first vote count the results are 48% for the Republican, 49% for the Democrat and 3% for the Libertarian. Suppose finally the Libertarian candidate's votes are then allocated according to second choice picks, and the Republican gets all 3%. The Republican accordingly wins the election 51% – 49%.

This system has been said to be more democratic, though it is simply another way to organize counting rules. It is also said to bring about more choice, less polarization, fewer negative ads, less money in politics and perhaps a winning lottery number as well. The system may have some utility for multiple-candidate local races but it is difficult to see why many of the promised results would materialize. It would be especially problematical at the presidential level, given the existence of the electoral college. In all, this strikes me as a solution in search of a problem, and is in no way connected to the actual problems bedeviling Congress today.

Finally, it seems to me that there is one way in which the primary system has indeed brought real changes to Congress. It has radically changed the incentive system for members of Congress. Candidates are no longer fully dependent on state or local political party leaders. They run their own campaigns from beginning to end. They set up their own campaign apparatus; they raise their own money; they establish their own policy positions; and they employ their own press staff to handle media relations.

Moreover, most national, state and local political party leaders remain neutral in primary contests. Where they do not, it is because there is a strong favorite or someone with special connections to the party. And where they do not, it is usually a source of recrimination and hard feelings from other primary candidates.

> **The primary system has brought real changes. It has radically changed the incentive system for members of Congress.**

Candidates who win primary contests then utilize whatever ground operation the party has in place, and to this extent parties are helpful to their nominees. State and local parties maintain databases of voters and volunteers. But in a very real way, political party leaders answer to the candidates rather than the candidates answering to party leaders.

This is very different from the time when party leaders played a large, if not the sole role in choosing the party's nominees.

Newly elected members of Congress come to Washington owing very little to their party's leaders. They are independent of state and local party leadership control. If they choose to run for re-election, as most members do, they can more or less count on the endorsement of their state or district party leaders. There is no need for members of Congress to fall in line with party leaders. They are not dependent on party leaders for their re-nominations.

This has created a far more independent breed of members of Congress. No longer do members have their rough edges rounded off, so to speak. They are their own masters. They are still dependent on congressional leaders for committee assignments—especially in the House of Representatives—but congressional leaders are often cautious about punishing members of their parties. This a far cry from parliamentary democracies, where parties can more or less dictate issue positions to their members.

It is also a far cry from members of Congress having to answer to local party leaders. Members are beholden to their constituents, of course, but this dependence is not mediated through the political parties. There is simply no guarantee that any member of Congress will toe the party line on any given vote, including very important votes. Members are influenced by peer pressure, but certainly not controlled by it.

This independence is especially characteristic of majority party members. There is a tendency of minority party members in Congress to hang together if doing so can thwart the wishes of the majority. But it is not at all unusual for majority party members to desert their partisan colleagues. This was the case, for example, with John McCain's vote on repealing Obamacare.

The primary process has reinforced, if not actually created, the atomism that characterizes today's Congress. Each member is an island unto himself or herself. One could reasonably argue that this is a genuine improvement over the decisions of unelected party bosses in smoke-filled back rooms. What is less debatable is that the primary system has loosened one external rein over members of Congress and made the institution of Congress that much less manageable.

II. HOW OUR LAWS ARE MADE

II HOW PLAYS ARE MADE

The Congressional Record

There Are No Blondes in China

I settle in and await my first assignment on Capitol Hill. It is not
long in coming. My Senator hands me a sheaf of papers which another
Senator had given to him. The papers were a brief account of a
congressional delegation trip to China which had been written by his
colleague's wife. My Senator said that as a favor to his colleague he
had agreed to enter the account in the *Congressional Record*. In a sure
sign that this was a different era, the Senator's colleague was from the
other side of the aisle.

My Senator asks me to write a brief introduction to the travelogue,
and to offer some kind words which his colleague and his colleague's
wife would appreciate.

I go to work and read the account. The year was 1978 and travel to
China was still rare in those days. I was certain I would learn a lot. The
Senator's wife detailed the delegation's arrival in China and her first
impressions. Then, off to a dinner with a high-ranking official in
China's Ministry of Foreign Affairs. Then an obligatory tour of the
Great Wall. And so on for a full week of activities.

As it turned out, the account was written in the style of a suspense
novel. At each event the Senator's wife hinted that there was
something very different about China, but she could not put her finger
on it. What could it be? The omnipresent government? The culture?
The food? Lots to choose from.

The suspense built. As I neared the end of the travelogue, I was
deeply curious. What was so very different about China? What was so

enigmatic that she could not put her finger on it? What fundamental social/political/cultural/philosophical difference kept pressing upon her?

At last the delegation reached the airport for the flight back home. And then it dawned on her. Hit her like a ton of bricks actually. Bowled her right over. She finally identified what had nagged at her during the entire trip. She realized she was the only blonde in China.

What was I to write about this? Could I commend her insight? How to express her shrewd intuition about this too-little appreciated fact of world politics? How to handle this? Something positive of course, but what?

Again the thought flashed through my mind that perhaps working on Capitol Hill had not been my best idea. At last I found my voice— grateful that publicly it would be my Senator's voice—and drafted a friendly, if slightly ironic introduction. It seemed to please everyone. I was beginning to hone the tools of my new profession.

****

What are we to make of this publication, the *Congressional Record?* Before delving into this question, we might first note that the response of my Senator to his colleague's request reflects a long-standing tradition of respect for fellow members of the Senate. This tradition extends to rules that do not permit impugning the motives of Senators on the floor of the Senate chamber. The House is less formal about its traditions, but it too operates on the more or less default position that no one should speak ill of his or her colleagues. There seems to me nothing wrong, and much that is valuable in these rules and traditions.

As to the *Record,* there is more to be said and some of it is mixed. *The Congressional Record* is a digest of all of the activities of the House and Senate. It includes announcements of committee hearings, communications from the other body, communications from the president, and more. It also includes all of the roll call votes and other actions the House and Senate take to adopt legislation. It includes a word-for-word account of every word uttered on the floor of either body. And finally, it includes remarks by Senators and Congressmen which are not delivered on the floor of their respective chambers, as well as any other material a member might wish to enter, including items that have absolutely no bearing on what transpires in Congress. This latter is well illustrated by the *Record* insert I drafted about the delegation trip to China.

There is one minor caveat to the claim that the *Record* contains words actually spoken on the House and Senate floors. After a member speaks, his or her staff is given a brief period of time to revise these remarks. This is not usually necessary when a member reads from a prepared text. But when a member speaks extemporaneously, it is often the case that these words—however moving when delivered orally—do not read well as a written text. This is to put it mildly. In order to prevent members from sounding illiterate, staff can clean up members' remarks in a way that makes them appear well-thought through and coherent. These revisions are not supposed to alter anything of substance—only of style—but of course there is no judge who sits over staff aides who edit their members' remarks.

It would be easy enough to make fun of the busywork and the cost to taxpayers of all that is included in the *Record*, especially as a good deal of it is errant nonsense. Without a doubt, the material in the *Record* which appears as "Extensions of Remarks" could be dropped entirely with no loss to the well-being of the republic. This material consists partly of words of a member of Congress that appear to have been, but have not actually been, spoken on the floor. These remarks are set off from what has actually been spoken on the floor, but in such a way that an uninformed reader would not know the difference. These remarks can be—and are—sent to constituents without a truth-in-labeling qualification.

The other matter included is of the sort I have already illustrated. These remarks are often puff pieces, inserted in order to flatter constituents or to assist in enhancing the standing of a member. Or a member's spouse, as we have seen. There is really no good reason—other than to offer one more way for legislators to make themselves look important and responsive—to retain this material in any record of the activities of the two chamber of Congress. Here is a place for simpler, less misleading, and slightly less expensive government.

As to the spoken record itself, there are good reasons to retain it. One reason is for what is called the "legislative history" of laws. It is hard to believe, I know, but not every bill which is signed into law is written in such a way that its provisions are crystal clear. Occasionally the meaning of laws can be clarified by the context in which they were adopted— by speeches made during the introduction of legislation and by the debate which takes place during its consideration on the House and/ or Senate floors. This can be useful to members of Congress, to the executive branch which must implement the law, and to the courts which may have to adjudicate the constitutionality of legislation.

There is a lively debate about to what extent, and indeed even as to whether, courts should look at the legislative history behind laws. After all, legislators may be mistaken about what their laws actually say; they may intend one result, and perhaps the laws which they actually write express a different one altogether. In that case, shouldn't the executive branch and the courts rely on the plain English words of a law as opposed to going behind those words and imputing certain meanings to them?

Seeking an intent which is not clearly expressed in the plain words of laws is a slippery slope and can quickly go far afield. It should be entirely discouraged. But a prudent look at the legislative history of a bill can help to interpret a law's words. After all, "originalists" who believe that the Constitution does not and should not change, aim to determine the meaning of the framers' words. This they do by looking at the framers' context—Madison's Notes on the Constitutional Convention, for example, or the accepted meaning of words as they were used in 1787. Why should it be permissible to look at context when seeking the meaning of the Constitution but impermissible to apply that same approach to the meaning of legislation? A limited, prudent use of legislative history in genuinely unclear cases—as opposed to abstract speculation to achieve an end one is seeking in advance—seems a reasonable tool for branches of government which must decipher the laws Congress passes.

The value of a record of what occurs on the House and Senate floors goes much deeper. The framers included in the Constitution the requirement that each house "shall keep a Journal of its Proceedings, and from time to time shall publish the Same, excepting such Parts as may in their Judgment require Secrecy." This was not intended to be a frivolous requirement. It was grouped with a number of constitutional provisions which all aim at the same goal: to ensure transparency about what occurs in Congress. Other related provisions include the requirement for Congress to meet at least once each year; to establish a fixed date when Congress shall convene; to allow neither house to adjourn for more than three days without the consent of the other; and to prohibit either house from moving to a different location than where Congress is sitting.

> The constitutional requirement that each house "shall keep a Journal of its Proceedings" was not a frivolous requirement. It was grouped with a number of constitutional provisions which all aim at the same goal: to ensure transparency about what about what occurs in Congress.

Each of these provisions aims to make Congress at least transparent, if not accountable. As James Wilson of Pennsylvania said during the Constitutional Convention, "The people have a right to know what their Agents are doing or have done;" it should not be an option for the legislature to "conceal their proceedings." Moreover, as Wilson pointed out, a provision requiring Congress to keep a record of its actions was already enshrined in the Articles of Confederation.

Both houses of Congress have kept records of their actions since 1789. These are contained in the Journals of the House of Representatives and the Senate, respectively. These journals are different from the *Congressional Record*. These journals do not contain a verbatim record of what occurs on the House and Senate floors. They contain motions, votes, and bills and amendments which have been adopted. These journals were supplemented by reporters who sat in on congressional debates and offered their versions of what was said. Sometimes these supplements were accurate and sometimes members accused the press of distorting or altogether falsifying their statements. In 1873 the Congress decided to create an official record of what was said on the floors of the two chambers, bringing into existence the *Congressional Record*. This was in part a result of improved technology which made possible accurate rendering of the words of members. That technology is of course much improved today, and it seems to me that the framers of the Constitution would in no way object to a full and accurate record of congressional debates.

There is every good reason to maintain a clear record of congressional debates, now increasingly presented in searchable formats. Who could reasonably object to the transparency this delivers to citizens about what their representatives are doing? As to retaining the extraneous material inserted by members of Congress to suggest they are engaged in debates in which they have not been present, or to commend their constituents for achievements great and small, or to commend themselves and their colleagues—this surely is altogether dispensable.

The Qualities of Members of Congress

"I Want to Offer an Amendment"

"Please come see me if I can be helpful in any way," I said. After becoming staff director of the Senate Foreign Relations Committee I met with each Senator on the majority side of the Committee. Although my entire staff and I technically were employed by the Chairman, I wanted to be sure that members knew we worked for all members of the Committee. As a former administrative assistant I understood that members had certain political needs and I wanted there to be no gap between members and their personal staffs and those of us on the Committee staff. We would have an open door.

It was not long before one Senator took me up on my offer. He asked if the Foreign Relations Committee would be "marking up" (debating and adopting legislation to send to the Senate floor) legislation the following week. Yes, I said, the Committee would be considering foreign assistance legislation the following Tuesday, perhaps extending into Wednesday as well.

The Senator said that he wanted to offer an amendment to the bill. I thanked him for letting me know and asked him what his amendment aimed to do.

He repeated that he wanted to offer an amendment. I thanked him again and asked about the general topic of his amendment. Our legislative counsel was present at the meeting and I volunteered his services. If we could know the intent of the amendment perhaps we could help draft appropriate legislative language and also draft some "talking points" to help him explain the amendment to other Committee members.

He thanked me and repeated yet again that he wanted to offer an amendment. I guess I was rather slow on the uptake, but it gradually dawned on me: the Senator wanted to offer an amendment, any amendment, and he didn't much care what it was. He wanted to be seen as an engaged, effective legislator, no doubt to offer his constituents back home a glowing report of the good work he was doing on their behalf. He wanted us to provide an amendment for him to offer.

Here I did something that I did only rarely, and probably should not have done in this instance. Several of us had been meeting regularly with the Chairman during the previous weeks to develop the "chairman's mark." This is the base bill which is introduced by the chairman and which becomes the vehicle for considering amendments which might be offered in Committee. Many of the staff suggestions were accepted by the Chairman and we had crafted a solid, comprehensive bill. There were a few provisions we proposed to him, however, including one which I thought quite good, on which the Chairman demurred. "Let's leave that provision aside for now," he said.

The reader can no doubt see where this story is headed. I had ready at hand what I thought was an excellent provision, and I succumbed to temptation. I told our visiting Senator we had an excellent little amendment that we would send his staff, along with a brief explanation and a page of talking points. He seemed quite pleased.

The following Tuesday the Committee convened, the chairman introduced his bill, and Senators offered a variety of amendments to the chairman's mark. Our Senator was recognized; he carefully explained his amendment's merits and offered it for adoption.

At this point the chairman turned to me. Uh oh, I thought, I've been found out. But the Chairman asked what I thought of the amendment. I said I thought it was quite good and reinforced what we were trying to accomplish in the larger bill. He spun around and announced that the chair was prepared to accept the amendment, thus including it in the bill. There was no further discussion.

When the bill came to the Senate floor the amendment remained untouched. And when House and Senate conferees met to reconcile their bills (about which more later) I kept an eye out to protect my offspring. The amendment remained in the House-Senate conference report and the bill, including our little amendment, was signed into law by the president. All this was duly noted by our Senator, who took massive credit for his handiwork as a grizzled, veteran legislator.

****

Our Senator here is admittedly a bit of an outlier in the scheme of things, but he does beg the question: who are these people who represent us in Washington? The framers believed that they would be better able than the average citizen to "discern the true interest of their country." This was one of several reasons to prefer a republic over a direct democracy. Is this true today?

We might begin by noting that the formal educational level of members of Congress does surpass that of the general public. Ninety-four percent of House members have a college B.A. or equivalent, as do all one hundred Senators. Roughly 33% of the American people over age 25 have a comparable degree. These percentages have grown steadily over the years. In 1940, for example, only 4.6% of Americans over age 25 had college degrees. Members of Congress have always enjoyed, as they do today, more formal education than average citizens.

One might say, somewhat tongue in cheek, that the less educated are not adequately represented in the Congress. The framers of course would have seen this under-representation as an advantage, not a shortcoming. They were very little disposed to the concerns today which pass under the rubric of "identity politics." In *Federalist #35*,

Hamilton says "The idea of an actual representation of all classes of the people by persons of each class is altogether visionary." Unless specifically mandated by the Constitution, people left to their own preferences will never choose representatives of their own class in a proportional way.

It is also true that members of Congress are on the whole wealthier than average Americans. Although financial disclosure information required of members of Congress is deliberately vague, there is no doubt that members are wealthier than their constituents. In today's Congress, for example, 268 or slightly more than half of all members are millionaires. The comparable figure for the American people generally is less than nine percent.

In terms of life experience, members of Congress come mainly from the professions of law and politics. This is currently the case for 271 members of the House and 60 Senators. Whether this demonstrates they possess more discernment about the public good is not so clear; but they do possess greater rhetorical and persuasive skills. All other classes of people, including medicine, engineering, education, theology, commerce, arts and crafts and blue collar workers are vastly underrepresented in the makeup of the Congress. Fewer members of Congress today have served in the military than was the case in any of the post-World War II decades; today 101 members of the House and Senate have served in the military.

More members of Congress today come directly from the field of politics than ever before. Most have ascended to Congress from state and local offices. The share of Senators which comes from the House has remained roughly constant over time, though today it is at an all-time high of 55 members. Moreover, both Senators and members of the House have accumulated greater experience by serving longer within their respective bodies. The average tenure of members of Congress remained steady throughout most of the nineteenth century, increased slightly during the first half of the twentieth century and grew rapidly during the second half of the twentieth century. Over the past century the average tenure in the House has increased from four to ten years and in the Senate from five to thirteen years in the House.

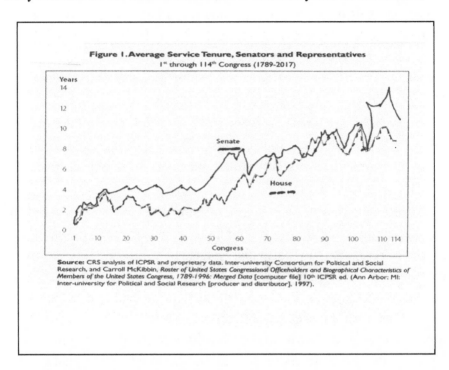

Figure 1. Average Service Tenure, Senators and Representatives
1st through 114th Congress (1789-2017)

Source: CRS analysis of ICPSR and proprietary data. Inter-university Consortium for Political and Social Research, and Carroll McKibbin, *Roster of United States Congressional Officeholders and Biographical Characteristics of Members of the United States Congress, 1789-1996: Merged Data* [computer file] 10th ICPSR ed. (Ann Arbor, MI: Inter-university for Political and Social Research [producer and distributor]. 1997).

Several factors account for longer tenure in today's Congress. One is that resignations from Congress were far more prevalent up until the second half of the twentieth century. Why this should be so is subject to speculation. Travel back and forth between one's state or district and Washington is certainly easier today. The benefits that accompany serving in Congress are greater today as well. And finally, it is worth noting that Congress today deals with a far larger share of issues that affect everyday Americans than ever before. As has been mentioned, while today's Congress is deeply engaged in health care policy, for most of the history of the republic health care was not addressed in any manner by Washington.

Second, the share of members of Congress who run for re-election and are defeated has declined. This share remained fairly constant throughout much of American history but declined significantly during the second half of the twentieth century. Perhaps this is partly a result of more clever strategies to create "safe" seats by gerrymandering congressional borders. This cannot be the entire answer, however, as the share of Senators defeated in re-election bids has also declined and state boundaries have remained unchanged over time.

Today's longer tenure is also partially a result of the fact that like all Americans, members of Congress are living longer. Most of the longest serving Senators and House members have served in recent decades or are serving now.

Perhaps a remark about congressional term limits would be appropriate here. At a time when tenure in the House and Senate was shorter, there was no particular interest in limiting the terms of members. In the contemporary period interest in this idea has grown apace with the lengthening tenure of members. There is nothing wrong on its face with the idea of congressional term limits. There was no limit on presidential terms in the Constitution, but this was changed in 1951 by the XXII amendment. This amendment was arguably very modest in its impact, as only one president had ever served more than two terms in the first place, and I know of no persuasive argument that the quality of presidential leadership has been better or worse since the adoption of this amendment.

Would term limits improve the Congress? The argument usually revolves around balancing experience against permanent entrench-ment. One could multiply arguments on both sides of this question, but it is unclear to me that term limits would make much more difference to the operation of the Congress than it has to the operation of the presidency. I have yet to see a persuasive argument for limiting voters' choices (by excluding members who had reached the end of their term limits). If one sent term-limited members to Congress as it is structured today we would very likely see the same results we see today.

Is there a difference between Senators and members of the House? The framers of the Constitution supposed there would be, suggesting that the office of Senator requires a "greater extent of information and stability of character." Indeed, this is one reason the framers invested the power to consent to treaties (or not) in the Senate. On the whole, the education level of Senators is slightly higher than House members; Senators on the whole are slightly wealthier than House members; Senators serve slightly longer tenures than House members, and Senators are slightly older than House members (the average age today being 61, compared with 57 for House members). In this sense one could argue that the framers guessed rightly about Senators, even though their mode of election has changed.

As has been said, the House has always been a major source of newly elected Senators. Since 1789 12,179 individuals have served in Congress, 1,963 of which have served in the Senate. Of these Senators 669, or roughly one-third, have also served in the House. Once it was not unusual for a Senator to move to the House. This does not happen today; the last Senator to go on to serve in the House was Claude Pepper of Florida, who died in 1989.

What can we conclude from all this? It is the case that members of Congress are somewhat better educated, somewhat more successful financially, somewhat better established in their communities and somewhat more proficient with words than the average American. These formal characteristics serve to distinguish members of Congress from voters, though it is easy to overstate their importance. Having a slightly higher IQ does not in and of itself make members of Congress good legislators. After all, as Madison says in *Federalist #57*, it is not only the wisdom to discern the common good that is required, it is also "the virtue to pursue" the common good. And as he says in *Federalist #10,* intelligence can be used not only for good but also for corrupt

purposes. Abstract intelligence can be used for good or ill, and if used
for ill, its "effect may be inverted." And on this score it would be a
very difficult case to make indeed, to argue that members of Congress
display more virtue than the average American citizen.

> **It is impossible to observe any superior level of virtue in American legislators. Their moral standing is no higher than average Americans, and it is often the case that their slightly higher abstract intelligence magnifies the moral shortcomings of American society.**

To the contrary, it seems that members of Congress more or less
reflect the prevailing ethical norms of American society. This should
not be too surprising, as they are elected by this society. It is
impossible to observe any superior level of virtue in American
legislators. Their moral standing is no higher, and it is often the case
that their slightly higher abstract intelligence more than reflects the
moral shortcomings of American society.

Many of the traditional guard rails of virtue seem to have given
way. A short-term, entitlement mentality has often been said to
characterize Americans today. The same is true, and even magnified
among legislators. This can be observed across the board, but perhaps
there is no better example than federal deficit spending. For most of
American history the United States government did not spend more
money than it raised. The only exceptions were during times like the
Civil War or World War II, when the country faced existential threats.
George Washington's counsel in his Farewell Address to avoid the
accumulation of debt so as not to "ungenerously throw upon posterity
the burden which we ourselves ought to bear," was largely observed
until the last four or five decades. In that relatively brief time we have
gone from the expectation of balanced budgets, to a Keynesian notion

of cyclical deficits and surpluses, to today's notion that budgets never need to be balanced. And yet in poll after poll American citizens suggest that balancing the budget is very important.

Since there are no short-term ill effects of massive and regular deficit spending, there is every reason to assume that Congress will continue down this course regardless of what the American people prefer—until the consequences take effect.

Select Federal Deficits and Federal Debt		
Year	Surplus or deficit (in millions)	Federal Debt (in millions)
1789-1849	70	N/A
1850-1900	-991	"
1910	-18	"
1920	291	"
1930	738	"
1940	-2,920	50,696
1950	-3,119	256,853
1960	301	290,525
1970	2,842	380,921
1980	-73,830	909,041
1990	-221,036	3,206,290
2000	236,241	5,628,700
2005	-318,346	7,905,300
2010	-1,294,373	13,528,807
2015	-438,496	18,120,106
2020 (est)	-487,953	22,503,321

The problem today is not that we are sending to Congress people with inadequate intellectual abilities, but that we are sending to Congress people who simply reflect—and do not challenge—the short-term entitlement spirit of today's America. Today's legislators are no worse, but neither are they any more virtuous than the Americans who send them to Washington. The most one could reasonably hope is that once these legislators arrive, they will not be made worse than they were when they came. Unfortunately this is not the case.

Our institutions, and especially the Senate, magnify the ill effects of short-term entitlement thinking. Congress is a more partisan body than are the American people. It has structured a winner-take-all system in which the winning party's congressional leaders, committee chairs and staff all are deeply advantaged, no matter the closeness of electoral outcomes. Its party leaders are often more partisan than their membership, being chosen by the majority of members who come from relatively safe seats on the political left or right. Under the seniority system its chairmen come from the safest of all seats. Its members have created processes which if not consciously designed to do so, have the effect of mystifying nearly everything about their actions. And they have created myriad rules and procedures which entitle members of Congress, and especially Senators, to delay even the most obviously needed policies.

In *Federalist #62* Madison offers a preview of what might come to pass if virtue does not accompany intelligence in policy-making: "It will be of little avail to the people that the laws are made by men of their own choice if the laws be so voluminous that they cannot be read, or so incoherent that they cannot be understood." If we cannot elect legislators of superior virtue—and there is no reason to think we can— the most that can be hoped is that Congress might reform itself.

Here it might only be noted that many creative and well-intentioned congressional reform proposals really have nothing to do with the actual problems of congressional organization. They address the manner in which members are elected or how long they can stay; but they do not address the underlying problem, which is the creation—by the Congress— of a set of rules and procedures designed more for the convenience of members of Congress than to advance the public good.

Congressional Legislation

Naming a Post Office

I was sitting at my desk minding my own business. Senator Lugar had gone off to dinner and I had sent the rest of the staff home for what promised to be a long evening on the Senate floor. I was fielding phone calls and monitoring the debate on the Senate floor. In those days Senate debates were not televised and one listened through a little squawk box. Over time one learned to feel the rhythm of Senate proceedings and to recognize the voices of most of the Senators.

My phone rang. It was the chief of staff to the Postmaster General, asking to speak to the Senator about an urgent matter. I explained that he was unavailable. "Can I help?" He asked if I could locate the Senator, because this was quite an important matter. Having no clue what could possibly be so urgent about a postal matter I said, no, at this moment I was the best he could do.

He relented. "Well, then, maybe you can help." He explained that Senator Exon from Nebraska would soon come to the Senate floor and ask for unanimous consent to pass a bill to name a post office. Naming a post office? I still did not sense the urgency.

He went on to explain that Senator Exon proposed to name the post office after a union organizer. I was given to understand that this union organizer was also a flouter of post office rules and regulations across the board, including wearing his hair shoulder length. Apparently one day his hair got caught in the rollers of a massive sorting machine and he was killed. The Post Office was dead set against honoring this kind of behavior by naming a post office after him.

Could I possibly call over to the Senate floor on behalf of my Senator, and object to a unanimous consent agreement to allow Senator Exon to proceed? This would give the Post Office time to inform all Senators of their position and hopefully deter the amendment from being offered. I considered this. As a rule, I did not like making decisions in my Senator's name without his knowledge. But perhaps this case was an exception. Senator Lugar was no particular fan of government unions, which is why I suppose the Post Office reached out to him in the first place. I supposed he would oppose the Exon bill and here, it seemed, was one of those rare instances when the Senate was in danger of acting too quickly rather than too slowly.

So I agreed. I called the cloakroom and indicated my Senator's objection to unanimous consent which would allow Senator Exon to proceed. I hoped very much that Senator Lugar would return from dinner before I heard anything further about this.

No such luck. Several minutes later I recognized Senator Exon's voice on the squawk box. To put it mildly, he was irate. He said that a Senator had put a "hold" on his legislation, which was outrageous. After all, he only wanted to name a post office. More ominously, he announced that he knew who was behind this perfidy. This, I thought, was disastrous—these holds are supposed to be secret. How had he discovered who was preventing him from naming his post office? How had I been found out? Worse yet, my Senator would be blamed for this, all the while having known nothing about it.

"I know who is behind this," thundered Senator Exon. I braced myself for the worst. "It is General Motors," he announced accusingly. General Motors, I thought? Those bastards. Where in the world had Senator Exon come up with that? Apparently Senator Exon was in a running feud with General Motors on an altogether different issue, and he simply assumed they were behind this effort to frustrate him.

That, I thought, was a close one. And happily, when Senator Lugar returned from dinner and heard the story, he was mildly amused by the entire event.

****

A bill to name a post office is not all that unusual. In fact, there is almost no subject under the sun that is too unusual to be the subject of a House or Senate bill. In addition to serious legislation that runs across all areas of foreign and domestic policy, bills are introduced to commend individuals or organizations, to name days or months in honor of worthy causes, or to express the "sense" of the House or the Senate about almost any topic imaginable. There is one piece of good news here. Congress has largely ceased to pass what are known as "private bills," which are bills to address a problem or an injustice faced by an individual U. S. citizen. These were very popular from the middle of the nineteenth century through the middle of the twentieth century. They have steadily declined ever since and Congress now passes only a handful of these bills in each congressional session.

But plenty of bills are still introduced in each session of Congress. The number of bills introduced in the House of Representatives peaked in the 1960s and early 1970s; 18,000-20,000 bills were introduced during each two year Congress. This averages to more than 40 bills for each member of the House. As one might expect from a smaller chamber, fewer bills are introduced in the Senate. The number of bills introduced in the Senate each Congress has remained relatively flat at 3,000-4,000. An average Senator introduces about 35 bills during each two year Congress.

The percentage of bills which actually pass each house is far smaller. Roughly 20% of legislation introduced in the late 1940s and early 1950s passed the House. The trend has been steadily downward since then, to an average of roughly 10% over the last decade. The trend in the Senate has been much the same. More than 50% of all bills introduced in the late 1940s and 1950s passed the Senate. Today that number is also in the range of 10%.

To become a law, however, a bill must pass both chambers. Historically only about 4-5% of all bills introduced in either house have been passed by both houses and enacted into law. Today that number is slightly lower; 296 of 10,637 total bills, or 3%, were enacted in the 113th Congress and 329 of 12,663, or 3%, were enacted in the 114th Congress. At the same time, bills enacted into law have grown in length. From the late 1940s through the 1960s bills enacted into law averaged two to three pages in length. Today that number is 15-16 pages. One cannot tell too much from this statistic alone, however, since many bills enacted into law are very brief. Many of these are the honorific bills referred to above. For substantive legislation the trend has clearly been toward enacting fewer and fewer bills which are longer and longer in length. The Affordable Care Act, for example, ran to 906 pages.

Why are fewer bills becoming law these days? Much of the reason can be traced to a decline in bipartisanship. As measured by the Lugar Center, bipartisanship has been in steep decline since 1999. The absence of bipartisanship compels both chambers, but especially the Senate, to roll more and more provisions into comprehensive bills. It is very difficult to get a vote in the Senate on any but the most non-controversial free-standing legislation, because such legislation is likely to be filibustered by one party or the other. That puts a premium on including what would otherwise be free-standing bills into larger, often "must-pass" legislation.

It is well-known that in polls today the Congress fares very poorly. Job approval ratings for Congress are at historic lows, hovering today around 13%. Throughout much of the post-World War II period, job approval ratings for Congress were in the range of 40-50%. Congress' approval rating briefly spiked to 84% in the immediate aftermath of 9/11, at a time when both members of Congress and the American people stood together and displayed a brief, but very deep, sense of unity. After 9/11 congressional approval ratings rapidly returned to the 40% range and then dipped to the 30% range and finally to 20%. There was a brief spike to the mid-30% range after Barack Obama's election in 2009, but the trend has been downward into the teens ever since.

What are we to make of these abysmal poll numbers? First, there appears to be no significant difference in polls regarding the House versus the Senate. The American people do not disaggregate their unhappiness with Congress to blame one house more than the other. It would be fair to say that the House is getting a bit of a bum rap here. Its rules make it easier to pass legislation and it tends to send far more bills to the Senate than the Senate sends to the House. There are at the moment of this writing more than 250 House-passed bills waiting for Senate action. Bills which are not enacted into law are more often the result of Senate inaction than House inaction. And for this reason bills that are enacted into law tend to be based more closely on the positions of the Senate than the House. There are of course important exceptions to this general pattern. For example, the 2013 "gang of eight" immigration reform bill passed the Senate but was never taken up by the House. But the overall pattern is clear.

This pattern would be no surprise to the authors of the Constitution, who saw the Senate as an institution designed to check the work of the House. And no reasonable person would make the argument that it is *ipso facto* better to enact more bills rather than fewer bills into law. It depends of course on what the bills do. But it is evident that with regard to deficit financing, entitlement spending, immigration policy, trade policy and war powers the Congress has been largely missing in action.

We have already considered the impact of direct election of Senators. As mentioned in a previous chapter, it has changed the character of Senators a bit. Having come to the Senate on their own, as it were, they are not as much consensus-oriented as Senators who were chosen by state legislators, and who thus tended to have had their edges rounded off a bit. One would not want to make too much of this, however, when one looks at some of the individuals chosen by state legislatures in an earlier age, not to mention the knockdown, drag-out battles to choose them in the first place.

It is also interesting to note a seeming paradox about congressional approval ratings. While Congress as a whole is rated very poorly, this does not extend to voters' view of their own House or Senate members. Voters' own representatives or Senators poll far better, hardly ever falling below 40% and more often polling above 50%. There are rare exceptions of course (such as Arizona Senator Jeff Flake who was polling at 18% before he decided not to seek re-election), but most incumbents poll well. This should not be too surprising, since with rare exceptions each member of the House and Senate was elected with more than 50% of the vote. And roughly 96% of incumbent members of Congress who choose to run again are regularly re-elected.

Clearly the institution of Congress is not prospering. What after all is an institution? It is the establishment of certain forms or rules into which behavior and decision-making is channeled. It is a way to channel outcomes that are better than would occur without them. Think about traffic lights. Their location, their timing and everything about them is perfectly arbitrary. They can be irritating. Yet they channel traffic in a way that is far better than it would be in their absence.

Congress is clearly not doing this in an optimal way. Is there anyone who thinks that his or her member of Congress or Senator is made better by being a part of the institution of Congress? To the contrary, it often seems as if otherwise normal people who go to Washington become the least admirable blowhards and self-promoters. Rather than ennobling them, Congress seems to be debasing its members. This, and the poll results I have outlined above, point to an institution which is failing.

> **It often seems as if otherwise normal people who go to Washington become the least admirable blowhards and self-promoters.**

For reasons mentioned above, much of the problem resides in the Senate. Can this be fixed? Can this be fixed without the lengthy and uncertain process of a constitutional amendment? There is no shortage of proposals to do so. Most, however, aim at externalities like fund-raising and term limits.

To my mind it makes far more sense to modify the rules and procedures in place which shape today's Senate. The good news is that no new constitutional amendment or law is required to do this. What is required is an end to the gradual accretion of powers and "rights" of Senators which were never envisioned in the Constitution.

The bad news is that it is very difficult to get any institution to reform itself, and this is true in spades for today's Senate. Congress has the authority to reform the other branches of government and from time to time it uses that authority. It creates new cabinet departments and reorganizes existing ones. It adds or subtracts from the number of judges in the federal system and it establishes the regions in which they operate. But it is very difficult for Congress to address its own shortcomings. The landscape is littered with proposals for congressional reform which have never been enacted. They are usually too sweeping to gain traction or too abstract to address specific and obvious flaws in congressional procedures.

The framers understood that a diverse and diffuse body like Congress would suffer from inevitable faults. The problem of accountability, in which no one seems able to be held responsible for ill-advised proposals or consistently poor results, is chief among them. In thinking about reforming the Senate we are not talking about achieving perfection. We are talking about reversing the slow accretion of powers and rights which Senators have so generously accorded to themselves.

Senate Procedures

Not Everyone has Said It...

As one might suppose from the preceding chapter, the Senate is a fractious place where the commodity most often consumed is time itself. This is not to say the Senate cannot act quickly when it wishes to. The magic of what is called "unanimous consent" can work wonders. I once witnessed a miraculous event in which the Senate—which was prepared to act on legislation which under its rules required a three day layover—"deemed it to be the following day" and passed the bill. The laws of nature are but a minor impediment to a Senate determined to act.

In most cases, however, the opposite problem obtains: Senate action makes molasses in January look like a raging river. Perhaps one case will illustrate this. Senator Dole was Majority Leader and as such, he decided what would and would not be considered on the Senate floor. He asked how much time I thought we would need to pass a complex, several hundred page piece of legislation. I stretched the truth a bit—or better said, compacted it a bit—and estimated two days. Based on that slim assurance he graciously allowed the Foreign Relations Committee two days of Senate floor time.

Toward evening on the second day, Senator Dole asked me how we were doing. How many more amendments had been filed and were we on course to finish by the end of the second day? I checked my list of amendments. Which amendments remained? Could we get their sponsors to allow us to accept them without discussion, or amend them to make them acceptable, or best of all to withdraw their amendments altogether? I told Senator Dole there were 12 amendments remaining and I still thought we could finish that evening.

He stroked his tie and said he was going to dinner. "Keep whittling away at the amendments," he instructed, and said he would check back later.

About an hour later Senator Dole reappeared on the Senate floor and asked what progress we had made. My answer: there was good news and bad news. The good news was that we had worked through seven amendments, leaving only five on the list to consider. The bad news was that nine new amendments had been filed, leaving us with 14 to go. We had lost ground.

Senator Dole took the news in stride, predicting that the later the hour, the less important many of these earth-shaking amendments would seem to their sponsors. Not to mention their colleagues. Offering new amendments or extending debate late at night does not win popularity contests in the Senate cloakrooms. For context, the reader might think back to his or her student days. When a professor finishes a lecture and asks if there are any questions before class is dismissed, the student who eagerly raises his hand at that late hour risks the undying wrath of his colleagues.

What is deeply, profoundly important at three p.m. often seems far less important at 11 p.m. Senator Dole was correct, as usual, and we finished the bill that evening.

****

The main problem with the Senate today is its glacial pace of operation. This is nicely captured in the saying about Senate debates that "everything that can be said has been said, but not everyone has said it." The framers established the Senate—or at least rationalized its existence—as a body to slow the passage of legislation. In Madison's words the Senate would check "the impulse of sudden and violent passions" which might emerge in the House of Representatives, the body closest to the people.

Apparently Senators do not think the structure put in place by the framers is sufficient to check the House. They have set up myriad additional procedures which extend far beyond what the framers ever imagined in order to slow the business of the Senate. These exist at both the committee level and on the Senate floor. One symbol of this occurs at a confirmation hearing for an important nominee. Every committee member on both sides of the aisle must be heard. On occasion Senators' opening statements consume the entire first day of a confirmation hearing. The nominee sits politely before the committee as Senators preen for the television cameras. A reader unfamiliar with Washington might get a sense of this by imagining himself at a condominium board or homeowners' meeting. Here the clock stands still; if only one could deem it to be tomorrow.

> **Apparently Senators do not think the structure put in place by the framers is sufficient to check the House. They have set up myriad additional procedures which extend far beyond what the framers ever imagined in order to slow the business of the Senate.**

Senators have a variety of tools with which to delay action at the committee level. Senators can ask for delays in voting on legislation or nominees. Often they coordinate their delays and even circumvent committee rules that limit such delays. Senators can file reams of written questions which they expect nominees to answer before proceeding with their nominations. Senators can demand that committee hearings end altogether if they run more than two hours after the Senate comes into session for the day.

Delays over judicial nominees can even precede a committee hearing. The Senate established a tradition which allows home-state Senators to signal their opposition to federal judicial nominees. This tradition was established on the once reasonable, but now dubious notion that home-state Senators know more about such nominees than do their colleagues. Given modern communications, the internet, Facebook and the pervasiveness of Senate staff, this is certainly no longer true. Senate tradition allows home-state Senators to hold up a nominee by refusing to return a "blue slip," which is essentially a hall pass for a judicial nominee. These days blue slips are no longer used to highlight personal issues with a judicial nominee, but to oppose nominees on ideological, partisan grounds. There is no excuse for this tradition to continue, and Senator Grassley has been correct in scaling this back.

On the Senate floor many procedures are employed by Senators either to delay action or to mislead their constituents, or both. One is the practice of voting successive times on more or less the same question, thus chewing up time and also allowing members to carefully position themselves on both sides of an issue.

Not long after I arrived in the Senate I had my first opportunity to venture onto the Senate floor. Staff assistants to Senators with a clear role in legislation on the Senate floor can sit in the back corners of the chamber. I felt a certain sense of awe, a feeling which I never lost.

The legislation under consideration by the Senate that day was the foreign aid bill. When a vote on final passage occurs, Senators often walk just far enough into the chamber to be seen by the Senate clerk. They cast an "aye" or a "no," sometimes with just a thumbs up or down gesture, turn and depart. No time to speak with other members and certainly not to the lowly staff huddled in the corner.

Except for one Senator. Senator Dole from Kansas ambled by our corner. "Well," he announced to no one in particular, "I voted no." He went on to add, "This is the tenth straight time I've voted against foreign aid." He chuckled and stroked his tie in his signature fashion. This I thought was a bit odd, as Senator Dole seemed to be committed to an internationalist point of view. He took a few steps, paused, and said, "Of course if they ever really needed my vote I'd vote for it." He chuckled again and left.

Now here, I thought, was an interesting fellow. He voted the way most of his Kansas constituents would likely approve. But here was also someone who, if it mattered, would put policy interests ahead of his own political interests. This did not then, nor does it now, strike me as particularly venal.

I had a different feeling about a more recent case. Senator John Kerry of Massachusetts said famously about his vote on a supplemental appropriations bill, "I actually did vote for the $87 billion before I voted against it." Here, it seems, is the very definition of hypocrisy; here was a blatant attempt to eat one's cake and have it too. Here was an attempt to vote on opposite sides of the very same bill, not in the interest of good policy or even good politics but in the self-serving interest of seeming to be all things to all people.

In his account of the Grand Academy of Lugado, Jonathan Swift proposed one means to ensure good legislation. After every Senator delivers his opinion and argues on behalf of a piece of legislation, Swift says, he should then be required to vote against it. This, he argued, would redound to the benefit of the public. It is hard to know what he would make of Senator Kerry's actions.

Another version of this practice can be found in the motion to "table" legislation. To table legislation is to end debate, drop it and move on. But it is also an excellent way to disguise, or at least to minimize the visibility of a Senator's vote. Senators can argue that they never voted against a particular bill or amendment; they simply voted to table it. For this reason, Senators who are trying to make a political point on a given vote, often seek an "up or down" vote rather than a vote on a tabling motion. If a tabling motion fails (thus demonstrating support for the bill or amendment), the underlying bill or amendment is usually adopted by unanimous consent. This dispenses with any need for a roll call vote. Who can say how anyone really voted?

The most powerful tool for Senate delay is of course the filibuster, which requires more than a simple majority for the Senate to proceed. There is nothing in the Constitution about the Senate requiring a supermajority to pass legislation or to confirm nominees. Indeed, the requirement for supermajority votes is carefully limited and specifically defined in the Constitution: Senate consent to the ratification of treaties; Senate votes on impeachment; overriding a presidential veto; and constitutional amendments. Interestingly, both Madison and Hamilton speak directly about this. In discussing the 2/3s requirement relating to treaties, Hamilton makes a broad point in *Federalist #75:* "It has been shown . . . that all provisions which require more than the majority of any body to its resolutions have a direct tendency to embarrass the operations of the government and an indirect one to subject the sense of the majority to that of the minority." He says in *Federalist #22* that If a "pertinacious minority" can control the majority, the result is "tedious delays, continual negotiation and intrigue, and contemptible compromises of the public good." This sounds about right.

It might not be surprising that as a strong advocate of energetic government, Hamilton would take such a position. But Madison does so as well. In defending the basic majoritarian structure of Congress Madison says in *Federalist #58*:

> It has been said that more than a majority ought to have been required for a quorum; and in particular cases, if not in all, more than a majority of a quorum for a decision. That some advantages might have resulted from such a precaution cannot be denied. It might have been an additional shield to some particular interests, and another obstacle generally to hasty and partial measures. But these considerations are outweighed by the inconveniences in the opposite scale. In all cases where

justice or the general good might require new laws to be passed, or active measures to be pursued, the fundamental principle of free government would be reversed.

The filibuster and its attendant supermajority requirement to pass legislation or to confirm nominees has not always been an integral part of the Senate's operation. It was used only sporadically in the nineteenth and early twentieth century. It was deployed more frequently from the mid-twentieth century onward, and especially after 1970. In 1970 Senate Majority Leader Mike Mansfield instituted a "two-track" process. Under this arrangement filibusters would no longer bring the Senate to a halt until they were resolved. Henceforth filibusters would work in such a way that the Senate could move on to other business all the while a filibuster, or more likely a threatened filibuster, was holding up legislation. This had a predictable effect, namely, to make the threat of a filibuster and its attendant supermajority requirement a part of normal Senate business. We now have a "gentleman's filibuster" in which Senators only need indicate their intent to filibuster rather than to speak at great length on the Senate floor. If the Majority Leader does not have 60 votes to end a filibuster he will likely not take up a piece of legislation in the first place. The number of filibusters and threatened filibusters has exploded since 1970, and the Senate operates far differently today than it did throughout most of its history.

Indeed, a given piece of legislation faces not only one, but two possible filibusters. Under Senate rules Senators can filibuster the motion to proceed to a bill as well as the bill itself. In other words, a minority of Senators can prevent not only passage of a bill, but also prevent the Senate from even debating it.

This has put the Senate in a bind, and the past half century has seen a reluctant, but steady movement to rein in filibusters. In 1949 the Senate required 2/3s of the total number of Senators, that is 67 Senators, to break a filibuster. In 1959 the Senate lowered that threshold to 2/3s of Senators who are present and voting. In 1975, the Senate lowered the threshold again, requiring only 60 Senators to break a filibuster. In 2013 Majority Leader Harry Reid abolished the 60 vote threshold for all nominees except justices of the Supreme Court. And in 2017 Majority Leader Mitch McConnell eliminated the 60 vote threshold for Supreme Court justices. Even still, there remains in place a Senate rule to permit up to 30 hours of debate on each and every nominee before the Senate. What in any nominee's background could possibly require 30 hours of debate? This rule is a stalling tactic pure and simple, and should be amended to substantially reduce this period of time.

Each of these steps was an attempt to rein in the filibuster to allow the Senate to do its work more efficiently. Today the 60 vote requirement remains in place for both the motion to proceed to bills and for passage of legislation. There is doubtless a genuine need to balance majority rule with protections for the minority. As a creature of the Senate I can understand the hesitation in eliminating the filibuster altogether. The Senate should certainly eliminate the two track system and/or eliminate the filibuster on the motion to proceed to consider legislation. This would be simple and defensible. But the more I think about it, it strikes me there is really no reason to maintain a 60 vote requirement for any legislation. The Senate should abolish the 60 vote requirement to end a filibuster and return to majority rule.

Would this result in removing an important brake on Senate action? The framers did not seem to think so. In fact, it seems to me that returning to simple majority votes for legislation would tend to make Senators' votes more responsible, not less. One less source of evasion and unaccountability would be available to Senators. And the need for House/Senate agreement and a presidential signature to enact a law would remain firmly in place.

If none of the current delaying tactics avails, and if Senators actually have to vote on legislation, there are still ways for them to explain away their votes. Since bills are larger now and contain more provisions, one can explain a yes or no vote based on any single provision within a comprehensive bill. Even where this is not the case, evasion is still possible. Perhaps there is no better example than Hillary Clinton's latter day explanation of her vote in favor of the Iraq War in 2003. When this vote became politically inexpedient some years later, she said that she did not really vote for the war, but voted only as a bluff so Saddam Hussein knew the U. S. was serious. All Senators knew at the time that this was a vote for or against war. In any event, I do not suppose that bluffing about going to war is a very good idea.

> **Senate rules and traditions that permit endless delays are invariably justified as good government. In fact, they are no such thing. They are accommodations to an ever growing list of "rights" which Senators somehow mysteriously possess. There is no more entitled group in America today than the United States Senate.**

Senate rules and traditions that permit endless delays are invariably justified as good government, fully in the mode of the framers' intent to assure careful and deliberate lawmaking. This is an argument which seems particularly important to conservatives. Why not retain each and every way to slow down the operation of the federal government? Would this not preserve the liberties of the American people?

In fact, Senate rules and traditions have nothing whatever to do with the intentions of the Constitution's framers and they are not necessary to preserve American liberties. They are accommodations to an ever growing list of "rights" which Senators somehow mysteriously possess. America today is often said to suffer from an excess of entitlement. There is no more entitled group in America today than the United States Senate.

The Role of Fortune in Politics

A Promotion

In the fall of 1984 Senator Lugar was poised for a new assignment. He would either be elected majority leader, become chairman of the Foreign Relations Committee or become chairman of the Agriculture Committee. Soon enough, Senator Dole's election as majority leader foreclosed that option.

Senator Helms, the conservative Senator from North Carolina, wanted to chair the Foreign Relations Committee. Having more seniority than Senator Lugar, he was free to do so. But it was his misfortune—perhaps rare mistake—to have announced to his rural North Carolina constituents that if elected, he would chair the Agriculture Committee. Once elected, he tried every which way to escape this self-created dilemma, but in the end could find no honorable way to do so. Sometimes campaign promises can be dangerous.

Senator Lugar became chairman of the Foreign Relations Committee. It turned out that like most normal Americans, his Hoosier constituents had not the slightest idea what was the job of Senate majority leader. Chairing the Foreign Relations Committee, however, had some real cache. So we declared victory. We enjoyed a few heady days of celebration. After all, Senator Lugar had ascended from the most junior member of the minority party to chairman of an important committee in a record-breaking six years.

More practical matters soon intervened, however, including who would be the new staff director of the Committee. The staff director would be responsible for hiring and firing the Committee staff and helping to construct the legislative agenda of the Committee. Mitch Daniels had already indicated his intent to join the Reagan White House as political advisor. Since I had handled Senator Lugar's work on the Committee for many years I thought I would be a reasonable choice—and truth be told, I wanted the job. But this was for Senator Lugar to decide and other voices were urging him to find a better-known, more senior foreign policy expert for the job.

One such person who had another idea was Senator Helms himself. Having consigned himself to agriculture issues for the time being, he remained crafty as always; if he could persuade Senator Lugar to hire his recommended staff director, he could still play an outsized role on the Foreign Relations Committee.

I happened to learn all this while sitting in Senator Lugar's office. While we were discussing an unrelated issue the Senator's scheduler entered to say that Senator Helms was on the phone. After a brief hesitation—talking with Senator Helms was not his favorite pastime—Senator Lugar said to put the call through. The purpose of Senator Helms' call quickly became apparent, even hearing only one side of the conversation. Had Senator Lugar decided on a new staff director for the Committee? If not, Senator Helms had exactly the right person to recommend.

It was my good fortune to be sitting there at that moment. Ever suspicious of Senator Helms, Senator Lugar sensed immediately that this recommendation would not be a good idea. He responded, "Well, Jesse, thanks much for your thoughtful recommendation. I appreciate it very much, but as it happens I already have someone in mind for the job." Senator Helms apparently then asked who, forcing the issue. Senator Lugar replied that it was his own administrative assistant, Jeff Bergner. Realizing he had been trumped, Senator Helms responded graciously that I was a solid choice and that he looked forward to working with me.

That is how I learned about my promotion. To this day, I have never had the nerve to ask Senator Lugar whether this had already been settled in his mind or whether he blurted out my name just because I was sitting there. As with most occasions of good fortune, it is wise not to inquire too deeply. And it is certainly never wise to assume that one deserves whatever good fortune comes one's way

****

Not surprisingly, this career-changing event has caused me to muse from time to time about the role of fortune in our lives. Such speculation of course has been with us since humanity's earliest days. To what degree can we control our lives? To what degree is our fate determined by unknowable and unpredictable forces?

Machiavelli concludes amusingly in *The Prince* that fortune is the arbiter of half our actions, but that "she permits us to direct the other half, or perhaps a little less, ourselves." Machiavelli confronts the conventional wisdom of his time; he suggests there is a greater role for human direction than supposed, and he offers some rules about how to achieve that. In particular, he says fortune favors those who are bold and not hesitant; to be controlled, fortune must be "beaten."

John Jay expresses a similar thought in his discussion of treaties in *Federalist #64*. There he says that "they who have turned their attention to the affairs of men must have perceived that there are tides in them; tides very irregular in their duration, strength, and direction, and seldom found to run twice exactly in the same manner or measure." To profit by these tides Jay says "there are moments to be seized as they pass."

Today's conventional wisdom ascribes a far smaller role to fortune. We tend to understand the world not as controlled by fortune but by necessity. If the world is governed by necessity, we can in principle learn the laws by which this necessity operates. Indeed, it is a fundamental conceit of the modern world that we can learn the laws by which politics operates and thus control the world.

We tend in this way to shade the meaning of "fortune" into "fate." Fortune suggests an unknowable randomness, perhaps affected by the unpredictable interventions of a supernatural power; fate suggests an unalterable destiny—unalterable but perhaps knowable. Perhaps what we call fortune is simply not knowing how things work; perhaps what we call fortune is ignorance of true causes.

If we know the laws by which fate or necessity directs politics, we can use these laws to make predictions (theory) and to affect outcomes (practice). This is the thrust of all modern thought, not only of contemporary social science but also of the great historical systems like those of Marx and his successors. According to these modern seers we can in principle know the future scientifically; the great forces like modes of production and social classes can be understood and we can know how history will unfold.

Though this sort of comprehensive, totalizing view has never found very fertile soil in America, we can hear its dim echoes in contemporary political discourse. This is what is suggested when partisans refer to being "on the right side of history." Or what is meant by saying that the "arc of history bends" in a certain way. Accordingly, it is said, we should position ourselves on the side of whatever is called "progress." We surely would not want to fail by trying to go "backward." How one might truly know what is forward or backward is never said. Perhaps these once purportedly scientific theories have today become purely rhetorical tools used to control the language of political debate.

Every version of the scientific study of politics has struggled with its failure to grasp the unpredictable complexity of political life. How could a socialist revolution take place in a backward, barely capitalist nation like tsarist Russia? The theory would not predict it. This led to all manner of tortured explanations concerning the "vanguard of the proletariat" and its dozens of imitators up to this very day. The only common characteristic of these intellectual contortions seems to be that no member of the actual proletariat is ever involved in them.

If there is comprehensive knowledge of the whole in politics—knowledge which would largely eliminate fortune or chance—I have never seen it. It is my experience over a long career in politics that many surprising and unexpected things happen. I will demur on whether or not they are fated, but they do seem to me unable to be predicted. Monday morning quarterbacks—or in the case of American elections, Wednesday morning quarterbacks—offer all manner of post-facto explanations and self-affirming after-the-fact predictions. But many things happen that no reasonable person could be expected to foresee.

I offer three rules to guide how one thinks about the role of fortune in politics. First, do not assume that you know everything. Doubt a little of your own infallibility. Doubt too of others who come across as self-certain and who suggest they know everything. That others may know more than you would not be surprising. But politics is the most complex of all human activities and it would be surprising if others knew everything. Be especially wary of those who attempt to conform their ideas with reality not by altering their ideas, but by torturing reality to conform to them. This is the hallmark of totalitarianism.

Second, be open to the idea that there is some part of life that you can control. Whether it is half or less, as Machiavelli surmises, it seems fair to say that fortune does not control everything. This is well-captured in phrases like "fortune favors the well-prepared" or "fortune favors the bold." If you risk nothing, you are unlikely to succeed. This is the gravamen of what Machiavelli says: fortune favors those who act boldly. We can increase the odds of success by our actions. We can master fortune to a degree, although we never know in advance to what extent that is true.

Finally, there is the question of desert. If you are the recipient of either good or bad fortune, do not assume that you deserve it.

Assuming you deserve bad fortune which has befallen you is a recipe for failure. Far better to learn what you can from misfortune, which is admittedly often difficult. But it seems even more difficult for people who experience good fortune to learn anything at all. If good luck falls in your lap, do not make the mistake of thinking you deserve it. There is scarcely a more unpleasant and tedious person than one who assumes that every aspect of his good fortune is a straight line result of his own intelligence and hard work.

> **If you are the recipient of either good or bad fortune, do not assume that you deserve it.**

Take fortune in stride whether it is good or bad. As Goethe says, "whatever comes to pass [one] may consider that it happens to him as a man, and not as one specially fortunate or unfortunate."

I had worked with most of the then-current staff of the Committee for years. The chairman and I decided to err on the side of new blood rather than institutional memory. One afternoon I fired all but one of the current professional staff in order to begin with a clean slate. I made no pretension that I deserved to do this, nor that they deserved to be on the receiving end. I was apologetic about it rather than glorying in it. This of course did not change anything materially for those who were fired, but it was a more honest way to begin.

Going forward, we had a plate full of new legislative opportunities and an excellent new staff to address them. We began with a comprehensive series of hearings on the state of the world, inviting every former secretary of state and other important contributors to testify. In doing this, we stole shamelessly from the model that Senator Henry "Scoop" Jackson had provided when he became chairman of the Senate Armed Services Committee two decades earlier. With more than our fair share of luck, we were off and running.

The Separate Worlds
of the House and Senate

The Far Side of the Universe is Only 75 Yards Away

The Scotch was excellent. I toasted my new friend. I had come to that afternoon through a circuitous path.

We had the good fortune to pass through the Senate that rarest of all legislative accomplishments: a bipartisan bill, and a foreign aid bill at that. After taking a day or two to enjoy our success, a new thought occurred to me. What happens next? We were the proverbial dog that caught the ambulance. What now?

How do we advance this Senate-passed legislation to become law? This would require cooperation with the House of Representatives, about which I had not given one moment's thought. This, I learned, was not all that unusual, as the two houses of Congress operate on very different tracks.

A bit of investigating revealed that the House had passed its own version of the foreign assistance bill. I wondered if there was a higher power that would somehow drop down and bring the two chambers together. For that matter, why hadn't we already heard from the House?

I decided to find out. My counterpart on the House Foreign Affairs Committee was Jack Brady, a tough and fearsome veteran of many House struggles. I didn't know him at all. Further, he represented the other political party, which at that time controlled the House. I called him and introduced myself.

I said, "Since we have both passed legislation, perhaps we should get together to discuss a conference between the two committees." "Yeah?" he growled. This was clearly not going well. "Well, you know, a meeting to see where we both stand, something like that," I suggested. "Yeah?" he growled again. My charm offensive was obviously not working.

"Yes, I could come over and meet you," I said. A long silence. What new offense had I given? At last he said, "Really? You will come over here?" "Sure," I said, "why not?" As if to reassure himself, he asked again "You'll come over to the House side?" "Sure, it's not that far." His tone softened. "Well," he said, "not a single one of the SOBs who preceded you would ever come over here. They always made me come over to the House of Lords."

Unwittingly I had apparently violated years of Senate precedent. My ignorance seemed to be working to good advantage, however, and I said, "Well, I have no idea about that, but I'm happy to come over to your place."

In an even friendlier tone he asked "Do you like Scotch?" I allowed that I did enjoy a glass or two from time to time. We set up a meeting for three p. m. the following Friday and thus began one of the happiest relationships of my Senate tenure. Jack Brady was a hard-drinking curmudgeon. He was direct to a fault, but totally honest. I found his instincts fully mainstream and not especially partisan.

One Scotch led to another that afternoon and we mapped out a series of staff meetings to begin to reconcile the hundreds of differences between our two bills. When our respective staffs could not agree with one another, somehow we could. In the purest form of the art of the deal, we traded back and forth programs worth tens of millions of dollars. This of course is easier to do with someone else's money. In the end we were able to reconcile all but a handful of differences (the Nicaraguan Sandinistas being a perennial) which required committee members to meet in a formal conference.

We conspired together on many other occasions. One such occasion involved yet another issue where the House and Senate positions were at odds. Jack said that both he and his chairman, Dante Fascell of Florida, opposed their own committee's provision. He proposed a set-piece exchange between the two chairmen: Chairman Fascell would say he needed to retain the House provision; Chairman Lugar would say the Senate was dead set against it; and Chairman Fascell would reluctantly relent, explaining to his committee members that he had fought the good fight to protect their provision.

I outlined this to my chairman, though apparently not very clearly. When Chairman Fascell demanded that the Senate recede to the House provision, Chairman Lugar said, "Oh, I didn't know you felt so strongly about this, Dante. Perhaps we can work something out." Jack glared at me. Chairman Fascell looked at me quizzically. It took some fast talking to get things back on track.

****

The House of Representatives publication entitled *History, Art & Archives* begins this way: "The two houses of Congress generally work separately...." This is an understatement, to put it mildly. The House and Senate, though located only 75 yards across the Capitol from one another, are different worlds. How infrequently the two bodies interact with one another struck me as a surprise. Both chambers pass bills with no assurance, except in rare cases, that they will be acted upon by the other body. The House sends to the Senate far more bills than the Senate sends to the House. This is a result of House rules which permit easier passage of bills. George Washington likened the Senate to a saucer which allows a drink to cool; House members see the Senate more as a place where their bills go to die. As mentioned above, in 2018 there were upward of 250 House-passed bills which the Senate failed even to consider, much less to pass.

> **The House and Senate, though located only 75 yards across the Capitol from one another, are different worlds.**

It is well known that the Constitution establishes differences between the House and Senate. Senate and House members' terms of office are different. The requirements of age and citizenship to be elected to the House or Senate are different. The House of Representatives has the power to originate revenue bills. And the Senate has the power to confirm executive branch officials and to consent to the ratification of treaties—or not.

But there are other constitutional provisions that are even more important in ensuring the independence of the two bodies from one another. One is that each house is given the power "to be the Judge of the Elections, Returns and Qualifications of its own members." Another is that each house "may determine the Rules of its Proceedings," including punishing or expelling its members. Neither house interferes in any way with the processes and procedures of the other. Each runs according to its own rhythms and each is free to establish or to change its rules at any time, without any input from the other chamber.

There is only one formal constitutional limitation on the independence of the two chambers. The Constitution requires that "Neither House, during the session of Congress, shall, without the consent of the other, adjourn for more than three days, nor to any other Place than that in which the two Houses shall be sitting." This provision was included in order to prevent one house from thwarting the will of the other by simply refusing to meet. Such a tactic is not wholly implausible; we witnessed it several years ago when Wisconsin state Democratic delegates fled to Illinois so their presence could not be compelled to vote on a provision passed by the other house.

Each chamber clings tightly to its constitutional authority to set its own rules. This tenacity has spilled over into another area not addressed by the Constitution. The legislative branch must be funded by congressional appropriations just like any other part of the federal government. This is not an insignificant amount of money, amounting these days to roughly $4.5 billion for the coming fiscal year. How does Congress set a budget for itself? The legislative branch appropriation bill consists of three parts—funding for the House, funding for the Senate and funding for joint congressional branch organizations like the Library of Congress, the Architect of the Capitol, the Government Accountability Office and the Congressional Budget Office. The section establishing funding levels for the House is set by the House and the section establishing funding levels for the Senate is set by the Senate. There is no constitutional, legal or rule-based provision that forbids one chamber from interfering in the budget of the other, but this is simply not done. Neither chamber wants to risk the intervention of the other in setting its own budget. Each chamber is the judge of its own budget.

As a practical matter, there are really only a handful of ways in which the House and Senate interact with one another. One is the familiar joint meeting of Congress in which both chambers assemble to listen to the president or a distinguished foreign leader. The first of these joint meetings occurred in 1789. On such occasions, however, neither body is really working, much less interacting with their colleagues from the other body. They are simply listening to what is being spoken; they are not acting in any way, much less together. Congress also meets jointly every four years to count electoral votes for the presidency. But again, this is largely a formality and besides certifying the outcome, no work is done by either body, much less both together.

A second kind of interaction is more meaningful. House and Senate leadership and their staffs meet together informally from time to time. This occurs more frequently toward the end of congressional sessions when each body is considering legislation like the annual appropriations bills, which must be completed in one way or another. Occasionally House and Senate leaders check with one another to gauge the seriousness of the other body about a particular piece of legislation. House members in particular become tired of having to "walk the plank" and take hard votes if the Senate will not take up their legislation anyway.

Finally, the most significant direct interactions between the House and the Senate take place during conference committees which try to reconcile bills passed in their respective chambers. Conference committees are usually, but not always, made up of members from the committees which have shepherded their respective bills through their chambers. It is very rare that any but the simplest, shortest bills emerge exactly the same from the House and Senate. On occasion, one house may decide simply to accept the language of the other because its leadership believes that further amendments will kill the bill altogether. This is what happened, for example, when the House accepted the Senate's language on the Affordable Care Act in 2010. On the whole, though, without House/Senate conferences very little legislation would ever be sent to the president.

These three interactions describe pretty much the complete extent of coordination, leave aside cooperation, between the House and Senate. There are, however, two outside groups which provide an additional degree of coordination between the houses. The first is the president and his administration. Presidents meet frequently with House and Senate leaders in meetings with their own party leadership or in bipartisan leadership meetings. Presidents have an interest in securing the assent of both houses for legislation which they favor. President Trump, for example, met regularly with House and Senate leaders in order to press both houses to act on tax reform legislation.

Lobbyists play a similar role. Lobbyists who seek to pass laws or amendments on behalf of their clients know that passage in both chambers is necessary. They aim to secure sponsors and advocates for their legislative initiatives in both houses. Occasionally members of one house will reach out to a member or members of the other house in order to introduce what is called "companion legislation." More often than not, lobbyists are behind these efforts.

Here is a story that illustrates the different worlds which the House and Senate inhabit. Until 1980 Democrats enjoyed uninterrupted control of both the House and the Senate for 26 straight years. Over this period a sense of complacency about control of Congress set in with both Democrats and Republicans. Many practices that might have benefitted from alternating party control were adopted, usually at the expense of the minority. Committee ratios and committee staff ratios were set at levels highly favorable to the majority. Many small corruptions developed over time.

When Republicans surprisingly won control of the Senate in the 1980 elections, they discovered the extent of these practices. On one major committee, Republican staff members had been allocated three parking spaces. They assumed—but did not know—that Democratic staff members had allocated to themselves at least six parking spaces, consistent with the ratio of majority and minority staff. Given the long accretion of Democratic power, perhaps Democratic staff had as many as eight or nine parking spaces. They were surprised to learn the true number—79 Democratic parking spaces. This is not an argument against Democratic control of Congress per se, but it is an argument that occasional changes of power can have a cleansing effect.

When Republicans took control of the Senate in January of 1981, their beleaguered House colleagues came to them with a proposal. House minority Republicans were vastly underrepresented on House committees. Why didn't Senate Republicans use their leverage to get a better deal for their fellow House Republicans? If Senate Republicans were to threaten their Democratic Senate colleagues with unfair treatment, perhaps that would entice House Democrats to treat their Republican minority more fairly.

You would have thought this proposal had dropped down from Mars. Senate Republicans were incredulous. Doing such a thing would require favoring their House counterparts over their Senate colleagues. Worse yet, it would entwine House and Senate rules in a new and unprecedented way. This was impossible. Unthinkable. The idea was, as they say both on crime shows and in Washington, dead on arrival.

Presidential Vetoes and Congressional Overrides

Stealing the Bill

Well, I thought to myself, this is probably not the best place in the world for me to be right now. I was being roundly denounced on the Senate floor by the so-called lion of the Senate, Senator Ted Kennedy. How I came to be there is a bit of a story.

In the mid-1980s there was considerable turmoil throughout the country about South Africa's racial system of apartheid. Demands grew for the U. S government to sanction South Africa. Indeed, both the House and the Senate passed bills to put in place economic sanctions against South Africa in 1985. These bills enjoyed overwhelming bipartisan support; our committee had reported out a sanctions bill which passed the Senate by a vote of 80-12.

After protracted negotiations, House and Senate conferees agreed on a joint bill to send to the president. Having passed its bill first, the House acted first on the newly agreed joint bill. The House passed it and sent it to the Senate where it was "held at the desk" for the Senate's consideration.

Both Majority Leader Dole and Foreign Relations Committee Chairman Lugar supported the agreed bill and intended to pass it in the Senate. Before Senate consideration, however, President Reagan agreed to adopt most of the provisions of the legislation in the form of an executive order. Reagan had threatened to veto South Africa sanctions legislation, but he reluctantly agreed to adopt its substance as an executive order, that is, in a fashion that would provide flexibility for the executive branch. He too opposed apartheid; in fact, he had appointed the first black American ambassador to South Africa to make just this point. President Reagan thought, however, that the inflexibility of legislated economic sanctions would end up hurting most the very people in South Africa we were all aiming to help.

Senators Dole and Lugar sought the president's support throughout the legislative process. They believed that a joint position of the House, the Senate and the president would make the strongest possible statement. Once President Reagan acted, they were prepared to wait and gauge the effect of his executive order.

Senator Kennedy, however, had other ideas. He wanted to bring the bill to the Senate floor that very afternoon. Somehow Majority Leader Dole had gotten wind of Senator Kennedy's intention to come to the Senate floor, gain recognition from the chair and move to consideration of the bill.

Herewith a bit of difficult but necessary inside baseball. No Senate rule exists to prevent any Senator from moving to consider a bill—but this is simply never done. Calling up legislation is by longstanding precedent the job of the majority leader. This is the majority leader's greatest power: to decide what does and does not come to the Senate floor, and when.

Senator Dole convened a small meeting in the well of the Senate. How could he stop Senator Kennedy? Surely the parliamentarian could recommend a strategy. The parliamentarian responded that there was no Senate rule to prevent it. Senator Dole pressed further. The parliamentarian thought for a minute and said, "Well, there may be one way." Senator Dole warmed. The parliamentarian explained that a bill must be "at the desk" to be called up. "What do you mean?" asked Senator Dole (betraying the truth that often the Senate parliamentarian is the only person in the chamber who is thoroughly familiar with the Senate's arcane rules). Just that, the parliamentarian said.

"You mean the bill has to be physically present here at the desk?" Senator Dole asked. Yes, said the parliamentarian. Senator Dole asked to see the bill. The parliamentarian fished through his files and placed the several hundred page bill (Congress rarely does less) on the ledge next to Senator Dole.

"So if this bill is not here, Senator Kennedy can't call it up?" asked Senator Dole. The parliamentarian nodded. "Has it ever happened that a bill disappeared from the desk?" asked Senator Dole. The parliamentarian said not recently, but that once it was quite a common practice. When southern Democratic committee chairmen would leave town, sometimes for weeks on end, they would collect all the legislation their committees had reported to the Senate floor, stuff it in their briefcases and take it with them. They were not about to see their own bills used as a vehicle for civil rights legislation in their absence.

Senator Dole was thoroughly warming up to the situation. He took the bill off the ledge where it rested, held it for about five seconds and said to Senator Lugar, "Here, Dick, do something with this." Senator Lugar, obviously a bit uncomfortable with this stratagem, held the bill for a nanosecond and said, "Here, Jeff, do something with this." Senator Dole ambled off chuckling to himself, Senator Lugar announced he was heading upstairs for an intelligence briefing, and I stood wondering what I should do with the bill.

My first thought was to take it home and show it to my wife and children. After all, here was a piece of history in the making. I reconsidered. There had been no time to print the bill, so it contained all the handwritten additions and deletions we had negotiated. What if I were in a car accident which destroyed the only extant copy of the bill? I could imagine the Washington Post headline the following morning. I decided the course of wisdom was to lock the bill in my office safe with other classified documents, after which I joined Senator Lugar at the briefing.

Before long, a staff aide approached Senator Lugar. He turned and pointed to me. My razor sharp political instincts told me this was probably not good. The aide said the parliamentarian wanted to see me. I entered the Senate chamber and noticed that Senator Kennedy had just been recognized to speak. Apparently the parliamentarian was getting cold feet about the course he had recommended. He asked if I had the South Africa bill. I said "Yes, you know I do." He handed me a prepared typewritten receipt saying that I had possession of the bill and asked me to sign it. Seeing no reason not to, as I did indeed have the bill, I signed the receipt and turned to go.

By now Senator Kennedy had risen to the highest reaches of the high dudgeon for which he was well-known. His face was florid and veins bulged from his neck. "Someone has stolen the South Africa bill," he shouted. "This is unconscionable. We will get to the bottom of this. We will find out who has the bill." Once again my shrewd political instincts kicked in and I headed for the relative safety of the classified briefing upstairs.

All went as intended from that point forward. Senators Dole and Lugar prevailed upon Senators to give the executive order a chance to work. They knew the legislation was always available if it were subsequently required and that it had a decent chance of passing over the president's veto (which it eventually did the following year).

When the legislative heat died down, I quietly returned the bill to the desk of the Senate. For whatever reason, the parliamentarian was none too pleased with me, though I saw myself as an innocent in this whole escapade. I returned the bill to him and stood motionless. "What do you want?" he asked testily. Since I no longer had the bill, I wanted my signed receipt back. He took out the receipt, ceremoniously ripped it in half, and handed it to me.

That afternoon my staff and I enjoyed a (self) congratulatory drink. After all, we had played a role in bringing sanctions to bear against the apartheid government of South Africa. And in the process we had reminded Senator Kennedy that he was not the majority leader. My stock with Senator Dole reached a new high.

My staff was wildly amused by the torn receipt. They taped it together, framed it and hung it on my office wall. When news of this spread to Senator Kennedy's staff, the framed receipt become an ongoing target for thievery. We redoubled our vigilance and strengthened our office security. I still have the receipt today.

****

What shall we make of this episode? We might note—as we have already done—the arcane rules and procedures of the House and Senate. But it was the president's veto threat that triggered this entire escapade, and it is worth a moment to reflect on this presidential power.

Although never mentioned by name in the Constitution, the presidential veto is another of the many compromises embodied in that document. Article I spells out this power. It states that every bill passed by both houses of Congress must be presented to the president before it can become a law. The president can disapprove such a bill— veto it—and return it to Congress along with his objections to the bill. Congress can, if it is willing and able, pass this bill into law over a presidential veto with a 2/3s recorded vote of both houses of Congress.

This provision reflected a compromise between providing the president an absolute veto over legislation (such as was possessed by the British crown) and providing no veto power to the president at all. In Federalist # 73 Hamilton, always a ready defender of executive power, refers to the veto as a necessary means of self-defense for the president. He also praises its virtue in ensuring yet another layer of approval for any new law, thus tilting the balance in favor of the status quo over change.

The framers thought the veto power would work in two ways, the first when employed to block the legislature. Indeed, Hamilton argued that the danger of the veto power was not that it would be used too often but too little. Has this been true? Since 1789 presidents have vetoed 2,572 bills, of which 1,505 were outright vetoes and 1,067 so-called pocket vetoes. This averages to about 11 vetoes per year or around 44 vetoes per presidential term. Presidential vetoes, however, have been employed very unevenly by presidents. Grover Cleveland issued 414 vetoes, the most in any presidential term (many of these were vetoes of private relief bills mentioned above). There was also a period of higher-than-average presidential vetoes in the 1930s through the 1950s; Franklin Roosevelt issued 635 vetoes, Harry Truman 250 and Dwight Eisenhower 181. In recent years vetoes have been used more sparingly, Clinton issuing 37 vetoes, George W. Bush 12 and Barack Obama 12.

Overrides of presidential vetoes have not been rare, but they have been infrequent. Of total presidential vetoes only 110, or about 7%, have been overridden by Congress. As one might suppose, a higher percentage of vetoes has been overridden in periods of partisan disagreement between Congress and the president. Andrew Johnson, for example, had 15 of his 21 vetoes, or 71%, overridden by the Republican Congress during the stormy post-civil war years. More recently, President Clinton had 5% of his vetoes overridden; George W. Bush 33%; and Barack Obama 8%. Overall, one would have to conclude that the presidential veto is a very effective tool for presidents to use against Congress: presidents get their way roughly 93% of the time. As a general matter, it is not easy to override a presidential veto, especially on a foreign policy issue where presidents have historically been given greater deference by Congress. That is why the congressional override of President Reagan's veto of South Africa sanctions legislation was such an unusual occurrence. More recently, we have seen another example in Congress' override of President Trump's veto of sanctions legislation against Russia, North Korea and Iran.

The veto power also works in a second, more silent way. A presidential veto threat can cause Congress to alter legislation it is considering in order to gain the signature of the president. Indeed, on occasion either house of Congress—or either political party—actively seeks a presidential veto threat in order to bolster its negotiating position. There is no record of how many times presidents—or their staffs—have deployed veto threats against legislation, but I have seen it often during my own career and my sense is that this occurs regularly each year. Veto threats are also a very potent tool for presidents.

In a narrowly tailored piece of legislation with one purpose—such as the War Powers Resolution of 1973—a presidential veto would likely be addressed against the core point of the legislation. In a large, multipurpose piece of legislation, however, the president and his advisors might have deep concerns about only one or several of hundreds of provisions in the bill. Often these large bills are spending bills which contain policy riders along with the bill's appropriations. This results in what is essentially a game of "chicken." Congress inserts provisions in a large bill which the president opposes along with many provisions he favors, thus daring the president to veto the bill. The president, on the other hand, utilizes a veto threat to lead Congress to withdraw the provisions in question because it wishes to retain the balance of its own legislative handiwork.

This is highly relevant these days, because Congress has tended to pass fewer, but much more comprehensive bills. This is certainly true with regard to the annual appropriations legislation, where all but a handful of departments' budgets are rolled into one large year-end bill, often called a continuing resolution. Since Congress has found it more and more difficult to pass legislation of any sort, sponsors of legislation try to include their provisions in one of the few legislative vehicles that come along. This is why so few bills have been vetoed by recent presidents.

Although there is nothing wrong with passing fewer and larger bills from a constitutional standpoint, this new reality has intensified the game of chicken between Congress and the president. Presidents have objected over and over again to being confronted with massive all-or-nothing bills to fund the government. They have argued that the nation would benefit from the adoption of a line item veto, in which the president can pick and choose among the provisions of a large bill, retaining some and vetoing others. It is not hard to see why presidents favor a line item veto: it would magnify their power significantly, and especially in the area of the Congress' strongest power, namely, the so-called power of the purse.

For reasons which are hard to comprehend from a standpoint of institutional self-interest, Congress actually passed a line item veto bill in 1996, providing presidents with just this authority. Happily, the Supreme Court saved Congress from itself in 1998, ruling 6-3 that the line item veto was unconstitutional.

It is difficult to know what to say about Congress' voluntary abdication of its own powers. A line item veto might in the short term reduce federal spending, and that is one reason that fiscal hawks in Congress support it. But the reality of such a provision would likely look far different. We would see the Congress larding up legislation with provisions, and especially spending provisions, which it knew the president would excise from the bill with his line item veto scalpel. Members of Congress could and would trumpet that they tirelessly supported additional spending for programs to benefit their constituents, knowing all along that the mean-spirited president would cut them out of the bill. A better name for the Line Item Veto Act would be The Congressional Irresponsibility Act.

A better name for the Line Item Veto Act would be The Congressional Irresponsibility Act.

The Supreme Court's clear ruling against the line item veto has not deterred Congress from trying out ever new ways to give its power to the president. A hybrid, watered-down version—which its sponsors thought might pass constitutional muster—was tried out again in 2006. Happily, this did not succeed either.

Nor has the Court's ruling deterred presidents from seeking ways to gain a practical equivalent of the line item veto. In response to the large, multipurpose bills the president receives from Congress, presidents have vastly expanded the use of a tool called a "signing statement." This is a lazy man's version of the line item veto.

Signing statements have existed going back at least to the Monroe administration. Though usually explaining and commending legislation, there are examples of signing statements from early in our history which reject certain provisions of laws which presidents have signed. But the widespread use of signing statements to express presidential objections, challenges or hints that they will not administer selected portions of laws which they have just signed is a relatively recent practice. It dates roughly to the Reagan presidency, when Reagan issued 250 signing statements, 86 of which expressed objections or concerns about provisions in the legislation. President George H. W. Bush issued 228 signing statements, of which 107 expressed objections; President Clinton issued 381, of which 70 expressed objections; and George W. Bush issued 152, of which 118 expressed objections. Barack Obama criticized the use of signing statements during the 2008 campaign but proceeded to use them in the very first year of his presidency and every year thereafter.

Many times the reason offered for a signing statement is a presidential concern about the constitutionality of one or more provisions of a bill they sign. There is an argument that presidents need not, and ought not, implement laws which they believe are unconstitutional. This has been a long-standing claim of presidents including, for example, in regard to the War Powers Resolution, which no president has understood to be constitutional. Then again, the War Powers Resolution was not signed by President Nixon, but passed over his veto. There is nothing in the Constitution, however, that makes presidents the judge of this question and certainly nothing that suggests they are free to pick and choose among provisions of the law as they see fit. It is one thing to express a view of the constitutionality of a law which was on the books when a president enters into office, but quite another to express such a view about legislation which the president has actually just signed.

We can date the rapid growth of presidential signing statements to the time Congress began to send the president comprehensive, multipurpose legislation. Signing statements do not always relate to such bills, but very often they do. In this sense, signing statements are one more unhappy result of ongoing congressional irresponsibility. If the Congress sent the president smaller, more narrowly tailored bills, he would have a cleaner opportunity to use his veto power. There would be far less need to resort to the short cut of a presidential threat not to implement certain provisions to which he objects. If presidents' objections are really founded in constitutional concerns, they should not sign such legislation. But presidents do, knowing they can finesse the issue and that Congress is unlikely to do anything about it.

> **We can date the rapid growth of presidential signing statements from the time Congress began to send the president comprehensive, multipurpose legislation.**

Perhaps it would not be out of order to make a final observation about vetoes. Congress hit upon a new idea in 1932, when it created the "legislative veto." Congress passed a law to authorize the president to reorganize the executive branch, subject to a congressional veto of his action if it disagreed with the president's plan. For a question relating to the organization of the president's executive branch, one could see why this might be a reasonable course of action. But

Congress soon enough expanded this practice to laws across the board, which addressed many issues both foreign and domestic. In doing so, Congress reversed the process spelled out in the Constitution. In the Constitution the Congress proposes and the president disposes; with a legislative veto the president acts first, subject to a possible congressional veto.

> **To cede to the president the right to act first in a given sphere is to cede the core responsibility of legislating.**

From its initial use regarding executive branch reorganization, Congress proceeded to expand vastly the use of the legislative veto. Provisions of both domestic and foreign policy legislation were made subject to a legislative veto. Legislative vetoes were constructed as two-house vetoes or one-house vetoes. In some cases legislative vetoes were constructed in such a way that individual congressional committees exercised this power.

To all of this presidents expressed no objection. Presidents were more than happy to trade a potential legislative veto of their decisions if they could set the agenda themselves. Presidents understood that Congress had granted to them what are undoubtedly legislative powers. Both Congress and presidents were pleased to agree for half a century on the use of the legislative veto process.

But simply because the legislative and executive branches agree on a given procedure—or bill—does not make it consistent with the Constitution. Once again the Supreme Court saved Congress from itself by finding the so-called legislative veto unconstitutional in 1983. To cede to the president the right to act first in a given sphere is to cede the core responsibility of legislating. The time-worn explanatory model of the separation of powers, in which the legislative and executive branches contend for power at each other's expense, seems wildly off the mark today. As often as not, we find Congress all too willing and eager to cede its responsibilities to the executive branch voluntarily.

III. THE PEOPLE SPEAK ... AND HOW

The Qualities of the American Electorate

This is a Matter for the FBI

I wandered out to the outer office of my Senator's suite. As I did, I heard a knock on the door to the suite. It was unusual for the door to be closed, so as I walked to open it I yelled "come in." The door opened and in walked a man. I use the word "walk" advisedly, for in fact he was on his knees, with his shoes protruding out from beneath his knees. He made his way past me—slowly—and when he came to our receptionist's desk he set his chin on her desk.

Even by the standards of constituent visits to our office this was highly unusual. In the event of problems, receptionists had buzzers installed under their desks to alert the Capitol Hill police. Since I was at hand, however, I thought I would handle this constituent myself. "Can I help you," I asked as if nothing were out of the ordinary. He said—naturally—that he wanted to speak with the Senator personally about a serious problem. That there was a serious problem here, I had no doubt. That my Senator was the person to solve it was less clear.

I explained that the Senator was not available but as his chief of staff perhaps I could help him. He was skeptical, but he agreed. I took him to a nearby conference table. "Now," I said, "how can I help you?"

The gentleman—who was indeed a constituent from Indiana—said that he was having a problem with the FBI. I listened. The FBI, he explained, had somehow installed listening devices in his teeth. The FBI was spying on him day and night. Worse yet, in recent weeks these devices were actually speaking to him, sending him messages of various sorts.

The kind of assistance this gentleman needed was obviously beyond our office's capabilities and I suggested various avenues to assist him. Had he visited his doctor about this problem? Was he seeing a medical professional in Indiana on a regular basis? If not, could we assist in referring him to one? How about a dentist?

The gentleman became a bit animated about my responses. He said loudly and impatiently that he had an intelligence-related issue, not a medical problem. Our conversation continued in this vein for another 15 minutes. I was taxing my imagination to discover some way to be helpful. He said that I did not seem to be taking his problem seriously. What did I intend to do about it? How could he get the FBI to stop this?

Devoid of further ideas, I then did what I am sure I ought not to have done. I told him that since we were unable to help him, perhaps he should take this matter up with the FBI directly. This was my very first idea that struck him positively. How might he do that, he asked?

I explained that the FBI was part of the Justice Department and that Justice was the place to begin. He asked for directions, which I helpfully provided to him. He reassumed his kneeling position and scurried out the door.

In fairness to my own judgment, this didn't seem to me an entirely satisfactory resolution of the problem. But truth be told, I was doubtful there was such a resolution. In any event, he was no longer in our office.

Having moved on to a host of other issues, I put this encounter out of mind until mid-afternoon. At that point my assistant announced that I had a phone call from the Justice Department. I hesitantly picked up the phone and heard the outrage: "BERGNER, what are you doing sending this guy over here?" Apparently, armed with a reference from our office, he had talked his way into the Justice Department.

Admittedly, security was not as tight in pre-9/11 days, but this was still quite an impressive feat. My friend at the Justice Department continued his rant for a full five minutes. When he came up for air, I explained patiently that after all the Justice Department did have jurisdiction over the FBI. I was going to ask why Justice couldn't control its rogue agency, but this seemed a bridge too far.

The rest of the story remains shrouded in mystery. I have no idea whether he entered the Justice Department on his knees. Nor whether the Justice Department was at all helpful to our constituent. Nor did I ever hear from him again.

****

We have seen in many of the foregoing tales that our government officials are not the god-like creatures they sometimes present themselves to be. They are often short-sighted and devoid of any sense of the broader public good. They often confuse ideology with genuine thinking. To cover all this, they create a myriad of procedural tricks. They posture, they preen and they are often more interested in appearing to do the right thing than actually doing the right thing.

How do we get a government like this? How do these people come to rule over us? Here we must recall that we are a representative democracy; we elect these people ourselves. They have not assumed power by way of a coup; they have been freely chosen by we the people. There are of course allegations that the people are not able to choose freely because the system is "rigged." This we will touch upon in the following chapter. But in plain English, we have a relatively open system in which there are very few legal bars to either voting or running for public office. It is far easier to construct an elaborate conspiratorial theory about who runs America than it is to look directly at the American public which is choosing its leaders.

The gentleman who entered our Senate office is of course an outlier. But it would be strange, and hardly to be expected, if the quality and character of our representatives did not bear some relationship to the quality and character of the American people who elect them. Let us here consider a few—depressing—facts. Much has been written about the general decline of Americans' knowledge. SAT and ACT test scores have been declining for decades, and have been re-tooled in order to prevent the appearance of further decline.

Study after study displays an extraordinarily low number of students who meet "minimum proficiency" standards of learning.

Comparisons with comparable foreign students are more discouraging yet. This is not the place to wallow in these depressing numbers. But when vast majorities of students cannot locate large and well-known countries on a map, or guess even remotely when Lincoln was president, or fail to understand the first thing about what is and is not contained in the Bill of Rights, there is an obvious problem.

While the numbers are low across the entire spectrum of learning, including reading, grammar, mathematics, history and science, the study of history fares especially poorly. It seems that for many Americans little of consequence has happened in the past; in Orwell's words "nothing exists except an endless present." The statue outside the National Archives reads (with apologies to Shakespeare) "What is Past is Prologue;" for many Americans today what is past is simply past.

In response to these dismal results it is sometimes said that today's schools are teaching kids not to learn facts but "how to think." Were this only true. There is no evidence at all that it is true, as Americans' scores are also very low compared with foreigners on problem-solving and analysis, leave aside genuine thinking. It has never been clear to me what one can think about if one does not know anything about which to think. The truth about all this was crisply expressed by Robert Frost who said of educators that "by thinking, they meant stocking up with radical ideas, by learning they meant stocking up with conservative ideas."

Americans are by no means stupid, but they are certainly ignorant. In fairness, this raises a surprisingly difficult question: what does it matter? What if most Americans cannot recount elementary historical facts, mathematical equations or scientific concepts? What does this have to do with electing competent public officials? What if a far higher share of Americans knew that Lincoln was elected president in 1860 and not 1960? Would the quality of America's government officials improve? Americans who know more might be less easily duped, but would this result in better government? How would more knowledge of history, mathematics, language and science result in better government? Is it not the job of government to govern the American people regardless of the level on which they are operating?

The framers of the Constitution believed elected representatives would be better than the electors. But there are limits. Immanuel Kant said that a properly constructed form of government would work even for a nation of devils. This is a deeply, even wildly optimistic assertion about the power of human reason to create good institutions. It has never been borne out in practice, however, and the framers of the American Constitution certainly did not subscribe to it. To the contrary, the framers argued to a man that only an educated citizenry is capable of self-government. Though well-constructed institutions can certainly help to produce better decisions than would occur in their absence, there are obvious limits to this. Like all humans, Americans are somewhere between devils and angels and their choice of officials, their vigilance against corruption and their reasonable hopes for the future are vital to a free and decent government.

To argue that citizens should possess more factual knowledge or more abstract thinking ability somewhat misses the point. What the framers argued for was education in virtue, or moral virtue, to use an old-fashioned term. For them an education which conduces to moral virtue is necessary to preserve liberty. Here of course we confront the real problem. At a time when educators doubt that there is such a thing as moral virtue, it is of course very hard to teach it. Perhaps the closest we could reasonably expect to come to teaching moral virtue today is to teach what was once called "civics." Civics is not simply instruction in names and dates and the other data of history. It is instruction about the nature of our government and why it was founded as it was; it is instruction about the nature of self-government and what are a citizen's rights and duties under such a system. To be tendentious, maybe it is even about why self-government is better than any other form of government.

To teach the notion of citizenship is an important way in which to reinforce what all Americans share. It reinforces a sense of unity, of participation in the whole. It is more fashionable today to refer to Americans in terms of their genders, their ethnicities and their other distinguishing differences. Civics teaches that Americans are citizens, not simply sub-group members. As such it teaches participation in the whole.

Civics will inevitably teach history as a part of its enterprise, but less for its own sake than to deepen Americans' understanding of the spirit which informs historical events. Civics might discuss at length the institution of human slavery which marked the first 75 years of our nation. This is not a subject to be elided. But it might also discuss why 364,000 union soldiers, 90% of whom were white, gave their lives to end slavery. All of this takes us into risky political territory these days. There is justified fear that even raising the meaning of citizenship, or heaven forbid the notion of duties, will result in loss of one's job or public humiliation. We have traveled a long way in the direction of identity politics and its narratives of division. Civics teaches a narrative of unity and of the whole, and is a necessary corrective.

Requiring that high school graduates be able to pass the citizenship test for immigrants is no panacea. It would, however, offer a beginning point for understanding the uniqueness of our nation and why so many people who want to come here understand that uniqueness better than do many natural born citizens.

None of this will be good news for people who believe the problem of governance resides entirely in Washington. Of course the problem resides there in what is sometimes called the swamp. But it resides there in part because Americans have filled up the swamp themselves. It is easy to lay off the problems of American government on what happens in Washington. Why is there so much bitterness, division and partisanship in Washington? Perhaps because there is so much bitterness, division and partisanship among the American people.

There are surely institutional fixes to be made in Washington and especially to the Congress. A Congress with a 13% approval rating should not be hard to improve upon. Numerous suggestions to improve the functioning of Congress, and especially the Senate, will be made in this text. But politicians are, if nothing else, very good at putting their finger to the wind and sensing accurately political realities. Among the various forms of self-entitlement which abound today is the expectation that we are entitled to a better government without having to reform the American electorate. Perhaps this is the scariest thought of all: as a people we may be getting exactly the government we deserve.

> **Among the various forms of self-entitlement which abound today is the expectation that we are entitled to a better government without having to reform the American electorate. Perhaps this is the scariest thought of all: as a people we may be getting exactly the government we deserve.**

The Role of Money in Politics

Oriental Rugs and Orchids

My wife and I were escorted into the Palm Beach mansion's front hall. There we were met by our host, replete in a remarkably suave outfit including dining slippers. We were here because I had set up a small fundraising dinner for Senator Lugar.

We were greeted by the other guests: our host's wife; our host's brother and his wife; businessman and philanthropist Max Fisher and his wife; and Milton Petrie (owner of 1700 women's clothing stores) and his wife. Altogether a distinguished group of stratospheric wealth, of which I had no business being a part.

Before dinner we enjoyed drinks in a massive sitting room which I was certain I had seen in the pages of *Architectural Digest*. The conversation ranged across numerous topics, the principal one being how very difficult it was to find high quality oriental rugs of a size appropriate to such a room. For orientation, we were not talking 9' by 12' rugs here. We were talking more like 24' by 36.' The guests lamented the small number of options and traded recommendations about who might sell high quality rugs of this size. Needless to say, I was not an active participant in this conversation.

We sat down to dinner at an intimate table setting for twelve. Again the conversation ranged widely, but finally settled on the topic of what each guest did for amusement. When not searching for oversized oriental rugs, what did everyone do for fun? In middle class lingo, what were everyone's "hobbies?" After several interventions our host's wife spoke. She said that she enjoyed collecting orchids.

This seemed a bit rarified, but an altogether understandable pastime. After all, we had an orchid plant on our kitchen window sill that someone had given us.

She added, however, that because many orchid varieties are exceedingly rare the only way to do this properly is—wait for this—by helicopter. She would be flown at low altitudes in her family helicopter in order to spot a rare variety. If the helicopter could put down nearby the orchid could be collected immediately. If not, a note of its location was made and staff would follow up afterward.

I have to admit that my initial notion of mentioning my stamp collection now seemed wildly out of place. This was quite simply a different world than the one I normally inhabited. When Scott Fitzgerald said to Hemingway that the rich are different from you and me, Hemingway is reputed to have responded yes, they have more money. This being a wonderfully ironic understatement.

****

Not everyone is captured in the description of average Americans in the previous chapter. There is a segment of Americans which is powerful, influential and generally well-informed. Not all of these people are wealthy—some are subject matter experts or public figures—but most are. Success in almost any career endeavor in America—including, it seems, some contemporary versions of theology—tends to make one wealthy, if not also healthy and wise.

Wealthy Americans are often said to be gaming the system for their own benefit. They are corrupting the democratic system with boatloads of money. Is this true?

There is no doubt that the wealthy are big contributors to political campaigns at all levels of government, and especially the federal government. The statistics are quite stark. Roughly 800,000 Americans contributed more than $200 each to political campaigns in the last election cycle. Approximately one one-hundredth of one per cent of Americans contribute 40% of all political funds. And one-fourth of one percent of Americans contribute a full 68% of all political funds. Moreover, expenditures on political campaigns have grown rapidly in recent years; total political spending in the 2016 election cycle was twice what it was in 2000.

These statistics mirror to some extent the income and wealth levels of Americans. The share of income comprised by the upper one per cent stood at roughly 20% in 2016, and the share of wealth at about twice that, at nearly 40%. The income of the top 20% of Americans comprised 50% of all income and the top 20% held close to 90% of the nation's wealth. These statistics also track the share of federal income taxes paid by wealthy Americans. The top one per cent of earners pays 38% of all income taxes and the top 25% pay roughly 86%. The bottom 60% of American wage earners pay roughly 2% of all income taxes, with the bottom 1% being net recipients of federal money through the Earned Income Tax Credit.

What are we to make of all this? It is taken almost as gospel that there is too much money in politics today. A recent poll showed roughly 90% of Americans agreed with that sentiment. Money is said to be "corrupting" our political system and "undermining our democracy." Though this is often asserted as too obvious to require evidence, the fact is that concrete evidence for this is somewhat hard to come by. In precisely what way is money corrupting our politics? It turns out that as soon as one becomes specific about how money is said to be corrupting our system, evidence to support this claim is dubious at best. A well-known critic of money in politics admits this in saying that money's effects are "manifold, subtle and hard to pin down."

> **As soon as one becomes specific about how money is said to be corrupting our system, evidence to support this claim is dubious at best.**

For one thing, spending more money in a political campaign does not guarantee victory. Examples of this abound. Indeed, in the 2016 presidential campaign money seemed to work perversely against the candidates. In the Republican primary, supporters of Jeb Bush spent a total of $160 million dollars to achieve almost no positive result and Jeb Bush dropped out early. In the Democratic primary, Hillary Clinton vastly outspent Bernie Sanders in the early days of the campaign. Sanders caught fire at that point and began to outraise Hillary Clinton, only to see her lock up the Democratic nomination just as his fundraising was surging. And in the general election Hillary Clinton outspent Donald Trump by nearly twice, $768 million to Trump's $398 million, a margin which was magnified by the additional funds provided by political and issue campaign organizations. One can also point to numerous congressional races in which this holds true as well, perhaps none more clearly so than Dave Brat's upset win over Republican House Majority Leader Eric Cantor in Virginia.

These are anecdotal cases and anecdotal cases never prove much. It would be foolish to deny that other things being equal—which they never are—it is helpful for candidates to spend more money than less. It would be strange to imagine that candidates would exert so much effort to raise money if it were not helpful in some way. Large contributions from wealthy donors are especially helpful in the early days of campaigns run by lesser-known candidates. It is always possible, I suppose, that candidates are misled by their own fundraisers about the importance of campaign money, since their consultants and fundraisers are the biggest beneficiaries of money in politics. But one would have to assume that candidates across the board are being hoodwinked by clever staff aides to believe this.

It seems clear—to me at least—that large contributions to congressional candidates which are carefully targeted to achieve a narrow result can be effective. An industry whose fate is controlled by a subcommittee chairman can come together to provide an enormous financial edge to that candidate. This does not guarantee success, of course, but it probably helps. And it does bring with it certain access to the winner after the election.

Contributions to candidates based on ideological preferences seem less clearly financially beneficial to contributors. Individuals, PACs, unions or trade associations which give largely to one political party or the other are less likely to secure measurable financial benefits from their contributions. But there are many other reasons to make large contributions. Perhaps contributors broadly favor a certain view of the role of government in America or perhaps they want to feel they are "doing the right thing." These contributors receive psychological benefits. Perhaps contributors like to be publicly visible at high dollar events with candidates and their fellow big dollar contributors. Or perhaps they are seeking a job, maybe an ambassadorship, in a new administration. There are many rewards to political giving, not all of which are financial.

A final reason advanced for the claim there is too much money in politics is that it compels candidates, and somehow especially incumbents to spend too much time fundraising. It is hard to know what to make of this claim. In reality this concern bothers mostly incumbents, who would understandably like to raise large amounts of money without having to work at it. Who else does this concern? Are we really to suppose that incumbents would be spending all their new found free time legislating wise policies for the nation?

Our current laws regulating campaign fundraising consist of some modest limits on campaign contributions coupled with a general philosophy of transparency. Funds received and expended by political campaigns and party organizations must be reported and are made public. This is not true of outside "issue" groups which raise money to advance issues which just happen to conform precisely to the policy positions of candidates. This so-called "dark money" is the subject of much debate and I see no reason why some or all of this should not fall under the same transparency rules that govern other political fundraising.

The Federal Election Commission (FEC) was created to oversee political campaign fundraising. It would be hard to imagine a more toothless organization. The board of the FEC is comprised of three Republican and three Democratic commissioners, thus guaranteeing a blocking number on any controversial or partisan matter. The information which the FEC receives about candidates' fundraising is not independently derived but is provided by the candidates themselves. Certain types of in-kind expenditures, employed especially by labor unions, are outside the purview of the FEC. And various forms of in-kind advertising on the internet are largely outside the current scope of the FEC as well. Sanctions for violations of campaign finance laws occur long after elections have concluded, making them irrelevant to the outcome of elections. The FEC is a perfect example of self-regulation by the two major political parties, with just about the results one would expect from such an arrangement.

One solution offered to the problem of big money in politics—if indeed it is a problem—is public funding. Public funding proposals usually contain very low dollar limits on political contributions, to be matched by government (i.e., taxpayer) funds. Sometimes these proposals call for only government funding. These proposals are advanced largely by the political left, as are policies to ensure easier access to voting. This apparently reflects some notion that there is an army of Americans who, if only the proper rules could be ordained, are thirsting to endorse big government policies. This may be true, but the opposite seems to me equally likely. If all eligible Americans ever voted at once, who knows what views might be expressed about balanced budgets, illegal immigration and abortion?

At any rate, at the current moment the political left seems to have muted its calls for public financing of elections. The idea remains a staple of the Democratic platform, but the passion seems to have gone out of the cause. Perhaps this is a result of the fact that Barack Obama far outspent his Republican opponents in 2008 and 2012 and Hillary Clinton far outspent Donald Trump in 2016.

Moreover, in 2008 Barack Obama decided not to accept federal matching funds which were available to presidential candidates. If a candidate accepts federal matching funds, he or she must abide by strict limits on private fundraising. Barack Obama had been a long-time supporter of public funding. In 2008, however, he made the calculation—correctly—that he could do better by raising private money without limitations. His arguments were interesting though one would have to say far from persuasive. He argued that the presidential fundraising system was "broken" and in any event his many contributions from small donors established a "parallel public funding system." As it turned out, only 28% of his funds came from small donors, and far less of those occurred in the early days of his campaign.

Barack Obama's decision has killed the notion of public matching funds for presidential campaigns for the foreseeable future. No presidential candidate going forward will agree to this arrangement, and one can expect an increasing amount of money to find its way into presidential campaigns. Neither Hillary Clinton nor Donald Trump accepted federal matching funds in 2016. Nor did Bernie Sanders, who was also a long-time proponent of public financing of elections.

There is evidence that high dollar donors, which once skewed heavily Republican, are increasingly moving toward Democrats. The 1,000 largest individual political donors in the 2016 election cycle, for example, split about 60/ 40 for Republicans. Most wealthy Americans still derive their wealth from business enterprises, but the face of American business is changing; the largest companies in America like Google, Facebook, Amazon and other new age businesses all tilt heavily toward the Democratic Party.

All of the above speaks mainly to the competition between Democrats and Republicans. There is, however, a deeper and more interesting critique of money in politics: the entire system is "rigged." On this view it is not so much that one major party or the other benefits more from money in politics; it is that there are no essential differences between the parties. On this view, whether Republicans or Democrats control the presidency and Congress is seen as more or less irrelevant. What is meaningful is that the wealthy, the elite, the insiders, the political class wins every time regardless of which of the two political parties is temporarily on top. On this view the major political parties have more in common than what separates them.

This view has historically been a staple of the far left. It is a version of the Marxist notion that in capitalist society the "bourgeoisie" controls all the levers of power. This line of criticism has taken many forms since Marx, including many re-definitions of who makes up the oppressed class. No longer is it the proletariat but perhaps racial minorities or women or transgendered individuals. But all are in agreement that a ruling class which expresses its will through the government marginalizes the participation of those who are oppressed.

This is essentially the platform on which Ralph Nader based his critique of American politics. And it also served as Ralph Nader's post-facto justification for why he could not attract more than a miniscule slice of the electorate.

In the 2016 presidential campaign Bernie Sanders espoused a version of this view. But so too did Donald Trump and this view is finding increasing resonance on the political right. Between Bernie Sanders voters and Donald Trump voters, it seems that this view resonated with a healthy portion of the American electorate. Is it true that the insiders, the political class wins every election? To espouse this view one has to overlook some very real differences between the political parties today.

One would also have to advance a more persuasive notion than I have yet seen of what a decent alternative would look like. What would a government which reflected the actual "will of the people" look like? There are various so-called populist governments around the world which purport to represent the will of their people. The current Venezuelan government, for example, speaks as if its every action represents what is good for the vast majority of the Venezuelan people. These claims are wearing a bit thin, however, as the mismatch between the Venezuelan government's words and its performance becomes ever wider.

There are academic studies which purport to demonstrate that the preferences of average citizens are less able to steer the federal government than are the preferences of elites. This would not be surprising, though it would not account for the fact that the wealthy bear an ever greater share of the federal tax burden. Perhaps paying a greater share of the tax burden is simply a cost of business for wealthy Americans who continue to enjoy a growing share of income and wealth.

Academic studies usually conclude that this inequality poses a threat to majority rule in America. These studies often proffer the dark notion that somewhere the American dream has gone off the rails. In this regard it is perhaps worth remembering that the country was not established as a pure majoritarian enterprise in the first place.

It is difficult to know what to predict about today's populist view that the system is "rigged," as there are many cross-currents of public opinion to be reckoned with. Perhaps Republicans will continue to move toward becoming the party which represents American workers and Democrats toward the party of wealthy elites, intellectuals and minority groups. Perhaps Republicans will revert to their historic ideological commitment to conservatism and seek to represent small businesses and the free market generally. In a time of rapid political change longer term trends and realignments are hard to discern—

though a wise person would not bet against an outsized role for money in politics, no matter how it finds expression.

Political Party Conventions

Life is Good at the Del

I was sitting at my desk in my well-appointed lobbyist corner office when a call came in from Ed Meese. I was of course familiar with Mr. Meese, but I had never spoken with him. Why might he be calling me? An interesting adventure was about to begin.

He was calling on behalf of Mr. Larry Lawrence, he said, who had just been nominated by President Clinton to be Ambassador to Switzerland. He had somehow heard that I was knowledgeable about the Senate confirmation process and particularly the Foreign Relations Committee, before which Mr. Lawrence's nomination would come. Mr. Lawrence might need some special assistance, as he put it offhandedly, to gain the support of the Republicans on the Committee. Might I be willing to help?

He explained that although Mr. Lawrence was a Democrat, and a large financial donor to the Democratic Party at that, Mr. Lawrence had been helpful to Governor Reagan's administration in California. Moreover, he noted, Mr. Lawrence had been nominated as Ambassador to Switzerland, a post which traditionally goes to political appointees and often generous donors to the sitting president's party.

I saw no objection to this and agreed to help. The following week Mr. Lawrence and his wife Shelia came by to talk with me. I now understood what Mr. Meese was hinting to me. Larry Lawrence had been a highly successful businessman with many investments in California, not the least of which was the iconic Del Coronado Hotel in San Diego. At this particular juncture, however, if I might use a politically correct term, Mr. Lawrence was just a bit "past his prime." His wife Shelia was quite a striking figure, about thirty years younger than Mr. Lawrence. Well-known to Bill Clinton, she was quite the more dominant figure in this marriage. Each time I attempted to engage Mr. Lawrence, she spoke on his behalf.

My work was cut out for me. Over the course of the next several weeks I contacted a number of Republican Senators and staff assistants on the Foreign Relations Committee. Each time I emphasized the arguments that Ed Meese had offered: Ronald Reagan liked him, he had been helpful to Reagan, and, in any event, what could possibly go wrong in U. S.-Swiss relations?

In due course Mr. Lawrence, who excited no particular partisan or ideological animosity, was voted on favorably by the Foreign Relations Committee and soon after confirmed by the Senate.

Several weeks later I received an invitation to Mr. Lawrence's swearing-in ceremony at the State Department. These occasions, often conducted in the regal eighth floor Ben Franklin room, are always pleasant affairs bringing together family members, friends and new State Department colleagues. I happily accepted.

When I arrived by cab at the C Street entrance to the State Department, I sensed immediately that this would not be a standard, garden-variety swearing-in ceremony. There was valet parking at the State Department! This I have never seen before or since. As I entered the Ben Franklin room I was immediately struck by the décor—enormous eight foot urns of towering flowers dotted the room. The normal spartan refreshments—whose cost must be borne by the nominee and not the government—had been replaced by a full bar and passed canapés. Hollywood had come to the State Department—and it was pretty much fun.

The Lawrences went off to Switzerland and I expected to have no further contact with them. A problem arose for me, however, which was to change this. The Republican Convention was scheduled for San

Diego that year, and good lobbyists that we were, my partner and I planned to attend. The problem was that the Republican National Committee had blocked virtually every hotel room within a 50-mile radius of San Diego, and was metering them out to those who agreed to generously sponsor one or another of their lavish events.

It occurred to me that maybe we had another option, and as the reader has probably guessed by now, I was not above calling in a favor. I called the American embassy in Switzerland and asked to speak with Mr. Lawrence. When I was referred to a staff aide I explained that I was looking to book some rooms at the Del Coronado and wondered if Mr. Lawrence could help. We would of course pay for the rooms, if he could help by making rooms available to us. He said he would check with Mr. Lawrence.

Several days passed. I assumed my request had gotten lost in the maw of the embassy bureaucracy and that my clever gambit would fail. But the following day the phone rang and it was the general manager of the Del Coronado. Mr. Lawrence had asked him to please be helpful to us in any way he could. The general manager asked if their best, large third floor lanai suites overlooking the ocean—which they had held out from the grasp of the Republican National Committee—would do. These rooms, it turned out, comprised nearly 2,000 square feet and had been used by President Reagan for his summit meeting with Mexican President Lopez Portillo. I said I thought they would be just fine.

And so it happened that we presented an enigma to the convention's state delegations housed at the Del Coronado. How had we come by these extraordinary rooms? We entertained a good bit and were studiously vague about the source of our unparalleled access and power.

Though I never spoke again with Mr. Lawrence, his name did arise some years later. He passed away and was buried in Arlington Cemetery on the basis of his service in the U. S. Merchant Marine. But it turned out that, once again to be politically correct, his service record had been somewhat exaggerated. He was not eligible to be buried in Arlington Cemetery. His body was disinterred and removed from Arlington Cemetery, which is by no means an everyday occurrence. Mr. Lawrence, whose company I enjoyed on the several occasions we spoke at length, was larger than life. And larger than death, too, it seems. A most interesting character.

****

Our experience at the Del Coronado prompts a few observations about political party conventions. There is perhaps no purer American spectacle than a party convention. Here are gathered Americans from all across the nation, in full political regalia, virtues and vices on full display.

But do these conventions serve any important function in the political life of America? Historically, the purpose of party conventions has been threefold: to select a presidential and vice presidential nominee; to write a party platform; and to establish the rules for the following presidential nominating process.

It has been a long time since party conventions have actually chosen their presidential and vice presidential candidates. Not since the Republican Convention of 1976 has there been a convention of either major political party in which the presidential nominee was in doubt. Neither Gerald Ford nor Ronald Reagan had enough committed delegates to win the 1976 nomination when the convention began. Gerald Ford, however, prevailed on the first ballot. It has been four decades, or ten presidential election cycles, since even this modest level of drama has occurred.

This of course is the result of changes which were put into practice by both political parties. Democrats in 1968, unhappy that Hubert Humphrey had secured the nomination without participating in a single state primary, put a more or less universal primary process in place. Some of these state events are operated as caucuses rather than primary elections, but the intent is the same—to open the process to all members of the Democratic Party. So too with Republicans, who adopted a primary/caucus process in the rules of their 1972 convention.

The primary process has all but eliminated competition for the nomination at the political conventions. The potential drama of a so-called brokered convention is often hyped by a viewer-hungry media, but in practice there are good reasons why this does not happen. It is of course theoretically possible that a party's nominee will not have secured enough votes in the primary process to win the nomination—but if a candidate who has prevailed in the primaries should not receive his party's nomination, this would represent a slap in the face of the party's primary process and appear to be wholly undemocratic. It would not necessarily be wholly undemocratic, but appearance here is what counts. There is no reason to expect this to change in the future.

The same is true for vice presidential nominees. Conventions do not choose vice presidential nominees; they rubber stamp the choices of their presidential nominees. But even here the role of the convention has receded. Prospective presidential nominees once waited until the convention to name their running mates. This provided at least a small fraction of the drama that was missing from brokered conventions. In 1988, for example, George H. W. Bush waited until the first day of the Republican convention in New Orleans to announce his choice of Indiana Senator Dan Quayle as his running mate. The timing of this was not optimal, as it seemed to catch everyone including the vice presidential nominee himself off guard. Senator Quayle had no time to prepare for the onslaught of media questions he would face and his selection did not turn out to herald the bold generational move that the Bush campaign had predicted.

I was hosting a small fundraising breakfast for Senator Lugar the morning that Dan Quayle would be formally nominated by the 1988 convention. As the senior Senator from Indiana, Senator Lugar had been asked to be one of the people who put Senator Quayle's name into nomination. During our small informal fundraising breakfast, Senator Lugar received a call from the White House. This added a bit of drama to our breakfast. He took the call in an adjoining room. When he returned he told the group that Pakistani President Zia-ul-huq had been killed in the crash of a C-130 aircraft. The White House was calling to ask if Senator Lugar would co-chair the American delegation to the funeral.

Our breakfast participants were all quite pleased to see this small slice of history unfolding before their very eyes—and for only $1,000 a head at that. Senator Lugar told them he had asked the White House for an hour to consider the request. Because he would have to leave for Washington that day, serving on the delegation would conflict with putting Dan Quayle's name into nomination that evening.

As Senator Lugar and I rode down the elevator after our successful breakfast event, I asked him what he intended to do. He paused for a moment, clearly considering the options, and said, "Well, Pakistan seems like a long way to go ... I suppose I should do the speech." He remained in New Orleans and put the name of the junior Senator from Indiana into nomination that evening.

Vice presidential selections have not been named during party conventions since then. Since 1988 the prospective nominees of both parties have named their running mates in advance of the convention. Presidential candidates and their campaign operatives have decided that by naming the vice presidential running mate in advance, they can dominate one additional news cycle.

The second purpose of political conventions is to adopt a party platform. Rarely has there been an exercise which generates more heat and less light than the writing of party platforms. These documents are said to represent the heart of what the party stands for: they are the principles behind which the party stands and the policies which the party's nominee will seek to implement. They are thus fought over issue by issue, line by line. They seem to be especially important to the faction of the party which has lost out in the nominating process. Platform planks are often offered as a consolation prize to the losers in order to unify the party.

In reality party platforms are almost entirely meaningless. Presidential nominees are under no obligation to honor their party platforms and the historical record suggests that if and when nominees are elected, party platforms play little or no role in shaping the policies of the new administration. Party platform writing makes the wrangling at medieval church synods look consequential by comparison.

The third purpose of party conventions is to update party rules. This is not an insignificant activity. Rules changes which move state primaries forward or backward or which punish states for adopting unapproved procedures can affect the following cycle's nominating process. So too did the Democratic Party's rules change significantly in creating so-called super-delegates. Super-delegates were designed to prevent the Democratic Party from nominating a populist candidate outside the influence of Democratic officeholders and other assorted party dignitaries. This rule worked just as intended in 2016, helping Hillary Clinton to secure the Democratic nomination against the upstart candidate Bernie Sanders.

But a four day national convention with thousands of delegates is hardly necessary to amend party rules. Indeed, the process works pretty much as one might suspect; a small number of party officials makes all the relevant changes. This could surely be done by a small gathering of party officials and official state party delegates to the national party. Nothing would be lost, as the current rule-making process is a thoroughly non-democratic exercise anyway.

Political party conventions have become media events pure and simple. They are not designed to conduct serious business at all. They are not designed to select party nominees but to sell them. Often this sales job is referred to as a chance to "introduce" the candidates to the American public. This is more wish than reality, however, as most candidates are already known to the American public. What is really sought is a way to re-introduce their candidates, and in such a manner as to pretend that the various negatives the American public has already observed are no longer present. One can see why a candidate might wish for this unlikely outcome, and one can see why campaign operatives continue to promote this notion. I have seen no persuasive evidence, however, that any candidate of either party has ever been re-introduced in a helpful way.

> **Conventions are said to "introduce" nominees to the American public. What is really meant is to re-introduce them in such a manner as to pretend that the various negatives the American public has already observed are no longer present.**

Indeed, the entire supposition that conventions are successful vehicles in selling their candidates strikes me as somewhat fanciful. The four days of media events which comprise today's conventions are carefully scripted. Unknown speakers who represent small constituencies of the party speak during daytime hours when no one watches them. Better known speakers occupy coveted evening time slots when the audience is somewhat larger. These evening speakers tend to be a retinue of has-beens and never-weres, each of whom is allotted a brief moment to make however many self-serving points they can squeeze into the allotted time. Perhaps the only exception to this is Barack Obama's highly successful keynote speech at the 2004 Democratic convention—which ended up helping him far more than the then-current nominee. One would have to have a pretty low opinion of American voters to think that any of this would hold their interest, much less change their vote.

It is true that after each party convention the candidate gets a "bump" in his or her approval rating. This would not be surprising for any organization whose representatives monopolize four days and nights of national television. Yet when the smoke has cleared and both party conventions are in the rear view mirror, things seem to settle down pretty much as they were before these spectacles were presented. Only when the public begins to focus on the campaign in September is there meaningful movement in the polls. And only when the candidates square off against one another in televised debates do voters begin to gain a real measure of the candidates themselves.

All this said, party conventions are unlikely to disappear any time soon. Neither side will voluntarily give up on conventions if the other side does not. This would be to risk the opposition candidate getting a "bump" in the polls which their candidate does not. There is unlikely to be any unilateral convention disarmament.

Inertia itself seems to drive the process; planning for the 2020 conventions commenced shortly after the end of the 2016 conventions. Party conventions offer many planning and consulting opportunities for political operatives and party leaders throughout the off-years of the political cycle.

Finally, delegates seem to enjoy the conventions. Conventions feed the egos of delegates in an outsized, but very real way. Delegates can tell their friends they have been chosen to take part in a quadrennial American ritual. Delegates get to rub shoulders with party leaders and luminaries. Delegates can see themselves as part of a larger cause of which they are a part.

In recent political cycles television networks have cut back drastically how much of the conventions' proceedings they cover. This is surely a proper market-driven decision. But not until and unless television networks cease live coverage of conventions altogether will there likely be an end to party conventions.

This is all just fine. I have myself enjoyed some of the spectacle and the revelry of political party conventions. No one should be against fun. But no one should confuse what conventions do with serious political work.

IV. AFFAIRS OF STATE

Presidential Nominations and the Senate Confirmation Process

Cuban Reveries

I sat down at the witness table and adjusted my microphone. I was there for my Senate confirmation hearing to serve as Assistant Secretary of State for Legislative affairs. I pondered the road I had traveled to get there.

Many weeks earlier I had been nominated by the president, a process which itself had been extremely time-consuming. Once nominated, I felt reasonably confident about my prospects for Senate confirmation. After all, I had once served as staff director for this committee and my former boss, Senator Lugar, was once again the chairman of the committee. In light of his close friendship with the chairman, ranking member Joe Biden also seemed favorably disposed to me. To be sure, over the previous years I had written some forward-leaning articles on the use of force against Iran (free advice: write less if you ever wish to be confirmed), but I thought I could defend their inherent reasonableness.

My confidence turned out to be misplaced. The State Department official shepherding my Senate confirmation (my sherpa, as the insiders say) called to say "I think you have a big problem. Did you ever write an op ed article on Cuba?" Until that moment my Cuba op ed article in the Washington *Post* had completely slipped my mind. As required, I had gathered together reams of relevant background information about myself, including books and scholarly articles I had written. My op ed article had appeared fifteen years earlier, in 1990, and I had forgotten entirely about it.

Unfortunately for me, the Cuban American National Foundation in Miami had not forgotten about it. This is an organization committed to maintaining economic sanctions against Cuba. In a somewhat heretical piece given my party affiliation, I had observed that economic sanctions had not worked very well in bringing down the Castro government during its first 30 years. I argued that a better course would be to end our sanctions and flood Cuba with Americans and American businesses. This, I argued, might be more effective in bringing about an end to Castro's tyrannical rule. In fact, when I was nominated fifteen years later, in 2005, sanctions had been in effect for 45 years, and I had not changed my mind. Nor had anything changed for the better in Cuba.

The Cuban American National Foundation feared that a fifth columnist might try to subvert what was then the Bush administration's support for continuing sanctions. There was now a "hold" on my nomination and opposition to scheduling a confirmation hearing. It was my bad luck that at that moment there were two Florida Senators on the Foreign Relations Committee, one from each side of the aisle.

My shepherd at State said that I would have to meet with both Senators to try to peel back their holds on my nomination. I met first with Republican Senator Mel Martinez. He allowed that he saw no logical or policy problem with my argument—which both surprised and encouraged me—but that it put him in a very tough spot. The three Cuban-American House members from Florida, Ileana Ros-Lehtinen and the Diaz Balart brothers were emailing him every 15 minutes to oppose my nomination. If I could persuade them of my merits, he would be fine with me.

I met next with Democratic Senator Bill Nelson, who surprisingly said much the same thing. If I could convince the three House members, he would have no problem with my nomination.

I told my State Department guide that I had to meet with the three House members. He said flatly, "No." "Why?" I asked. He explained that it was Department policy not to meet with House members regarding Senate confirmations. It was bad enough, he said, that Senators interposed all sorts of unrelated demands on nominees without getting the House involved as well. After all, the House has no constitutional role in the confirmation process. While I understood the wisdom of this argument, I said that in this case there was really no choice. He finally relented, but I think only because if I were to make it through the Senate confirmation process I would eventually be his boss.

I met with the three House members. I explained that I was deeply opposed to Castro and that the question of sanctions was a tactical one. Happily, a number of my friends had weighed in on my behalf before the meeting. After a rigorous cross-examination, one of the Diaz Balart brothers declared me to be a "patriot" and announced they would ask the Florida Senators to allow my hearing to go forward. Before I had traveled the 20 blocks back to the State Department, both holds on my nomination had been lifted.

So now I sat at the witness table. I participated in a pre-arranged colloquy with one of the Florida Senators. I agreed I would not try to undermine the administration's policy on Cuban sanctions, which was easy enough to promise. I pledged to support the administration's policies, which after all was the chief part of my job description.

Senators alternated questioning across the aisle until at last they reached the most junior member of the minority party. This was an earnest new Senator named Barack Obama. Senator Obama announced that inasmuch as Senator Lugar supported me, he would do so as well. But he had a favor to ask. In a circumstance like this, the proper answer for a nominee (read supplicant) is "Of course, Senator. How can I help?"

I had said in my opening remarks that I once worked for the most junior member of the Committee's minority party. Senator Obama noted that within six years that member was now chairman of the Committee. Could I meet with his staff assistant after the hearing, he asked, and explain how I had made this speedy transition possible? His amusing question lightened the atmosphere of the hearing. But it only partially disguised the fact that he already had in mind a higher office than chairman of a Senate committee.

****

Why would anyone volunteer to go through the Senate confirmation process? Further, given how few nominees are actually rejected by the Senate, why should we have this process at all? Isn't this a lot of work for the nominee, the administration and the Senate, all for very little positive result?

These are all fair questions. We might begin by noting that the confirmation process is established in the Constitution:

> …[the president] shall nominate, and by and with the Advice and Consent of the Senate, shall appoint Ambassadors, other public Ministers and Consuls, Judges of the Supreme Court, and all other Officers of the United States, whose Appointments are not herein otherwise provided for, and which shall be established by Law.

This provision reflected, as do so many others in the Constitution, a thoughtful compromise. Presidents would not be free to fill up the executive branch as they pleased. Nor would Congress be able to choose any executive branch officials (a truly terrible idea). The Constitution created a hybrid, in which Congress could decide which appointments would require Senate confirmation and which it would leave to the sole discretion of the president. Congress is free to draw that line anywhere it chooses. Roughly speaking—in addition to the positions specifically named in the Constitution—Congress has drawn that line at the level of assistant secretaries and above.

The Senate can reject any presidential nominee it pleases, and for any reason at all. It can effectively reject nominees in three ways: by roll call vote; by threatening to reject or to delay a nominee, causing the nominee's name to be withdrawn; or by simply failing to act, as was the case with Obama Supreme Court nominee Merrick Garland. Even so, very few presidential nominees fail to be confirmed. Outright rejection by roll call vote is rarer still.

Only three cabinet nominees, including most recently in 1989 Senator John Tower of Texas, have been rejected by Senate roll call votes in the past hundred years. More are withdrawn, rather than face the prospect of a negative Senate vote, as was the case with former Senator Tom Daschle who was announced as the nominee for the Department of Health and Human Services. It is not unusual that nominations made toward the end of a president's term are not considered, especially if they are political appointees and not career government employees. Even with all these avenues to prevent confirmation, perhaps only two per cent of all nominees fail to be confirmed.

Given this outcome, is this time-consuming process worth all the effort? The framers were well aware that relatively few presidential nominees would be rejected. They saw another and stronger benefit to the confirmation process. Hamilton explains in *Federalist* #76 the real benefit of the confirmation requirement would be displayed by "a powerful, though, in general, a silent operation." The requirement of Senate confirmation would operate in advance, as it were, by leading the president to nominate more fit candidates than he might otherwise do. The president's choices would be motivated less by a spirit of favoritism and personal inclination than by a concern for his own reputation.

This seems to me generally, though not always true. Given some of the people presidents have nominated, one would not gather presidents always harbor a deep concern about their good name. I recall an instance in which I was not sure whether the ambassadorial nominee had a command of the language of the country where he was to serve—and the country was Great Britain.

On the other hand, there is little doubt that a looming Senate confirmation process is often a factor in choosing a nominee. Can the nominee be confirmed? At what political cost? These questions, for example, were a clear consideration in President Obama's decision not to nominate Susan Rice to be Secretary of State during his second term. Could she survive the obvious mistruths she had told about Benghazi on five national television shows? For that matter, why would President Obama want to dredge up the entire Benghazi scandal in an extended Senate debate?

The Senate has an unreviewable power to prevent confirmation of any nominee. To offset this power, the framers added an additional provision to tip the scales back in the president's direction. They gave the president the power "to fill up all Vacancies that may happen during the Recess of the Senate." This is known, not surprisingly, as a recess appointment. As the reader might guess, this power has not been without controversy. For example, President George W. Bush nominated Sam Fox, a wealthy St. Louis philanthropist and Republican donor, to be ambassador to Belgium. This would normally be a relatively straightforward nomination. Among his many contributions to worthy causes, however, Sam Fox had donated $50,000 dollars to the anti-John Kerry group called Swift Boat Veterans for Truth. Unfortunately for Mr. Fox, defeated presidential candidate John Kerry still served as a senior member of the Foreign Relations Committee which considered his nomination. Senator Kerry opposed Mr. Fox's nomination—cloaking his opposition in the charge of "bad judgment"—and rounded up enough Democratic votes to defeat Mr. Fox in committee.

Faced with this impending defeat, President Bush decided to withdraw the nomination. I delivered the withdrawal letter (I had never seen one before) to the committee just minutes before it was scheduled to vote on Mr. Fox's nomination. Senator Kerry seemed quite pleased that he had won the day. Unfortunately, he did not understand this was only the first act in a two act play. President Bush recess-appointed Mr. Fox during the very next Senate recess.

This did not go over well with Mr. Fox's detractors, including Senator Kerry. Majority Leader Reid responded by never allowing the Senate to go out of session long enough for the president to make another recess appointment. During the periods the Senate was out of session, a Senator from the Washington, DC environs would gavel an empty Senate to order and adjourn it within seconds. This ploy served its purpose.

Senator Obama approved of this tactic; President Obama, however, did not. As president he denounced the tactic as a fiction and recess-appointed three nominees to the National Labor Relations Board. This resulted in a law suit which eventually went all the way to the Supreme Court. The Court ruled 9-0 against the president, saying flatly that the president was not the judge of when the Senate is and is not in session. As Justice Breyer concluded, "The Senate is in session when it says it is." This was a reasonable decision, but one which came at the end of a process which has added recess appointments to the long list of government actions which have been thoroughly politicized.

How has the confirmation process worked over time? It would be wrong to romanticize the early years of the republic; it took only until August of 1789 for the Senate to reject one of President Washington's nominees. It would be fair to say, however, that in recent decades the confirmation process has become more politicized than ever before. As long as Senators considered mainly the personal merits of nominees— or even the hope to install their own favorites—the confirmation process functioned reasonably well.

In these days of intense partisanship the process has worked less well. Nominees over the past two or three decades have frequently been subjected to an additional layer of ideological scrutiny. It should not be surprising that nominees will tend to mirror the political philosophy of the president who nominates them. But Senators of the opposition party increasingly scour the background of nominees whom they oppose for ideological reasons. This in turn has resulted in ever more time-consuming due diligence by presidential staff to insure to the fullest extent possible that there are no background issues which might offer a pretext to reject a nominee.

Today even this mask has been peeled off. Senators declare openly they will oppose nominees for purely partisan, ideological reasons. As already mentioned, the traditional "blue slip" process whereby Senators can weigh in on judicial nominees from their states has been widely abused; well-qualified nominees are held up for openly ideological reasons. In the past year a new and even less defensible practice has emerged. Senators now feel free to question the religious views of nominees, a practice which seems to set them squarely against the constitutional provision that "no religious Test shall ever be required as a Qualification to any Office or Public Trust under the United States."

Given these developments Majority Leader Reid was wholly correct to abolish the 60-vote threshold for all nominees except Supreme Court justices. And Majority Leader Mitch McConnell was wholly correct to abolish that requirement for Supreme Court justices as well. The Senate is the judge of its own rules, to be sure. But nothing in the Constitution suggests there is the slightest reason to require a 60-vote supermajority to confirm nominees. Had the framers thought so, it would have been easy enough to include a supermajority requirement, as they did in the very same paragraph of the Constitution which sets forth a 2/3 vote to consent to the ratification of treaties. The 60-vote threshold was simply another precedent which crept into usage to accommodate the never-ending list of "rights" of United States Senators.

> **Nothing in the Constitution suggests there is the slightest reason to require a 60-vote supermajority to confirm nominees. Had the framers thought so, it would have been easy enough to include a supermajority requirement, as they did in the very same paragraph of the Constitution which sets forth a 2/3 vote to consent to the ratification of treaties.**

In further response to the excessive partisanship of our times, the Senate took a positive step in 2011 by streamlining the process for a number of positions subject to Senate confirmation (Senate Resolution 116). To my mind this process could be extended even further, eliminating additional positions from the requirement of Senate confirmation. There are still roughly 1,000 full-time confirmed positions, as well as part-time positions and military and Foreign Service officer promotion lists. This step would in no way reflect a criticism of the framers; to the contrary, the framers vested the authority to decide which positions require confirmation clearly in the Congress.

There are also many additional ways for Senators to delay a vote on presidential nominees. Tactics of delay at the committee level and on the Senate floor are used regularly by Senators. These have been raised to an art form today by minority party Senators who are on a campaign to "resist" the Trump administration. There is no justification for these delaying tactics; once again they exist only to cater to some mythological "rights" Senators are thought to possess.

After I had worked at the State Department for several years I received a request to meet with a delegation from the British House of

Commons. It seemed that the parliament was considering whether Britain should adopt some version of the American confirmation process for British cabinet officers. The State Department handles more high level confirmations than any other cabinet department—in addition to assistant secretaries and above, the Constitution specifically requires all ambassadors to be confirmed. Given that roughly 200 ambassadorial positions rotate every three years or so, the State Department has about 60 ambassadors to confirm each year. For that reason the White House recommended that the delegation speak with me.

I reserved the secretary of state's conference room in the secretary's 7th floor suite for this august delegation. I was not entirely sure what I would tell them about the American system. As fortune had it, however, I was a few minutes late to the meeting. As I rushed into the conference room, I set down on the table a 6-8 inch stack of papers that had been required for my own confirmation. These papers included all the forms required for the president to nominate me and all the forms required by the Senate to confirm me—largely the same information, but of course in different formats.

As I set the papers down I apologized for being late. The leader of the British delegation said with the usual British civility that it was no worry at all. He went on to add that judging from the stack of work I had brought along, I must be very busy. They would try to be brief.

I smiled politely and explained that this was not my current workload, but rather the forms I was required to fill out for my own nomination and confirmation. The delegation blanched. All this for just one nomination?

We had a very pleasant discussion afterward, but the damage had been done in that opening minute. Without intending to, I had killed the notion of a British parliamentary confirmation process in the crib. I have been awaiting calls from a generation of grateful British cabinet officials ever since.

The Federal Bureaucracy: Is there a Deep State?

A Christmas Party

Not long after I arrived at the State Department I received an invitation to a Christmas party. It seemed that one of my deputies held an annual Christmas party for the entire staff of my office and he hoped I might attend. My wife and I accepted.

The several Saturdays before Christmas are always a prime time for parties and my wife and I had also accepted another invitation for the same evening. Our plan was to attend the other event first and then swing by my new deputy's office party.

By the time we approached the office party it was well after nine p.m. and the always difficult parking challenge in suburban Washington was truly daunting. Every parking space was filled for blocks in front of our host's house. We parked a considerable distance away and trudged through the slushy snow toward our host's house.

As we did, we passed by all of the cars that belonged to my newly acquired staff. I noted with interest, perhaps even a hint of trepidation, the bumper stickers that appeared on nearly every car: "Kerry/ Edwards." "Kerry/Edwards." "Kerry/Edwards." Each offered a fading reminder of the presidential election that had taken place a year earlier.

The State Department is comprised of three kinds of employees: a small number of political appointees, Foreign Service officers and career civil servants. My new staff, it seemed, was populated almost entirely by members and advocates of one political party. This was not altogether surprising to me, though the direct visual confirmation of this reality seemed clarifying in the chilly December night air.

****

What, if anything, should we make of this? More generally, what is the composition of the federal work force? Is there a "deep state" which is relatively impervious to the shifting political views of presidential teams which come and go?

The notion of a "deep state" first gained currency in the analysis of developing countries which were not marked by a strong tradition of representative democracy. In such states, of which Pakistan, Egypt and Turkey might serve as examples, unelected bureaucrats wielded considerable power and pursued their own agendas no matter who served as the head of government. These elites often shared a common background; perhaps they were educated at elite universities or perhaps they bonded during long military careers. Heads of government might come and go, but this permanent class was able to frustrate plans of elected leaders in favor of its own agenda. When the deep state served as a check on elected governors, it was in this sense undemocratic, if not anti-democratic altogether. When it served during the rule of military officers or others who had seized power, there was not much democratic about any aspect of the government. In any event, the deep state often brought a degree of professionalism and stability to governments which were not well-versed in exercising power, whether democratically or otherwise.

The notion of a deep state raises important questions for democratic theory. If a president and vice president were elected and not allowed to replace a single member of the executive branch, how democratic would America be? Would elections matter if neither liberal nor conservative elected leaders were able to implement their policies over and against a permanent, entrenched bureaucracy? Here we would have a system which produces stability bordering on sclerosis, and the electorate would be largely unable to do anything about it. One has the feeling occasionally that West European parliamentary governments tend a bit in this direction.

With only a few limitations, the Constitution placed the effective power to hire and fire executive branch employees in the hands of the president. As the federal work force took shape in the first century of the American republic, a spoils system—patronage jobs—emerged. The winning political party replaced executive branch employees with its own people at any and all levels with its own partisans. The new swept out the old, without distinction as to the type of job or its level.

At the end of the nineteenth and beginning of the twentieth century, a new system was established. Progressive reformers put in place a system in which only top level employees turned over with the election of new presidents. This system was based on two notions, one surely correct and one highly debatable. What was surely correct is that lower level employees do not need to reflect the political views of their new chief executive. What difference does it make who sells stamps at the post office?

The second, debatable notion is that political appointees throughout the government would be replaced by professionals with no agenda of their own. These professionals would be experts in government management—what we call today public policy making— and expert training coupled with long experience would ensure capable administration of the government. A professional cadre of experts would assume much of the task of governance and, except at the highest levels of the executive branch, would remove governance from the hands of partisan amateurs.

These experts would differ from partisan amateurs, but also from average Americans. They would be smarter and would understand the requirements of governing better than do average Americans. They would bring professionalism to the task of governance. They would constitute what the German philosopher Hegel called a "universal class."

What was not well understood was the impact of progressive government upon the governors themselves. One can search the literature of civil service reformers, progressive intellectuals and other reformers and find little thought that the permanent bureaucracy would develop a set of interests of its own. Federal bureaucrats would possess more credentials and expertise, and they would bring professionalism, experience and continuity to the American government. All of this was reinforced by the constitutional premise that the executive branch was not to make law-like decisions, but only to execute the law. But there was no thought that permanent bureaucrats might develop a set of interests distinct from the American people as a whole.

Does America have a deep state? Is there an identifiable set of interests of executive branch civil servants which distinguish them from the American people as a whole? This has been much debated. Proponents of the view that there is no deep state in America acknowledge that civil service employees are insulated by legal protections, enjoy *de facto* tenure and operate according to their own guild codes of professional behavior. But they assert that the executive branch is too large, too diverse and too much comprised of middle class employees to qualify as a genuine deep state. The workings of the executive branch are transparent and "fair," and the permanent government is not a deep state but a "meritocratic technocracy, or as former FBI Director James Comey said recently, a "deep culture."

Is this true? We might begin by noting that we are long past the days, if they ever existed, in which the executive branch merely executes laws which Congress has passed, without itself engaging in law-making activities. From 1789 forward it has always been the case that the executive branch can make policy in the interstices of laws passed by Congress. This is only natural. But policy-making, as opposed to policy execution by the executive branch has vastly expanded in two ways. First, as Congress has expanded the reach of its concerns in American society and as Congress has also bundled legislative provisions into ever larger bills, cabinet departments have been given enormous latitude to determine the meaning of laws.

Second, the growth of independent agencies which have been established by successive Congresses has multiplied the ability of executive branch officials to make policy. Independent agencies by design are not only insulated from Congress, but are insulated in significant ways from the president as well. The president retains the ability to nominate the heads of independent agencies, and also to fire them, but the expectation is that presidents will not "interfere" with the supposedly independent and professional decision-making that occurs in these executive branch agencies.

We might note here the latest, quite extraordinary instance of congressional abdication which is the Consumer Financial Protection Bureau (CFPB). Against its long-standing tradition of jealousy to preserve its power of the purse, Congress created the CPFB as an agency with no need to receive congressional appropriations. The CFPB receives its funds from the Federal Reserve, a wholly novel and untested constitutional approach. One can easily imagine the degree of responsiveness to Congress that the CFPB feels under this arrangement. The CFPB operates more or less independently of both the Congress and the president. The 2017 struggle over a successor to the departed director of the CFPB is only the latest instance of CFPB hubris. It has been well said that the CFPB acts without law, outside the law and even against the law.

The permanent government thus enjoys a sufficient scope of action to qualify as a deep state. But are its decisions made in a way that is discernibly, regularly and reliably oriented toward certain ends? To count as a deep state the decisions of the executive bureaucracy must not be random, but must have an observable tendency in a certain direction. It seems the answer is yes.

The executive branch bureaucracy is marked by four interlocking characteristics: (1) a bias toward increasing the size and scope of government across every department and agency, no matter which party controls the White House or Congress; (2) a non-military workforce that skews overwhelmingly (though in different degrees in different departments) toward the liberal end of the political spectrum, and which is ideologically disposed to support this growth; (3) a broad support system of direct government funding for non-government liberal groups which reinforces the bias toward ever larger government; and (4) the development of a privileged set of rules and rewards for executive branch employees including compensation levels, bonuses, guaranteed job security, defined benefit retirement plans, administrative leave, and a different set of rules and standards by which to measure executive branch propriety than are used in the private sector.

This of course is not to say that every federal employee is a partisan, much less a liberal partisan, or that every decision is ideological in nature. They are not. But it is to say that the operation of the entire system is self-reinforcing. No census exists to determine the political affiliation of executive branch employees. But there is considerable anecdotal evidence to support the notion of a deep state marked by the characteristics outlined above. One form of evidence is a series of polls and surveys conducted by academics going back at least to the 1980s. These surveys reveal consistently, and over-whelmingly, a liberal orientation among non-DOD federal employees.

A second form of anecdotal evidence consists in the changing voting patterns of northern Virginia. Four decades ago short-hand conventional wisdom suggested that Democrats tended to live in Washington or suburban Maryland and Republicans tended to live in northern Virginia. Those days are long gone. As the federal government-dependent economy of northern Virginia has grown, the politics of northern Virginia have shifted markedly. Northern Virginia now provides reliably Democratic majorities in Virginia state-wide elections. So too at the presidential level. As the following chart illustrates, northern Virginia has moved increasingly in the Democratic direction:

Northern Virginia Presidential Vote, 1972-2012										
Year	1972	1976	1980	1984	1988	1992	1996	2000	2004	2008	2012
Dem.	33.7%	47.0%	34.0%	38.4%	39.6%	42.4%	46.9%	47.2%	**50.9%**	**58.5%**	**57.2%**
Rep.	**64.8%**	**50.9%**	**54.8%**	**61.2%**	**59.6%**	**43.0%**	**47.1%**	**49.1%**	43.8%	40.5%	41.3%
Other	1.5%	2.1%	11.1%	0.4%	0.8%	14.6%	6.0%	3.7%	0.8%	1.0%	1.5%

Source: Geoffrey Skelley, "Regional Voting Strength in Virginia from 1968 to Today," *Virginia Policy Review*

A third form of anecdotal evidence is federal employee union membership and political contributions. The large federal employee unions such as the National Treasury Employees Union, the American Federation of Government Employees and the National Federation of Federal Employees tilt overwhelmingly to the political left. In the 2016 election cycle, for example, federal union political contributions totaled $16 million, more than $14 million of which went to Democratic candidates. In a recent election cycle 94% of National Treasury Employees Union contributions went to Democrats, and the disparities were stark—for example, $156,000 to Democratic House candidates and $1,000 to Republican House candidates.

Federal unions also spent more than $10 million in declared lobbying fees to advance their agendas. Some agenda items included union-relevant pay and work rule issues, but many were other, loosely related liberal causes. It is not surprising that federal employee unions would favor Democratic candidates, who in turn favor the agendas of federal unions. But this is exactly the point; there is a permanent, interlocking set of interests here, and this is the very definition of a deep state.

One academic commentator who suggests there is no deep state in America makes an interesting, and somewhat revealing point. He argues that it is only presidents who are "insecure" who believe there is a deep state. Presidents who are "confident and secure" about themselves regard executive branch employees as a national treasure. Aside from the pop psychology, this conclusion seems to elide the fact that there is a predictable pattern of which presidents tend to struggle against the deep state and which do not. Republican presidents like Nixon, Reagan and Trump all have struggled with the federal bureaucracy; Democratic presidents, confident and secure about themselves, have not.

This is only natural. Republican presidents tend to favor smaller government (at least in theory) and are less sympathetic to the claims of the federal bureaucracy. Democratic presidents tend to support expansion of the scope of the federal government, higher pay for federal employees, and greater workforce protections and benefits. There is a natural, symbiotic overlap between Democrats and federal employees. If it is the essence of a deep state to provide continuity of orientation to the federal government no matter who is president, here we have a crystal clear example of the deep state.

> **If it is the essence of a deep state to provide continuity of orientation to the federal government no matter who is president, here we have a crystal clear example of the deep state.**

The Federal Budget Process

"You Can't Move a Wastebasket"

I waited in the outer office of Congressman Frank Wolf from Virginia. Once settled at the State Department, my first order of business was to pay a courtesy visit to the chairmen and ranking minority members of the House and Senate Foreign Operations Subcommittees. While the Department had plenty of business to conduct with the foreign affairs authorizing committees—especially the Senate Foreign Relations Committee—it was the appropriations subcommittees that had a stranglehold on our budget. These were people I knew less well than their counterparts on the foreign affairs committees.

I thought I would pay a quick visit to Chairman Wolf. My plan was to introduce myself, mention a few of our biggest concerns and offer to be helpful to him in any way I could. I assumed this would be a friendly 15 minute meeting. That turned out to be a very bad guess.

Chairman Wolf was loaded for bear. He was deeply passionate about the horrendous violence occurring in the Sudan. He looked for ways to confront the government of Sudan and its Janjaweed killers who had unleashed unspeakable atrocities against innocent men, women and children. This I knew in advance.

What I did not know, however, was that to make matters worse a former State Department employee had recently signed on to represent the government of Sudan as a Washington lobbyist. Chairman Wolf demanded to know what I intended to do about this. How was the State

Department going to address this outrage? To say that I was caught by surprise would be the grossest of understatements.

I responded that I was unaware of this matter and that I would look into it. Not good enough, he said. Gathering my wits, I said that I did not know the extent of the State Department's legal ability to limit its former employees' actions but that I would surely have a careful look at it and report back to him promptly.

Still not good enough. Until we fixed this problem, he said, he "would not allow us to move a wastebasket from one room in the State Department to another." I couldn't suppress the hint of a smile at this colorful threat from our financial overseer. This was a mistake.

Chairman wolf was not amused that I was amused. "Put in the video," he instructed a staff member. For the next ten minutes we watched a painful series of interviews with Sudanese women whose families had been killed, whose villages had been uprooted and whose bodies had been violated. It was a truly depressing spectacle.

When the video concluded, Chairman Wolf turned to me and, much to my surprise, asked in a friendly, conversational tone "Now what's on your mind?" I had brought with me a brief list of issues and funding concerns I had hoped to raise with the Chairman. But somehow the moment did not feel quite right. So I said that while I had some issues to discuss, in light of the video we had just seen they seemed somewhat minor and pale by comparison. Why didn't I check into his request about Sudan's lobbyist and raise the other items at our next meeting?

Demonstrating once again the maxim that it is better to be lucky than smart, this proved to be a home run. During the car ride back to the State Department I took a call from Chairman Wolf's staff aide. He said that the chairman had been very impressed by my good judgment and that he looked forward to our next conversation. In the meantime, I should feel free to let him know if he could be helpful.

This was not the last difficulty I would have with Chairman Wolf, whose behavior always seemed to me a bit mercurial. But we were in the game.

****

Having pondered the relationship between Congress and the executive branch from my post at the Foreign Relations Committee, I was now seeing this relationship from a brand new perspective. Although presidents and their cabinet departments have enormous power and considerable discretion in executing the laws, there is one area in which Congress, if it chooses to use it, has unparalleled power. That is power over money or what is often referred to as "the power of the purse." The executive branch cannot create money out of thin air (though the Obama administration made a good start at this with funds provided to health insurers under the Affordable Care Act); it must get the funds it expends from Congress. There is a good reason why the administration's annual funding proposal is called a budget request. It is a request, not a demand.

Although the annual budget process usually begins with an executive branch submission of a budget request, Congress is fully within its rights to ignore that request and begin anew, from the ground up. If it does so, the administration's request is rather unkindly referred to as "dead on arrival." There is no constitutionally privileged position for an administration's annual funding wish list. Congress can accept it, add to it, detract from it, or ignore it altogether. The president of course is free to veto funding legislation that is sent to him—but a veto does not produce any new money for the executive branch. Congress still retains its full power to fund or not to fund whatever it pleases. I discovered that for all the pleasures of my new job, when it came to funding the State Department's annual budget request, I was no more or less than a supplicant.

In recent decades, the annual budget process has taken several new twists—all for the worse. Congress has created a multi-step internal process for providing money to the executive branch. I am not certain that the average member of Congress could provide a coherent account of this process, including the difference between authorizations and appropriations of money. In a nutshell, authorizing committees are supposed to operate as policy committees. They are supposed to craft the outlines of the programs which the administration will execute and to provide an authorization, or permission, to spend monies on these programs. The appropriations committees are then supposed to follow behind and appropriate as much money for the following year as they think wise, in light of many competing budget priorities—but never more than the cap which has been authorized.

No part of this process is inviolable, nor can this process be found anywhere in the Constitution. The Constitution speaks only of appropriations and it states in Article I that no money shall be drawn from the Treasury "but in Consequence of Appropriations made by Law." The authorizing and appropriations committees are wholly the product of congressional rules governing the conduct of congressional business. They have no standing under the Constitution and no force of law. The appropriations committees themselves were formed in the mid-nineteenth century, to divide the work of raising and spending federal money between two separate committees in each house. The authorizing committees came into existence because extraneous policy provisions attached to appropriations bills were slowing the work of the annual appropriations process.

In recent years most of the authorizing committees have fallen into abeyance. Of the twelve annual appropriations bills to fund the government, only a handful enjoy regular annual authorizations— usually those of the Armed Services Committees, the Homeland Security Committees and the legislative appropriation. The House and Senate both have rules that require authorizations prior to appropriations, but these rules are weak and require a point of order to be raised in order to be effective. Congress has found it easier to ignore its own rules than to enforce them. This has resulted in a shift of power to the House and Senate Appropriations Committees, and effectively to their subcommittees which control the funding for their respective executive branch cabinet departments. Hence my role as a supplicant before Chairman Wolf's subcommittee and his Senate counterparts.

In the 1970s Congress added yet another layer of complexity to the annual budget process. It created budget committees in both the House and Senate, creating a third gauntlet for congressional spending decisions. The purpose of the budget committees is to put forward overall budget guidelines for spending and taxing. These committees are also purely creatures of House and Senate rules. Their budgets—if they actually pass them in any given year—are established by concurrent resolution, meaning they have no force of law. They are routinely ignored by both the authorizing and appropriations committees. About the only utility of the budget committees is to establish a process called reconciliation, which allows Congress to pass spending and tax bills with only a simple majority vote in the Senate. However, if as I have already recommended, the Senate were to eliminate its filibuster rule, there would be no real advantage of, or need for, the reconciliation process.

This multi-layered process has always struck me as needlessly complex. There is no reason in principle that Congress requires budget, authorizing and appropriations committees; this is at least one layer too many. This is demonstrated in practice by how often Congress shortcuts this three-layered process.

> **There is no reason in principle that Congress requires budget, authorizing and appropriations committees; this is at least one layer too many. This is demonstrated in practice by how often Congress shortcuts this three layer process.**

A reasonable way to proceed would be to establish a budget super-committee to make broad spending allocations by government function, and then allow separate, substantive committees to decide how to spend (appropriate) the money. This would mean blending the authorization and appropriations committees together. Each committee would then have total control over the authorization of new programs, the creation of policy legislation and annual appropriations within its jurisdiction.

This would of course limit the number of bites at the apple that members of Congress get on annual spending bills. Would this be a dangerous consolidation of power into each of these committees? Not at all. It would be fully consistent with the Constitution's requirement for Congress to appropriate money. It would undo the accretion of layers of obstruction that Congress has set up on its own through its internal system of rules. It seems to me far more likely to produce prudent behavior on the part of the authorizers/appropriators since there will be no committee coming behind them to tidy up their work. And there would also remain in place the requirement to reconcile House and Senate spending decisions as well as a potential presidential veto. The 9/11 Commission recommended the consolidation of the intelligence authorizing committees and their appropriating function, and I see no reason why this should not be extended across the board.

In an even deeper sign of current congressional dysfunction, even the appropriations committees cannot seem to do their work in the way prescribed by Congress' own rules. In lieu of twelve separate appropriation bills, one for each functional area of government, these days Congress often passes only a handful of separate bills. This current fiscal year the House has done better, and even the Senate has surpassed its usual low bar. In lieu of twelve separate bills, the remaining appropriation bills are rolled into one large bill which funds most of the federal government. And even this bill does not pass as a carefully debated bill whose provisions are crafted anew, but as a so-called continuing resolution. The continuing resolution continues funding at the previous year's levels, with whatever alterations upon which Congress can agree. And even this usually requires one or more short-term continuing resolutions before a final bill can be enacted to fund the government for the balance of the fiscal year.

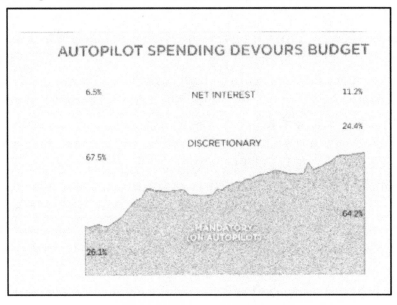

Source: OMB   Heritage.org

Finally, it would be remiss not to mention the creation and rapid growth of so-called mandatory spending or entitlement programs. Programs like Social Security and Medicare are not debated and renewed by Congress each year. The money for these programs is not appropriated at all, and lies outside the scope of the appropriations committees. These programs run on autopilot, funded by permanent authorizations which are shaped by formulas which establish each year's payment levels. There is no act of Congress, for example, that establishes that X dollars will be spent on Social Security in any given year. How much is spent is a straight function of how many people are eligible multiplied by whatever the benefit formula establishes for that year. Of an almost four trillion dollar federal budget, Congress appropriates only about 1.3 trillion dollars, or roughly 1/3; the remainder lies outside the appropriations process altogether. It is no wonder the federal government is deeply in debt.

The obvious, public and repeated inability of Congress to act— even in the area of its principal responsibility to appropriate money for the government—has caused some observers to favor a strong executive. It is not difficult to see why. This is not the place to outline all the reasons why this is not a good solution. Suffice to say that the executive branch is itself far from perfect and substituting its judgment for that of Congress is no guarantee that wise policy will emerge in Washington. This question has arisen over the use of congressional "earmarks," narrowly targeted funds which one or more member of Congress includes in broader legislation. It is true that these provisions are often special pleading, pure and simple, for programs or institutions that will benefit members' states or districts. These are often very insular in nature and do not necessarily pass the smell test for good government. But the alternative is to allow bureaucratic—and presumably disinterested bureaucratic—preferences to rule. I hope the reader will trust me when I say that these are not always the products of universal genius either.

Examples could be multiplied under this head. Perhaps one example—which mercifully was not seen through to conclusion—will serve to make the point. At a time when the government was debating the vexing problem of how to ensure the survivability of our land-based nuclear missiles against a potential Soviet first strike, many options were put forward. One which was supported by the Carter administration was called the "racetrack." Under this plan our land-based missiles would be constantly circulating around the country on rail cars. This was a proposal that would have required all the concrete the nation produces annually just to provide its infrastructure.

Confronted with the impracticality of this approach, Pentagon officials went to work on a substitute plan. One day Pentagon representatives came to brief me on a new, blockbuster solution.

Rather than disperse or continually move our missiles, we would bunch them together to protect them. We would base them on the south side of a mountain range in Wyoming that ran east and west, on the premise that a Soviet first strike would come across the North Pole, the shortest distance. The result of a Soviet attack would be fratricide of its incoming missiles, thus preserving our land-based deterrent.

As I listened to this my head spun. Here was a plan so indescribably implausible and ridiculous I could not believe my ears. What guarantee was there that Soviet submarine-based missiles would also come across the North Pole? And more to the point, what could conceivably survive the chaos and devastation that would be wreaked on that small site? Dr. Strangelove himself could not have authored a more bizarre plan than this. The name of the new proposal was "Densepack," and as far as I could tell its only virtue was that it was aptly named. There are times when a congressional check on the executive is very helpful.

The better course would be for Congress to reform itself and simplify its procedures to allow it to play the role the Constitution's framers intended. There is simply no justification for a budget process that begins by carving out 2/3s of all spending—and the fastest growing portion of federal spending at that—from regular congressional review and oversight. To be sure, it would be both unreasonable and politically impossible to subject social security and Medicare spending to annual spending caps. But to place these expenditures entirely on autopilot makes no sense either. Congress needs to review entitlement spending on a regular basis or we are likely to see a federal budget consumed entirely by these accounts.

Moreover, Congress needs to simplify the way it handles the remaining 1/3 of expenditures, the so-called discretionary accounts. These are not really discretionary expenditures either, as it is not possible that the Congress would fail to fund the defense budget or any other major federal functions. Knowing in advance that it must fund the entirety of the government, Congress should adopt procedures which will allow it to do so in a regular and predictable way.

Government Spending and Government Waste

Signaling

Once again the Egyptian ambassador was on the phone. Sounding desperate, he spilled out his concern that the House Appropriations Committee was threatening to cut Egypt's foreign aid from last year's level. The House appropriators were concerned about Egypt's human rights record and money for the Egyptian military was on the block.

What was the State Department going to do about this, he asked? This was a major crisis. He demanded that the State Department intervene forcefully to fix this problem. I might have been more moved by this if it had not been the sixth such call I had received in the past week from ambassadors worried about their foreign aid levels. I assured the ambassador that we supported the full request for Egypt which we had made, that we opposed any cuts, that we understood the importance of the issue, and that we were working on the problem.

This seemed to hold him at bay, though only for four days as I learned on the following Saturday. My wife and I had gone to a Christmas party with friends in Annapolis and for a few blessed moments I was able to set aside the year-end budget worries that seemed to be consuming every embassy official in Washington.

Somehow the Egyptian ambassador hunted me down in Annapolis. He was beyond mere desperation now, into full panic mode. He said he had learned the House Appropriation Committee had decided to cut Egypt's aid levels. It was almost too late to stop this. Nothing would do but that Secretary of State Condoleezza Rice must call the chairman and talk him out of this. We simply could not allow this to happen.

This was not the first time I had heard all this, so my inclination was not to bother Secretary Rice on a Saturday. This was all the more true as I knew somewhat more than the ambassador and I also thought the chairman might have a point. But something seemed different this time. The ambassador hinted that if deprived of funds, the Egyptian government might have to review how quickly U. S. warships would be able to transit the Suez Canal.

I weighed the alternatives and reluctantly agreed to call Secretary Rice. Unfortunately she was attending a conference in Paris where it was already early in the evening. The reader can guess how pleased she was to hear from me at that point. Nevertheless, she was—as always—unfailingly polite and diligent and agreed to call the chairman. If traffic in the Suez Canal were slowed, it would not be our fault.

****

It is interesting to note that in all my conversations with the Egyptian ambassador, the question of precisely how much money the Egyptian military needed to accomplish its goals never arose. Not once. Not once were the actual merits of the military assistance program ever discussed. The conversations were never about the substance of the matter, but about its optics. How would a cut in military assistance be taken by the Egyptian government?

Indeed, this question never arose on the American side either. The threatened cut by the appropriators was not based on a careful analysis of the requirements of the Egyptian military; it was intended to send a message. It too was all about optics. A cut in U. S. aid is meant to signal displeasure with the recipient government. This is what is behind a recent proposed reduction in foreign assistance to Pakistan; American officials are not pleased by Pakistan's unwillingness to combat terrorism forcefully along the Pakistani-Afghan border.

This process works the other way as well. An increase in foreign assistance is meant to convey American satisfaction with, or support for, a recipient government. I have sat around the table when the regional assistant secretaries at the State Department outline their wish list for the coming year. Do we like the recipient country more or less this year? Are they up or down? Are they generally supportive of American views or not?

There is another angle as well. How much military aid Egypt receives also reflects on the Egyptian ambassador. The ambassador would not like to report to Cairo that Egypt's aid is being cut on his watch. How much aid a country receives is a clear marker of how well a foreign ambassador is doing in Washington.

All of this can be captured under the rubric of "signaling." We are signaling through changes in our programs our pleasure or displeasure with recipient nations. Not every expenditure of U. S. tax dollars is determined this way; there are cases where funds provided reflect a thoughtful consideration of what is actually needed. But the reader would be surprised by how many funding decisions are based on the practice of signaling.

The State Department has nearly 75,000 American and foreign national employees. I often mused to myself that if I could cut 20% of the foreign aid budget without telling anyone, there were not 20 employees who would ever know it happened. This is especially true for countries like Egypt where there are billions of unspent dollars in the pipeline from previous years' appropriations. Perhaps we will learn something about the truth of this in the coming year, when foreign assistance will be significantly reduced for the first time in many years.

Lest the reader conclude that I have a special problem with American foreign assistance programs, I hasten to say that I do not. The issue of signaling which I have just described runs straight across the expenditure of funds in virtually every sector of the federal budget.

Signaling operates every bit as much for domestic programs as it does for foreign aid. And after all, foreign aid makes up only a very small share—roughly one per cent—of the annual federal budget.

Consider, for example, the food stamp program or SNAP—the Supplemental Nutrition Assistance Program. How does the debate over SNAP funding unfold in the Congress? Is it based on careful reflection about how much funding is required? About the proper level of incentives for persons funded under the program? About what are reasonable qualifications for eligibility under this program? About how to address issue of rampant fraud? One might like to think so.

But the reality is far different. Propose a minor cut in a program like SNAP with as much statistical support as can be garnered. Stand back and wait for the outrage. "You do not care about poor people." "How can you be so heartless?" "Children will die as a result of this." Every proposed cut in a program, no matter how minor, sends a signal; it says that you do not care about the recipients of that program. This is no different than what occurs in the realm of foreign aid. And by the way, I suppose there is a lesson here: since you will produce the same level of outrage no matter how minor a proposed cut, you might as well propose a large cut and save some real money.

This situation is true with regard to military spending as well. The customary call for additional military spending is rarely based on a detailed analysis of precisely how much funding the military requires. It is based on whether one supports the military or not. "How can you leave the country defenseless?" "You do not care about the troops." "You want to disarm America."

This kind of signaling takes place with regard to defense, education, health, agriculture, social programs and every other department of the government. The level of argumentation on behalf of government programs has the same characteristics everywhere. A senior citizen in tennis shoes who wants the government to "keep your hands off my social security" or a column by economist Paul

Krugman—these amount to pretty much the same kind of argumentation. If one were to conclude that some taxpayer money might be wasted in this process, one might well be correct.

There is a much deeper lesson here. Consider a program like SNAP. It would not really matter to the dynamic of signaling whether the program is funded at $70 billion, as it is now, or $60 billion or $80 billion. A proposed cut to a program like this will generate outrage at whatever level the program is funded. And here is the open secret of all government funding: there is no "correct" level at which programs should be funded. There is no correct level where every reasonable person would agree that less funding would be heartless and more funding would be wasteful. Such a holy grail does not exist. Every single government program is a rough hewn compromise hammered out between advocates who want to spend more and critics who want to spend less. Here we have reached the outer limits of the science of government. Government is, and always will be, a battle between competing priorities. This might seem obvious if one steps back from it, however much a social scientist might wish to squeeze the arbitrariness out of governance.

> **Here we have reached the outer limits of the science of government. Government is, and will always be, a battle between competing priorities.**

This provokes a comment about the concept of zero-based budgeting, a concept from do-gooders which arises from time to time. Who could object in principle to the underlying notion? Zero-based budgeting is budgeting which is not based on past years' budgets; it is a budget which is constructed from the ground up, based on a clear-eyed assessment of what is needed in the current year. In short, zero-based budgeting aims to create budgets which are rational.

During his 2008 presidential campaign Barack Obama said that his administration would rely on zero-based budgeting. He would not rely on the arbitrary numbers of the previous year's budget but would create a budget based on facts and genuine requirements. What he really seemed to mean was that he intended to cut agriculture programs which he did not much like.

How did this work out? It is not clear that Obama's proposal was serious or whether it was merely a campaign talking point to explain how he would balance the budget, especially given his many proposed new programs. Predictably, zero-based budgeting died a quiet death before the words of his inaugural address had reached the far end of the Washington mall. What are the odds that a ground-up examination of government programs would have resulted in less government spending? We all know the answer to that question.

There is no more salvation to be found in zero-based budgeting than in the hoary trope of cutting "waste, fraud and abuse." There is certainly genuine waste in all departments of government. If anyone doubts this, I can offer a first-hand story of abuse of the SNAP program from my latest visit to my nearby grocery store. There is certainly every good reason to seek out waste, fraud and abuse and to prosecute those who take part in it. But to think this will ever result in a significant alteration in the federal budget, or even save very much money, is a mistake. It has become almost an inside joke in Washington that cutting waste, fraud and abuse will fix the federal budget.

Zero-based budgeting—in addition to being impractical—aims to base spending decisions on a rational basis which is beyond where reason can legitimately take us. It is somewhat akin to running a legal system based on the notion that decisions by wise rulers should establish the guilt or innocence of defendants. We do not favor this. We operate our legal system entirely differently; it is not based on abstract reason but upon the tussle of advocacy. So too with government budgeting.

We should surely not fund a program this year just because it was funded last year. This results in programs like the legendary mohair program, which was funded for decades beyond the time when it made the slightest bit of sense. Yes, cut every bit of waste, fraud and abuse. But know in the end that the great bulk of government spending can never be shaped purely by reason, whether by the pseudo-science of zero-based budgeting or the scalpel of cutting waste, fraud and abuse. It will invariably result from a clash between advocates with differing priorities. And the battle lines will inevitably be drawn in one very clear place: how much did we spend last year, and should we spend more or less this year?

Perhaps it would be fitting to say a few additional words about the federal budget. We are now well into the seventh year of an economic expansion and the federal deficit for FY2018 currently stands at $668 billion. This is $82 billion more than the previous year's deficit of $586 billion. One might recall candidate Obama's assertion that the final George Bush budget deficit of roughly $480 billion was "unpatriotic." As a nation we seem to have moved from the notion of regularly balanced budgets, to the Keynesian notion of running deficits during economic contractions; to running deficits all the time, in good years and bad. Projections show that we are on course to add a total of roughly $10 trillion dollars to the federal debt over the next decade.

Why is this? We could analyze the budget in detail and learn (as we have shown above) that most new spending growth occurs in so-called entitlement programs like Social security, Medicare and Medicaid. Defense spending which in the 1950s and early 1960s amounted to roughly half of the federal budget now stands at 16%. Social Security, Medicare and Medicaid now account for half of all government spending. Without changes in their trajectory, these programs threaten to crowd out all other government programs.

We could also analyze the reasons why entitlement spending continues to grow at a rapid rate. The nation is aging. Priorities have changed. And entitlement programs have an in-built tendency to expand their coverage over time, both in terms of increased benefits and in terms of increased numbers of people covered by them.

At bottom, however, both annual deficits and the overall federal debt result from the fact that Americans seem to want big government but do not want to pay for it. Polls suggest that while Americans complain about big government generally they are reluctant to cut any specific programs, with the exception of foreign aid and some types of welfare. And polls make equally clear that Americans do not want their taxes raised.

How to deal with this problem? Republicans by and large want to decrease the tax burden on Americans. Democrats by and large want to increase spending. What is to be done? Critics of today's Congress lament the inability of the political parties to work together. Why can't the two parties work together to adopt a balanced package of spending cuts and tax increases? But the fact is that Congress has already found a bipartisan way to work together. If spending cannot be cut and taxes cannot be raised, there is one additional option: borrow the money.

> **Congress has already found a bipartisan way to work together. If spending cannot be cut and taxes cannot be raised, there is one additional option: borrow the money.**

This agreement is not written down and it is not the result of a formal pact, but it is very real nevertheless. Those who seek bipartisanship should be careful what they wish for. Bipartisanship can result in positive legislative accomplishments, but it can just as easily result in outcomes which are bad for the country. There is no reason that simply because both political parties agree on something, it has to be a good idea. Indeed, there are times in which both parties can agree on truly bad legislation. This is every bit as true as it is that simply because Congress and the president agree on a course of action, that course is either wise or constitutional. One might think again of the legislative veto, a favorite of both Congress and presidents, which the Supreme Court found to be unconstitutional in 1983.

We have a *de facto* bipartisan agreement on how to handle the imbalance between spending and taxing. It is a relatively painless solution, at least as long as interest rates remain low. It gives the American people both lower taxes and higher spending. We borrow the money and lay off the interest payments on future generations. Republicans can continue to operate on the old maxim of Senator Russell Long of Louisiana: "Don't tax you, don't tax me, tax the man behind the tree." And Democrats can continue to operate on the plane of moral outrage, asserting that any cut in social programs is a death sentence for their recipients.

There is no end in sight to this informal bipartisan agreement. Republicans remain committed to cutting taxes and Democrats remain committed to increasing spending. Indeed, the progressive wing of the Democratic Party seems to be moving ever more strongly in the direction of expanding government programs. And Donald Trump and a growing number of Republicans seem unwilling to take the political heat over proposing cuts in federal entitlement programs. Republicans seem to be increasingly comfortable with debt. Donald Trump has a long familiarity with debt, but this is a new development for congressional Republicans. Good politics all, but not necessarily wise policy.

The national love affair with debt can no doubt continue for some years to come. It is difficult to say when the massive $20 trillion debt will grow to the point where it becomes a genuine problem. It has already outlived many earlier predictions of disaster. But there will come a point at which this debt will leave policy makers with no good options. For this they will have our current policy makers, who will be long gone by then, to thank.

The Privileged Lives of Washington Officials

In the Bubble

As I pulled up to the gate at the German ambassador's residence on Foxhall Road, I could tell something was different. The normal ease of parking in the courtyard had given way to a rather stiff formality. The guard was just not sure anyone could park there. After much back and forth I prevailed on the guard, parked in the courtyard and headed inside to the pre-dinner reception.

What was different, I learned, was the imminent arrival of the vice president and all the security that such a visit entails. Sure enough, shortly afterward Vice President Biden arrived with a phalanx of secret service members.

He worked his way around the reception, greeting each small group of guests with his usual ease and familiarity. When he came to our group he greeted former Senator Nunn effusively. He said a warm hello to then-Senator Lautenberg. When he turned in my direction he brightened and said a bit too loudly "Heeeey, man, how are you?"

I said "I'm fine, Mr. Vice President." I went on to say that this was the first time I had occasion to call him Mr. Vice President. I added that I still thought of him from his Foreign Relations Committee days when he was "Mr. Chairman." "Yeah," he said, "that was a great gig, wasn't it?"

Perhaps emboldened by his easy manner, I then trod where perhaps I should not have. "Yes," I said, "back then you had a real job."

Audible breaths were drawn in around our little circle and a moment of uneasy silence ensued. Joe Biden laughed heartily, acknowledging that those were good days, and set everyone at ease.

Undeterred, I asked the vice president "Do you know why I said that?" "Why," he asked? "Because I'm retired and I say pretty much what I please these days." Vice President Biden laughed again. To the general amusement of the group, he said in an uncharacteristically understated way "So do I."

And indeed he does. And it is impossible not to appreciate the pure humanity of the man.

****

I have found that a carefully chosen irreverence serves well when speaking with important people. It is frequently said that high level officials live in a "bubble" and I think that is true.

It is not that high level officials are unaware of the wider world and the hopes and fears of ordinary mortals, though at times this can be true as well. Officials watch television, listen to the radio, and meet with an extraordinary range of people. They are bombarded with news summaries, intelligence briefings and numerous other sources of information throughout their day. They employ staff members who help to craft statements designed to resonate with ordinary people. There is no shortage of information which comes before high-ranking officials each and every day.

But even this information, as vast and daunting as it can be, often comes from within a bubble itself. For Washington officials there is always the looming horizon of what we might call, with emphasis, Conventional Wisdom. Washington is awash in conventional wisdom. It is not just that there is a common reservoir of facts; there is also a common reservoir of meanings and interpretations and a common reservoir of processes, procedures and things which are just "not done" by people in the know.

There is an echo chamber in Washington which, if officials could hear it, would be absolutely deafening. If one were to read the Washington *Post*, the New York *Times* and listen to the news on one of the three traditional major networks, one might assume one had read and heard all the news that is worth consuming. This is far from the case. One would miss half or more of what is occurring in the country and worse yet, one would have little guidance about how to interpret what one is hearing.

One sees this phenomenon clearly with Donald Trump. Here is a president who doesn't play by the rules of conventional wisdom. No effort has been spared to pound him into submission, but to date all efforts seem to have failed. Conventional wisdom therefore assumes that he does not understand what he is doing, indeed, that he might be mentally unbalanced. So deep does Washington conventional wisdom run that anyone who defies it is considered a bit crazy.

One might think that at least the intelligence briefings which high-level officials receive would be a corrective to conventional wisdom. But these tend to offer up their own version of the same. It is rare that the intelligence community offers a view which is novel or outside the box. To the contrary, their assessments tend to be watered down in an effort to achieve consensus. In this way they offer up views which are conventional or "safe," reinforcing the ethos that in Washington one must go along to get along.

The nature of the bubble in which the Washington political world lives is nicely illustrated in a little story which I offer here in an admission against interest. I was sitting in the anteroom of the office of the Secretary of Defense, waiting to meet with his chief of staff. There was quite a stir on the other end of the room, and a number of young female military officers were abuzz. They were talking with a gentleman and taking pictures of themselves with him.

One of the young women walked by me and I asked who was the man who had engaged their attention. She looked at me incredulously.

"You don't know? That's Michael Bolton." Further confirming my ignorance I said "Who's he?" Now she was certain that I had just dropped in from another planet. She explained that he was a world famous singer.

A few minutes later the chief of staff came by and said he would be with me in a few minutes. He stopped for a second and asked "Who's that?" I said "You don't know? That's Michael Bolton." "Who's he?" my friend responded. After I patiently and condescendingly explained, he disappeared into his office.

A few minutes later the Secretary of Defense entered. The Secretary said "Hi, Jeff, are you being helped?" I told him I was waiting to see his chief of staff. He turned to the far end of the room and asked "Who's that?" I said "You don't know? That's Michael Bolton." "Who's he?" he asked. I explained again, which turned out to be useful since Michael Bolton was on the Secretary's schedule for a five minute meeting to thank him for entertaining American troops.

> **Washington officials regularly receive a degree of deference not accorded to other human beings.**

Here we have in a nutshell the very powerful, but very insular world of Washington. But there are other and deeper manifestations of the bubble in which Washington officials live. Officials regularly receive a degree of deference not accorded to other human beings.

They are addressed as "Mr. President" or "Mr. Vice President" or "Madame Secretary" or "Mr. Chief Justice" or "Senator." They are known as "honorable." When they enter a room, people usually stand, and often they exit a room before anyone else. Even in this egalitarian republic which broke sharply with European traditions of nobility, these simple titles convey a sense of social hierarchy. These officials are often surrounded by physical security which further reinforces the sense of social distance.

Washington notables are also surrounded by staff members who share their points of view. They are accustomed to hearing praise from their staff for what are often quite pedestrian comments or observations. They are accustomed to their staff putting the best possible construction even on statements which are not very intelligent. This is quite different from what an ordinary mortal hears from his spouse or friends.

I recall an occasion when the vice president's staff was in full agreement with one another that the vice president was on the wrong side of a certain issue. They were determined to address him about this and to offer their unified criticism. Before they went in to see him they all took an oath—no backsliding, only the unvarnished truth. The door swung open, the vice president entered, and he asked "How's it going? How are we doing?" The response? "Just fine, Mr. vice president." "Just great." "Couldn't be better."

It is very easy to become accustomed to this and perhaps even to conclude that it is simple justice. One could speculate—though this is dangerous territory—that perhaps this is the reason sexual affairs seem so common. No doubt they occur in part, just because they can. Henry Kissinger famously said that power is an aphrodisiac. But perhaps too affairs bring with them a more normal, human form of connection.

At its worst, the bubble in which Washington officials are encased can lead to excesses and differential treatment far beyond any justification. After all, important people have serious work to do. They cannot be bothered with ordinary niceties that constrain the rest of us. "Why, we Senators are doing the nation's business. We cannot be expected to undertake the chores of daily life." "I am an important cabinet secretary. Of course I cannot be bothered to fly on a commercial aircraft." "I am voting on important matters. I cannot be expected to live like regular people. I need access to a dedicated doctor, a dedicated pharmacy and a dedicated barber." Or my personal favorite, dating back to the gasoline shortages of the 1970s. A subcabinet defense official explained why he broke every regulation propounded by his own administration about hoarding gasoline. "Well, I have an important job. I need it."

Still and all, it is my sense that there is always a lingering feeling on the part of American officials that there is something artificial and not entirely deserved about their treatment. Perhaps this is a vestige of the republican virtue of America's founding. This seems like an indicator of political health which one hopes will never disappear. For this reason, a bit of gentle irreverence toward public officials seems fair enough and is often appreciated by people within the Washington bubble. It somehow speaks to what is missing from their lives.

On one occasion my wife and I were enjoying breakfast at the Waldorf Astoria in New York. My wife said to me, "Isn't that the vice president?" "The vice president of what?" I asked. "Of the United States," she responded. I turned to look and indeed it was. "Does he know you," she asked? "Sure, why?" "Because he's headed this way." A moment later we were greeted by his signature "Heeey, man." Other guests looked up in surprise.

After brief introductions, I asked the vice president what he was doing in New York. "Are you up here at the United Nations giving away nuclear weapons to the Iranians?" He laughed and explained that he had come up for a speech his wife gave at Columbia and they had stayed the night to take in a play.

Not everyone is as open to this as Joe Biden. This might not have been the reaction of his successor as chairman of the Senate Foreign Relations Committee, a man often wrong but never in doubt. Perhaps those who have the hardest time breaking out of the bubble are the ones who need it most. Indeed, I would offer a simple test as a sure marker of the openness and liberality of a government: is it permitted to joke about, make fun of, or otherwise suggest the mere mortality of government officials?

Spouses in Washington

What Do You Mean We, Kemo Sabe?

Like most married men, I am in trouble at home from time to time. But never more so than on one ill-fated occasion soon after I joined the State Department.

My wife and I had moved in from the Virginia suburbs to a wonderful apartment on 24th and Pennsylvania Avenue. The apartment had been recommended by Randy Tobias, the then-Director of Foreign Assistance. Fortunately Randy was better at recommending apartments than dealing with the press. When he was later queried about his alleged dalliance with prostitutes, he said he could not remember any of their names. After all, he said, does anyone remember the name of his pizza delivery man? Randy was a good guide to Washington apartments, but not a public relations wizard.

The two balconies of our spacious apartment looked out on the Washington Monument and Georgetown. I could walk to work at the State Department and my wife was a short Metro ride from her volunteer work at the National Archives. We could walk downtown, to Georgetown and to the Kennedy Center. For the first time in our married lives, we joked, we were actually living like adults.

At the same time we were only about seven blocks from the White House and the worries inspired by 9/11 were not that far distant. To anyone preternaturally disposed to worry, a concern about a follow-on attack or a chemical or biological event was only natural. My ever-prepared wife had purchased potassium iodide pills to combat the danger of radiation to one's thyroid. A diffuse concern about terrorism is still present today among many Washingtonians and New Yorkers, but at that time it was palpable.

One evening my wife asked me a very fair and straight up question. Shouldn't we develop a plan for what to do in the event of another terrorist attack on Washington? In five of the worst chosen words of my life, which I regretted the moment they escaped my lips, I said "What do you mean we?" The surprise, the shock, the sense of betrayal rolled over her in waves. "Oh," she said, as she gathered that some plan was in place that involved me but not her. "Oh...."

I will say no more about this, other than that the potential threat of nuclear destruction has generated many sub-fields of activity for government planners and schemers. And it would be surprising if some thought had not been given to what is euphemistically called "continuity of government."

I knew at once I had made a mistake. And it was all the more foolish because I knew that the best laid plans were unlikely to survive for more than five minutes in a crisis. Are we really to suppose that senior government officials would desert their spouses and children en masse? Are we really to suppose that the deepest springs of human nature would cease to operate in a crisis? To the contrary, it has always seemed to me they would operate even more forcefully.

****

All of which brings me to say that Washington can be a very cruel place for spouses. This is not true for the president and his/ her spouse or for "power couples" like Senate Majority Leader Mitch McConnell and Transportation Secretary Elaine Chou. But the spouses of most Washington officials do not have an easy path. High level Washington officials work long and crazy hours, receive accolades all day long, and are in high demand at Washington social events. Spouses have no independent standing in this world and the equality of marriage is obliterated as spouses trail along either little noticed or ignored altogether.

> ## Washington can be a very cruel place for spouses.

This has been recognized by military and political groups, which have established clubs and other social outreach for spouses. The military services, as one might expect, are the best at this. Each service sponsors spouses' clubs which feature a variety of events and talks. The purpose is to create a sense of extended family for spouses of military officers.

Similar groups exist for the spouses of members of Congress. Both Republicans and Democrats offer events for the spouses of members of Congress. Some are bipartisan, while others are organized along partisan lines. There are also informal organizations which offer programs for the spouses of foreign diplomats who are serving in Washington. They experience many of the same difficulties which spouses of American diplomats often face when their spouses are posted abroad.

Likewise, on Congressional delegation trips abroad (CODELS) regular efforts are made to schedule programs for spouses of members of Congress. These schedules—usually comprised of shopping and museums—are created to fill the time when their government spouses are meeting with prime ministers and other foreign dignitaries.

This is more interesting today as women secure more and more leadership roles. What was once, for example, a Senate wives club is now a Senate spouses club. Husbands of members of Congress and diplomats participate regularly in the events of spouses' clubs and join in on spouses' schedules during congressional delegation trips.

Still and all, as valuable as these activities can be, they do not fill up the life of a spouse. Some spouses of members of Congress choose to remain behind in their state or district, especially if children are involved. It is no doubt difficult being apart so much, even though it might strike a casual observer that Congress is more often out of session than in session. But members of Congress whose families accompany them to Washington also have significant problems. Members of Congress often work long hours when Congress is in session, leaving home early in the morning and returning late in the evening. Houses are far more expensive in Washington than in the average member's state or district, and affordable housing is most likely located far outside of Washington. Children need to be transferred to new schools, necessitating either moving to desirable school districts or incurring the cost of private school. Remaining home in the district is not ideal, but it is certainly understandable.

For all these reasons Washington can be a tough place for a spouse. Perhaps nowhere is this more poignantly observed than at the venerable Washington dinner party. Here spouses are regularly introduced as "the wife of X" or "the husband of Y," suggesting their entire being is derivative. Here you are seated, usually at a table of eight, with your spouse across the table wedged between, say, an ambassador on one side and a government official on the other.

It happened more than once that a dinner companion would turn to my wife and ask the overarching, ubiquitous, all-determining Washington question: what do you do? If the answer did not include a fancy title or—horror of horrors—that she was raising children, the dinner companion would spin in his chair in search of more interesting quarry on his other side. These were never good evenings and gradually we attended fewer and fewer of these dinners.

This behavior always struck me as a bit of a shame, because there is much to be learned when you ask a dinner companion about his or her children. How do you balance the roles of work and children in your family? How did you pick the schools your children attend? What philosophies guide your child-raising? What do you want your children to become one day? These are all questions interesting in and of themselves and they often stimulate deeper conversation. But I guess they don't provide much to include in a cable sent back to an ambassador's home government.

Asking about children proved curiously interesting at a dinner I attended one evening in New York. I was seated next to a North Korean diplomat who represented his country at the United Nations. Knowing very little about North Korea—who knows much?—I looked forward to learning something new. I asked question after question about North Korea, about its government, about its government's policies and about the work of my dinner companion in New York. Nothing availed. He was guarded and non-communicative. He would say little or nothing in response to every topic I raised. This was a dead end conversation if ever there were one.

I tried a new tack. Did he have children? At this he brightened a bit, but still did not let down his guard. Yes, he said, he had two children, a boy and a girl. Unsurprisingly, they were both at home in North Korea, one of several ways the North Korean government employs to minimize the risk of diplomatic defections. What did his children do? How often did he get to see them? Gradually he began to let down his guard and to speak more openly. Suddenly he blurted out that he had learned his daughter had been arrested by his own government. He had not spoken with her, but he had learned this from a colleague.

He became visibly distraught. No, he said, he did not know why she had been arrested. He was uncertain where she was, perhaps a prison camp outside of Pyongyang. Did he hope to see her again one day? Yes, of course, but he didn't know if this would be possible.

Just as suddenly, he caught himself and regained his composure. Then he uttered the strangest comment of the evening. He was quite proud, he said, that he had been able to learn of his daughter's arrest. His high-level connections at home were good enough to provide him with this valuable knowledge. Not everyone in the North Korean government had that kind of high-level connection; not just anyone could learn such a thing.

I was not disappointed that evening. I learned a great deal at this dinner, more than I could have guessed. We all know that North Korea—the Hermit Kingdom—is a tyranny of the most complete and thoroughgoing kind likely to be possible on this earth. But to witness the psychological contortions and disfiguring of normal human impulses is really quite something to behold. And to see this on the part of an apparently well-trusted, high level North Korean official was more astonishing yet.

Not every dinner companion provides such an interesting, if deeply depressing, experience. Most do not and the frequent experiences of my wife are far more often the rule than the exception. There can occasionally be minor compensations. At an embassy dinner my wife was seated next to a well-known Washington reporter. Pretending not to know of her, my wife asked her what she did for a living. Perfect.

Despite all its purported glamour, Washington is not a very hospitable place for spouses. To the spouse of any newly minted Washington official, Dante's counsel is sound: *Lasciate ogni speranza, voi ch'entrate.*

V. EVIL LOBBYISTS

Lobbying for Corporations

"What's New?"

Washington lobbyists are often portrayed as Svengali-like, operating behind the scenes and pulling strings as they practice their dark arts. The truth is usually far more mundane.

We were busily engaged at the State Department trying to advance the U. S.-India Civil Nuclear Agreement through the Congress. We were everywhere on Capitol Hill seeking support for what was arguably one of the major foreign policy accomplishments of George W. Bush's second term. Secretary Rice testified; senior State Department and other administration officials conducted one-on-one meetings with key legislators; our staff met regularly with the staffs of the committees of jurisdiction; and whenever experts in the arcana of nuclear non-proliferation policy were needed we produced them.

All of this effort was theoretically being assisted by a team of crack Washington lobbyists who represented major American corporations which supported the agreement. This team would convene every other week with its corporate sponsors to review the bidding. Had additional members of Congress agreed to support the agreement? Had we lost any members? Which members were shaky? What work needed to be done?

I could always tell when a lobbyist team meeting was approaching. I would receive a series of phone calls from lobbying team members. A former Senator who had gone on to greener pastures was one of dozens of lobbyists representing the business community—and paid very handsomely for his work by the way. His cheerful voice would come on the line. "What's new?" he would unfailingly ask. Then he would ask, always politely and with a sense of discretion, if I would share with him our current understanding of the legislative situation. When was the next key meeting in the House? What were the prospects for committee passage? Which members did we think could use additional persuasion?

Over the following days I would receive similar calls from every lobbyist with whom I was personally acquainted. I have to confess I was often tempted to offer wildly conflicting information to the different team members just to see what happened. I didn't, but I did withhold some nuggets from those of whom I was less fond.

Why all these calls? Each was in preparation for the upcoming lobbyist team meeting. The goal of this meeting was ostensibly to report on the team's work. One way to do this, of course, would be to expend some shoe leather actually meeting with members of Congress and their staffs. And some of this did happen. But it was far easier to ask me where things stood and then report this information with both solemnity and a hint of intrigue to the gathered corporate assembly. Needless to say, this was not advancing the ball very far toward the goal of passing the U. S.-India Civil nuclear Agreement. But it did serve, as we used to say, to make the purveyors of this information look "big" in front of their corporate clients. Having once been a lobbyist myself, I was not unfamiliar with this process.

****

Much of what passes for lobbying in Washington consists of passing around bits of information, always hoping to be the most current on what is happening in Washington. This is a function not unlike that of the press. Almost invariably, members of Congress, staff assistants and executive branch officials are better informed than their high-priced brethren in the lobbying world. After all, they are the people who are actually making things happen.

Perhaps one example will serve to illustrate the point. My former business partner, who even today is one of Washington's most unforgettable characters, excelled in the art of information one-upsmanship. On one occasion he took our newest employee with him to a major lobbyist meeting on an issue of great importance to the business community. Roughly 20 lobbyists and corporate clients were gathered around a conference table for an early eight a. m. legislative strategy meeting. Before entering the conference room my partner advised our newest employee to let him do the talking.

Predictably, the lobbyists went around the table, each puffing himself up with some tidbit of information. One had heard that a key Senator supported the legislation. Another had heard a rumor that a House-Senate conference would soon be scheduled. And so it went. My partner waited strategically before intervening. At last he said authoritatively that not much he had heard that morning made sense to him. His view of the situation was very different. How did he know? With a flourish he announced that he had seen the vice president earlier that morning. This was a trump card, to be sure, and his view carried the day. Surely he was an invaluable, even indispensable member of the lobbying team. No cutbacks or downsizing would jeopardize his continuing presence on the team, not only on this issue but on other issues yet to unfold.

On the way back from the meeting our newest employee expressed his amazement. When had my partner had time to meet with the vice president that morning? After all, the lobbyist team meeting began at eight a. m. "Meet with the vice president?" my partner asked. "I didn't meet with the vice president. I said I saw the vice president. And I did. I saw him on television this morning. He was being interviewed on an early morning network talk show. I saw him while I was shaving."

Why do corporations employ Washington lobbyists? In some cases—which I will discuss in the next chapter—it is because lobbyists are good at what they do. But in most cases it is the purest possible example of a CYA strategy. An issue of major importance to a corporation comes up in Congress. The corporate affairs staff in Washington wants to assure the corporate vice president at headquarters that everything possible is being done to influence the outcome. The corporate vice president wants to assure the CEO that everything possible is being done. And the CEO wants to assure the board of directors that everything possible is being done.

Money becomes a minor factor in this chain of corporate self-defense. And in any event, the money does not come from the salary of the corporate representative, or the corporate vice president, or the CEO or the members of the board. The money comes from the corporation, and it is almost as easy to spend the money of a large public corporation as it is for Washington officials to spend the money of taxpayers. If the issue goes south for the corporation, who wants to admit that the issue was lost because not enough lobbying fire power was brought to bear? And if it is lost even after hiring a full complement of Washington lobbyists, well, everything that could be done had been done.

This process is not unique to the world of lobbying. It works in precisely the same way when large corporations hire well-known law firms. Well-known law firms provide a degree of protection against charges that corporations have not adequately defended their interests. Sure, corporations want to prevail in law suits, but if corporate officials hire the best and most expensive firms they cannot lose either way. And by the way, there is really not much difference between Washington law firms and Washington lobbying firms. They basically do the same kind of work, though lawyers are somehow able to avoid the apparent stigma of having to register as lobbyists. They are too professional to be sullied by that.

A somewhat similar process also takes place in the world of business consulting. I once spoke with an academic economist who consulted on the side for major U. S. corporations. My friend, who went on to become one of America's pre-eminent theoretical economists, told me this was the easiest money he ever made. He would be hired to provide counsel about a pending corporate decision: should corporation X expand into a new geographical region? He said that it was usually perfectly apparent what the answer to the question was supposed to be. His work, he said, consisted largely of changing interrogative sentences into declarative sentences, adding a bit of academic lingo along the way, and forwarding his recommendations along with a hefty consulting fee.

Why would a corporation pay a hefty consulting fee for this? Because it provides corporate officials with outside, expert validation for their decisions. If ever asked—or even if never asked—they could explain that their decisions had been validated by the work of a well-respected Ivy League economist.

Indeed, there are occasions when corporations must search around for, or even create outside validators because none are at hand. Where could one find a highly reputable, independent source of expertise to validate the positions taken by corporate officials? Perhaps one might commission a Washington think tank with a reputation for expertise in a particular area to do an "independent" study, paid for of course by the corporation itself. Or, in extreme cases, perhaps one or a group of corporations might have to create a new association out of whole cloth to provide outside validation for their point of view.

A great deal of corporate behavior in Washington and elsewhere consists in just this kind of activity. Indeed, I have been struck again and again by how little knowledge—and even more so by how little courage—is displayed by executives of large publicly held corporations. There are of course notable exceptions. But by and large corporate CEOs do not get where they are by being iconoclastic or swimming against the tide. They become CEOs largely by being survivors. They usually display less boldness and more caution; fewer stands on principle than avoidance of controversy; and less concern about how corporate dollars are spent than the standing of their reputations.

> **By and large corporate CEOs do not get where they are by being iconoclastic or swimming against the tide. They become CEOs largely by being survivors.**

The well-known Jeffrey Immelt of General Electric (GE) provides a clarifying example. Here was a CEO much praised and even named to Barack Obama's business advisory council. On the basis of what exactly? During his sixteen year tenure at GE, the company's stock declined from the high $40's when he took over in 2001 to just under $18 when he left. All the while he deployed a backup corporate jet on world trips in case his primary jet broke down.

Why are the CEOs of supposedly powerful corporations so easily cowed by public relations campaigns organized by a handful of people who employ computer tricks to magnify their size and import? Why can a handful of activists make the titans of American capitalism afraid of their own shadows? One might look at the standard career path of publicly held corporate CEOs for an answer.

This might also explain another apparent contradiction. Why is it that CEOs of publicly held corporations who take political jobs in Washington are generally so bad at them? Why is it that a CEO who has run an enormous corporation cannot seem to run successfully a government cabinet department or agency? The route up the corporate ladder in America trains CEOs to survive, if not prosper, in the business world. When suddenly thrust into a different world—and the world of politics is much, much different—CEOs have no such helpful career background to fall back upon. The tools which they employed in their businesses are only partially useful in the world of politics.

As Ronald Reagan proved, the skills of actors are more readily transferable to Washington. I recall an amusing occasion which illustrates this to a tee. President Reagan nominated the actor John Gavin to serve as ambassador to Mexico. Opposing political party staff thought they had been provided an occasion to embarrass the president. After all, John Gavin was also well-known as the Marlboro Man, the actor who played a cowboy in a series of ads for Marlboro cigarettes. Surely he would not be up to the task of a major ambassadorial post. As Mr. Gavin entered the committee hearing room, I watched him take in the scene—Senators seated above, staff behind, the press on the side, and the public in back. He sized this up the way an actor would a movie set—and proceeded to command the hearing.

Some CEOs are immediately "captured" by the Washington bureaucracies which they theoretically oversee; others flounder around looking for non-existent parallels with their former corporate world. In all events, one could count on one hand the number of former public corporation executives who have succeeded in Washington. Their skill sets are generally not transferrable to the world of politics.

The process works better the other way around; many are the examples of Washington political officials or military generals who succeed in the private sector. One thinks of George Shultz and Robert Gates and Donald Rumsfeld and Admiral McRaven, to name but a few of many possible examples.

I will share with readers for the first time my groundbreaking notion of "the glass floor." We have heard for many years about the glass ceiling, a kind of invisible barrier that keeps women from rising above it. Herewith the notion of the glass floor: when one rises to a certain level of fame in America one cannot fall beneath the glass floor, no matter how much or how badly one has screwed things up in one's previous assignment.

> **When one rises to a certain level of fame in America one cannot fall beneath the glass floor, no matter how much or how badly one has screwed things up in one's previous assignment.**

We see this with corporate executives who bounce from firm to firm and industry to industry; we see it with high level government officials who never seem to disappear, but find ever new posts in which to serve; and we see it with artists and entertainers who, no matter how abysmal their latest creation, always seem to return to the public limelight.

Perhaps there is no better poster child for the glass floor than the august, distinguished and highly regarded Robert Strange McNamara. Here was a "whiz kid" from the Ford Motor Company who was present at the creation of the Edsel, one of the most legendary failures in American corporate history. For this he was rewarded with the job of Secretary of Defense in the Kennedy administration. Here his misplaced technocratic approach helped sow the seeds for the only war America ever lost. For this he was in turn rewarded with the presidency of the World Bank where he presided over a massive increase in loans to poor countries. These loans were extended during the inflationary days of the Carter presidency; at 10%, 11%, 12% or even 13% these loans soon enough bankrupted countries around the world. This failed loan policy ultimately forced a re-thinking during the Reagan administration of the role of loans versus grants to impoverished countries.

These were not inconsequential mistakes of the sort most people make, like paying too much for a used car. These were world class blunders, for which there seems to be no price to pay other than the perpetuation of an unearned reputation for skill and good judgment.

Lobbying for Privately Held Companies

"How Did I Do?"

I briefed my client extensively about Senator Jesse Helms, with whom we were to meet to discuss a pressing agricultural issue facing his firm. As Chairman of the Senate Agriculture Committee, Senator Helms would be in a position to help. I covered all the fine points of Senator Helms' views on the issue at hand—what he had said about it, ways my client might approach it, and solutions that might be possible. My client listened patiently, but I had a sense this was all going in one ear and out the other.

Senator Helms greeted us warmly. He said several nice things about what great representation my client had in Washington, which I appreciated, and asked what he could do for us. My client said he would come to that in a moment but first he wanted to tell Senator Helms a little bit about himself.

My client explained that he came from a very wealthy, well-connected family in Cuba. His grandfather and father had established one of the largest sugar cane businesses in Cuba. All that had changed, however, when Fidel Castro took power. He and his family had been forced to flee, leaving behind their homes, their businesses and their worldly possessions. I noticed that Senator Helms was listening carefully.

My client went on to say that Castro moved frequently for security reasons, and used my client's family home as one of his temporary residences as he moved about. Another family property located in

Havana had been turned into a government museum. Senator Helms seemed entranced.

My client said that he and his brother and their families fled to America, where they deeply appreciated their reception and the freedoms they encountered here. By dint of hard work they scraped together enough money to buy several ancient sugar cane processing facilities which they moved to Florida. Their continuing diligence and work paid off and they purchased additional sugar cane growing land. They were now one of the largest sugar growing enterprises in America. Somewhat elided from this description was the substantial fortune they had transferred to an American bank when they arrived in America, but the sentiments were quite genuine. They had become American citizens, he said, and no one was more grateful for America's freedoms than he and his brother.

I thought Senator Helms was going to cry. My client was just the sort of person who made America exceptional, he said. He represented everything about American ideals in which Senator Helms himself believed. He was sorry to hear that Castro had expropriated his family homes and properties and hoped that one day he would get them back. Meanwhile, how could he help?

From there it was an easy segue to the issue at hand, and before long we had secured Senator Helms' full-throated agreement to help. We thanked him and stepped out into the hallway of the Dirksen Senate Office Building.

When the door closed behind us, my client turned to me and asked somewhat disingenuously, "How did I do?" The answer of course was obvious. He had hit upon a far more effective approach than my deep dive into the details of agricultural policy.

****

This meeting might serve to confirm two points. The first is that there is indeed such a thing as effective lobbying, lobbying which more than repays its rather extravagant fees. One could multiply many examples under this head. Here are a few for starters: specially carved out tax breaks for firms or industries; long-term patent protection extensions; favorable loan guarantees; agricultural price supports; carefully crafted anti-competitive laws or regulations; and direct appropriations of federal dollars. The list could go on.

All of this is to say that not all Washington lobbying consists of simply reporting on events as opposed to shaping them, a practice I described in the previous chapter. Perhaps there is no better example of effective lobbying than the case of Dennis Neill and Egypt. Dennis Neill's firm represented the government of Egypt at the time that Egypt signed the Camp David Accords and formally recognized the state of Israel. Having done so, Egypt received a substantial payment from the United States.

But Egypt was also promised, and had every reason to expect, ongoing foreign assistance of the kind which had been flowing to Israel for many years. The impulse of the Egyptian government was to compete with Israel for foreign assistance. Egypt had a much larger population, a far poorer population and an antiquated military; Egypt thought these factors should give it a leg up vis-à-vis Israel.

Dennis Neill patiently explained this was exactly wrong. There was no way to compete against Israel for foreign aid in the American Congress. Israel's relationships in the Congress were too strong. If Egypt sought to make this a zero-sum game it would lose every time. Far better to do the opposite: allow Israel to drive the appropriations train in the Congress and accept an informally agreed percentage—in the range of 2/3s—of what Israel receives each year. The more Israel receives, the more Egypt receives—and without a lot of legislative wrangling at that. This, he argued persuasively, was the better course.

In the four decades since the Camp David Accords were signed, Egypt has received both military and economic assistance totaling roughly $70 billion. There have been some bumps in the road when human rights or other concerns have arisen, but on the whole the process has worked very much the way Dennis Neill imagined. This is effective lobbying.

If there were not recurring examples of successful lobbying, the number of Washington lobbyists would be a lot smaller than it is. Today there are just shy of 11,000 registered lobbyists (and many more who should be registered) working in Washington, and while most of them cannot pretend to produce a payout in excess of their fees, those that do create the mythology that surrounds the entire business. After all, if there were no large lottery payouts from time to time, how many people would continue to buy tickets?

For this reason Washington lobbyists fight tooth and nail to protect their current billing model. As a rule they refuse to work on a success fee model of billing. It should be acknowledged here that there are legal prohibitions against success fees for securing federal appropriations. Lawmakers have thought this practice simply far too seedy to pass muster. But these laws reinforce the already strong impulse of lobbyists to resist success fee billing. There are many ways for legislative or regulatory goals to get bogged down. And the result of a lobbying campaign is often half a loaf or even one-fourth of a loaf. It is difficult, if not impossible, to foresee all the eventualities that might intervene in a legislative battle. As one of my partners said when approached by a potential client who proposed to pay us a success fee, "We don't get paid to win. We get paid to try." And that crystallizes the optimum lobbying strategy: always win, but never too quickly.

The second point that strikes me is that the owners of privately held companies, like my Cuban-American client, are far more talented than their publicly held corporate brethren. This makes a certain amount of intuitive sense. These people are generally entrepreneurs who have built their businesses from the ground up, as opposed to climbing the corporate ladder rung by rung. They tend to know their businesses better, to know their competitors better, and to have a deep, personal stake in their businesses.

> **Privately held corporation heads are generally entrepreneurs who have built their businesses from the ground up, as opposed to climbing the corporate ladder rung by rung. They tend to know their businesses better, to know their competitors better, and to have a deep, personal stake in their businesses.**

These qualities make them much more attentive to the rational expenditure of their business' money. At the end of the day, the profits of privately held companies belong to the owners. No money is likely to be wasted in CYA activities, since private owners have no bosses or independent boards of directors to which to report. This of course makes negotiating lobbying fees with owners of privately held businesses a bit more difficult; they want to be assured they are receiving value for money and that their Washington lobbyists are like any other division of their business, namely, a profit center. On the other hand, owners of private corporations are generally far more responsive than publicly held corporations' CEOs and are able to make decisions quickly. If a new legislative strategy is required or if their presence in Washington is required, they are usually quick to respond.

It has always struck me as an interesting experiment—unlikely to occur, but interesting—to see how congressional appropriators would respond to a similar set of incentives. As things stand now Congress spends other peoples' money. What difference does it make to a member of Congress if an appropriation is set at $60 million or $80 million? Especially if other members of Congress are actively seeking $80 million and agreeing to a larger number will produce a harmonious outcome? Why not agree with the other party and generate a degree of bipartisanship? After all, in the great scheme of federal spending there is very little difference between $60 million and $80 million.

What if legislators were required to fund a tiny portion of appropriated money themselves? As an example, let's say a legislator were required to deduct .00001% from his paycheck for agreeing to the additional $20 million? In this example, this would amount to $200. While I will confess up front that such a proposal is highly impractical—and probably wrong in many different ways—it seems to me that under such a system we would be enjoying regular budget surpluses instead of annual $800 billion deficits.

The structural imbalance of incentives is a problem that runs through not only government but all large institutions. Spending other peoples' money is easy to do. There are always reasons, and sometimes even good reasons, to spend additional money on worthy goals and programs. Leaders of large corporations may be offered incentive packages to achieve greater corporate profits, but the connection between the two is hardly ever direct. Union officials are equally profligate with their members' money, especially if membership dues are required and not dependent on their members' continuing judgment of the value of union activities. So too, with large not-for-profit entities like hospitals or universities. Indeed, we have constructed an entire health care system in which the connection between the patient who utilizes medical care and the billing and payment system for that care is beyond opaque. Every study of human behavior suggests that it would reduce costs and save money to require people who spend money to have some skin in the game.

Lobbying for Causes

Clubbing Baby Seals

Several of us were standing around chatting about various matters, waiting for a committee hearing to begin. Among us was Senator "Sam" Hayakawa of California. Once a brilliant linguist and academic administrator, he was now somewhat past his prime—though every bit as amusing as ever.

Senator Hayakawa had a tendency to drift off—sometimes obviously so—during committee hearings. Senator Helms, who sat on one side of him, and Senator Lugar, who sat on the other, worked out an informal arrangement to take turns nudging him awake. This, I think, is the only known instance of cooperation between Senator Helms and Senator Lugar.

This particular morning Senator Hayakawa arrived early and sat in his seat awaiting the chairman's arrival. A rather buxom young lady approached the dais where Senator Hayakawa was sitting. She stood to her full height and rested her large chest on the ledge directly in front of Senator Hayakawa. He looked up and peered over his glasses, displaying his well-known fondness for the female form.

One could not have guessed what happened next. "Senator," she said, "we need to outlaw the practice of clubbing baby seals to death." To say the least, this came from far out in left field at a hearing to address problems in the Middle East (what else?). What might the Senator say to this surprising intervention? Agree? Disagree? Ask for more information? Without missing a beat Senator Hayakawa said,

"And I was having such fun clubbing baby seals." Surprised and shocked in turn, she beat a hasty retreat.

****

What is one to make of this young woman's behavior? What could prompt someone to approach a United States Senator with such an agenda out of the blue, in such an obviously inappropriate time and place? The answer is that she represented a "cause." For a "cause" lobbyist there are no inappropriate times or places to discuss their issues. Their issues are deeply moral and thus not bounded by customary social niceties and decorum.

Conjure up the stereotype of a lobbyist. Here is a figure with cigar in mouth, wads of cash bulging from his pockets, the stuff of newspaper cartoons. These lobbyists are often pictured as seeking special favors for wealthy clients. Such lobbyists actually exist, more or less. But a surprising number of lobbyists in Washington represent single-issue advocacy or "cause" organizations. Some aim to restrict or to oppose restrictions on gun ownership; some to promote or to oppose abortion; some to represent animal rights; some to impose or to remove economic sanctions; and some to oppose the clubbing of baby seals. There are 1,800 single-issue lobbyists registered in Washington.

It is not that these groups are averse to money; indeed, they are constantly trying to raise more of it. But they aim to raise money in order to further their cause rather than to line their own pockets (at least usually). They are armed with a moral fervor, a zealotry for their causes which informs their work and their lives. It is a little difficult—though not impossible—to imbue a tax carve-out for a business client with deep moral fervor—but a "cause" is another matter altogether. What means could not be justified in order to stop the clubbing of baby seals? Or? Or?

Cause lobbyists find willing allies in the House and Senate. Politicians on the right and left become the legislative spokespeople for causes. They aim to pass legislation advocated by cause lobbyists.

When that is not possible, they aim to maneuver the House or Senate into votes that will put members "on record" for or against favored causes. The goal is to maneuver opposing members to vote against ending the clubbing of baby seals, carrying with their vote a shaming and a potential campaign issue down the road. Both sides of the aisle maneuver in this fashion, though it has been my experience that the Democrats do it better. Democrats seem to be the natural repository of moral outrage.

The field of economic sanctions is particularly fruitful for cause lobbying. There is no end of potential malefactors to be sanctioned at any given point in time—South Africa, Burma, Libya, Russia, Iran, Cuba, and North Korea, to name but a few of dozens of possible candidates. This is not the place for an extended evaluation of the effect of economic sanctions, which has been discussed in numerous books and scholarly articles. But perhaps an example from the case of Sudan will be clarifying.

> **The field of economic sanctions is particularly fruitful for cause lobbying. There is no end of potential malefactors to be sanctioned at any given point in time.**

I met one afternoon with the House committee staff that oversees foreign trade issues. "Have some M and Ms," I said, offering a small bag to each staff member. Lest the reader be concerned about my ethics, I was not exceeding the new and much-tightened gift limits that Congress has imposed on itself. The M and Ms were a prop designed to illustrate the problem I was there to discuss.

I was there to make a plea on behalf of my newest lobbying client, a small New Jersey firm which was about to be driven out of business. This was not the result of failing to offer a good product at a competitive price. To the contrary, it was the direct result of a legal action taken by the United States government. This action was, as I will explain, well-intentioned but entirely self-defeating.

There is an industrial product called gum arabic, which derives from the sap of acacia trees. These trees happen to grow almost exclusively across a swath of central Africa, a swath in which the country of Sudan is located. Herein lay the problem. Because of the massive human rights violations of the Sudanese government, already mentioned in a previous chapter, the United States government had placed economic sanctions against Sudan. It was no longer possible to import products from Sudan into the United States.

It turns out that gum arabic is a product with many uses. It causes certain materials to congeal and to bind themselves together. It is used, for example, to make the coloring of soft drinks uniform throughout. Without it, the orange coloring of a soft drink would sink to the bottom, a less than desirable look for marketers and consumers alike. It binds together the ink used in raised printing, of the sort that is often featured in fancy wedding invitations (at least before the age of evites) and business cards. And it is used to create the slightly harder exterior cover of slow-release pharmaceutical products and for the coating of candies like M and Ms. My M and Ms offered a visual demonstration of an everyday use of gum arabic.

As is so often the problem, many of America's friends and allies did not join the U. S. in sanctioning Sudan. In this case, the French in particular continued to import from Sudan all the gum acacia they needed, and then some. They would process the raw material just as did my small client from New Jersey. And—you guessed it—they would make it available for sale to American soft drink, printing, pharmaceutical and candy companies. At a considerably higher price of course. It's good to be a monopolist.

Was it evil to seek an exemption from well-intended sanctions against Sudan? Would this make one complicit in Sudanese government human rights violations? Well-intentioned as it was, U. S.

government policy created the following result: American end users were getting all the gum Arabic they wanted; French companies were making more money than ever; and American processors were going out of business. Worst of all, Sudan was selling as much gum acacia as it ever had. As they say, the road to hell ....

It might be a bit uncharitable to say so, but economic sanctions have always struck me as splitting the difference between doing something meaningful and doing nothing at all. Let's say a foreign government has taken an action or actions of which we do not approve. Perhaps it is developing nuclear weapons; perhaps it is oppressing some or all of its people; or perhaps it is invading a neighbor. We do not want to use military force to respond to the problem, a step which would surely solve the problem, though at a very high cost. But neither do we wish to be seen doing nothing. So we put in place economic sanctions, sometimes broad and punitive but more often—in the parlance of today—"targeted" sanctions. In Washington it is always good for whatever action one takes to be "targeted," whether it is sanctions, spending cuts or anything else. After all, no one wants to be accused of governing with a meat ax instead of a scalpel.

Occasionally, and over time, economic sanctions actually work. They arguably did so in the case of South Africa, in which the entire world joined the U. S. to sanction South Africa's apartheid government. Far more often, however, they achieve nothing close to what is advertised by their sponsors. This is particularly true of narrowly targeted sanctions; of sanctions against big and strong countries; of sanctions which are imposed only by the United States; and of sanctions which aim to bring about "regime change."

The example of Cuba which arose during my Senate confirmation is a good case in point. At the time my op ed article on Cuba appeared in the Washington *Post,* sanctions had been in place in one form or another for 30 years; at the time of my confirmation hearing in 2005 they had been in place for 45 years; and today they remain largely in place after 58 years. They have not seemed to have much effect on removing the Castro brothers and their self-appointed successor from power. This is not to say that eliminating sanctions will necessarily achieve that outcome either, at least immediately. But it is to say on a scale ranging from the success of a military invasion to doing nothing, sanctions seem to fall far closer to the do-nothing end of the scale.

I say this not to be churlish, as there are undoubtedly occasions worthy of such moral outrage I would support sanctions myself. But truth be told, sanctions are often less a tool of genuine foreign policy utility than another chance for members of Congress to preen and to demonstrate moral outrage, an activity which has grown into a substantial cottage industry in our nation's capital.

> **Sanctions are less a tool of genuine utility than another chance for members of Congress to preen and to demonstrate moral outrage, an activity which has grown into a substantial cottage industry in our nation's capital.**

Sanctions are a tool to express moral outrage, but they also reflect a split-the-difference approach, in this case between military invasion and doing nothing. There are many other examples of this split-the difference approach in Washington's legislative battles. There are occasions when neither side in a debate has the votes to secure victory. The result is often—banish the thought—a kind of compromise. One form which this takes is the well-worn executive branch "study" or "report." One side wishes to pass a new law; the other side opposes it. Neither can quite work its will. The result: both sides agree to study the question further. And who is usually tasked to do such a study? It is of course not the Congress itself; it is the executive branch. The executive branch is charged with conducting a study and reporting its results back to Congress. During the study process each side lobbies the executive branch to produce a study outcome that is favorable to its side, thus giving it a leg up in a future legislative battle.

This congressional compromise, which takes members of Congress about 60 seconds to enact, results in an enormous and generally useless expenditure of time for the executive branch. At any given time the executive branch is conducting hundreds of studies mandated by Congress. Worse yet, many of these are written into law not as one-time reports, but as recurring reports which are required once a year or even more frequently.

I once spearheaded a quixotic effort to streamline and eliminate reports which Congress had requested over the years in the foreign policy area. I sent a massive list of all required reports to each member of the Senate Foreign Relations Committee. I asked each member to please indicate which reports he or she would like to continue to receive. We would then include a provision in upcoming legislation to eliminate the rest. This after-the-fact sunset provision seemed to me to be the epitome of good government itself.

I immediately ran into a wall of resistance, largely from the staff members of Senators. Senators themselves scarcely ever looked at executive branch reports which were sent regularly to the Hill. In some cases, the original requesters of studies had retired from Congress or died of old age. After a bit of perseverance we did manage to remove what I think were roughly 20 outdated report requirements, some of which the executive branch was no longer even producing and none of which were ever missed by anyone in Congress.

It is often remarked that it is hard to beat something with nothing. It is especially hard to beat moral outrage with nothing. This, I think, has been noted by practitioners in the moral outrage industry. But even this can occasionally be taken too far. I recall a debate involving the legendary Senator Jacob "Jack" Javits from New York. In asking for my Senator's vote on a minor procedural matter, he said, "Dick, do it because of the holocaust." Hard to one-up that.

It would be tilting at windmills to expect an end to the moral outrage industry in Washington. But one might at least hope that its fruits do not needlessly hurt too many people or put too many American companies out of business in the process.

Registered Foreign Agents: Lobbying for Foreign Governments

The Blockhead

My partner and I were on a conference call with a client. I was explaining the legislative situation and discussing next steps. A second client called on the other phone in my office. The second client was the representative of a foreign embassy who needed to speak to us urgently. Though I had been the firm's point of contact with the foreign client, my partner suggested I continue with the first client. He would talk with the embassy representative.

This made me extremely nervous. Our second client represented the embassy of an East Asian country and I had always tended to their concerns with special care. After all, I was a foreign policy expert, skilled in handling the nuances of diplomacy.

Let us call our two contacts at the embassy Mr. Yin and Mr. Yang. Mr. Yang was a highly skillful diplomat, fully fluent in English, and who would later serve his country's president in a very senior national security post. Mr. Yin was none of these things. He was not the sharpest knife in the drawer; we observed his head was shaped like a helmet, in the manner of stories about infants whose heads had been shaped by shoeboxes. We nicknamed him "the blockhead."

It was Mr. Yin on the phone. My partner came on the line and said "Mr. Yin, how are you doing, buddy?" I cringed. This was not the argot of a seasoned foreign policy hand.

I was now listening to that call as well as handling my own. Mr. Yin explained that he had some questions about an election prognosis we had sent him. He was about to send our electoral projections to his government and needed some clarifications. "Shoot, buddy," my partner said. Mr. Yin noted that our report on the upcoming 34 Senate races predicted Republicans would win 15, Democrats 13 and the other six were too close to call. In his usual straight ahead manner, Mr. Yin asked "Who will win the six races?"

My partner hesitated a moment and then began spinning like a top. In two of the races the Republican candidate was a sitting governor with broad statewide name recognition, so perhaps they would have a slight edge. In a third case, the state had displayed a tendency to vote Democratic in recent cycles, so perhaps the Democratic candidate had an edge.

This seemed to satisfy Mr. Yin—up to a point. He persisted: "Who will win the other three races?" My partner explained in detail that these were genuine toss-ups; one couldn't really say. Mr. Yin asked again "Who will win the three races?"

By this time I had extricated myself from the first call and rushed over to help. "Well, Mr. Yin," my increasingly exasperated partner said, "We really can't say for sure." He went on to provide even more granular information about voting records, campaign expenditures and endorsements. But he said again that these races were just too close to call.

Again Mr. Yin: "Who will win the three races?" My partner, whose long suit was not patience, finally cracked. He blurted out "Damn it, Mr. Yin. This isn't your country. We don't know in advance who will win."

Silence. Six seconds. Eight seconds. Ten seconds. I saw visions of our valued client firing us on the spot. Then Mr. Yin laughed heartily. "Ha. Ha. Ha. Very funny. So you really don't know?" From that day forward, whenever he called our office Mr. Yin asked to speak with my partner.

****

In addition to representing publicly and privately held firms, trade associations and issue advocacy/cause clients, Washington lobbyists do a brisk business representing foreign clients. These include foreign governments, foreign corporations and foreign individuals, all of whom can and do have interests before the American government in much the same way as their American counterparts.

Sometimes foreign interests represent themselves in Washington. This is often the case with West European governments, whose embassy officials flatter themselves that they know more about the American political process than Americans do. But other times foreign interests are mystified by the complexity of our separation of powers, and really have no good idea where to start. Some foreign entities in nations which are ruled non-democratically are on the lookout for the secret levers of power in Washington. At home there is always one official who can "fix" any problem. Where is that locus of power in Washington?

Indeed, sometimes foreign governments are the worst defenders of their own interests. The United States-India Civil Nuclear Agreement, which the Indian embassy in Washington strongly supported, offers a good example. As a State Department official trying to persuade Congress to agree to this pact, I worked diligently to keep Indian embassy officials away from Capitol Hill. If there was a congressional concern about the agreement, it was that the executive branch had ceded too much ground in negotiations with India. To have the Indian embassy on Capitol Hill cheerleading for this agreement would have reinforced this impression. I never succeeded until I threatened to unleash American embassy officials in Delhi to sell the agreement to the Indian legislature, which in turn thought that Indian negotiators had ceded too much ground to the United States.

There is no legal bar against lobbyists representing foreign clients. But this kind of representation requires disclosure of lobbying activities. There are also disclosure requirements for lobbyists who represent domestic American clients—spelled out in the Lobbying Disclosure Act (LDA)—but the disclosures required for lobbyists representing foreign clients are more extensive.

The rules governing foreign representation are set out in the Foreign Agent Registration Act (FARA). This legislation, originally passed in 1938, was intended to address concerns about Nazi propaganda being circulated in the United States. The act was substantially amended in 1966, shifting the emphasis away from propaganda to work on behalf of the economic or political interests of foreign clients. "Foreign agents" are defined as individuals who seek to influence U. S. government policy on behalf of foreign principals.

Though the focus of the law has changed somewhat, its underlying purpose remains the same: to provide transparency about who is representing foreign clients, to what ends, and in which ways. The law requires regular reports by lobbyists on their activities and on the information which they disseminate on behalf of their clients. The goal is not prevention but transparency.

How has this law worked? In the past half century virtually no one has ever been prosecuted under FARA for failing to register as a foreign agent. There have been cases in which the Justice Department, which monitors FARA activities, has sought or threatened civil penalties, but not a single prosecution has occurred since the amended law took effect in 1966.

We might also mention the Logan Act in this context. The Logan Act, passed in 1799, criminalizes efforts undertaken by private American citizens to negotiate with foreign governments. This act was one of a number of measures including the subsequently repealed Alien and Sedition Acts, to combat excessive French influence in 1790s America. The act aimed to reinforce a monopoly of negotiating power for the executive branch, without its efforts being undercut by private citizens. It had two goals—prohibiting the attempt to "influence the measures or conduct of any foreign government" and prohibiting efforts "to defeat the measures of the United States."

There have been no prosecutions under the Logan Act since its passage in 1799. Two indictments have been brought under the act—in 1803 and 1853—and a number of passports have been revoked due to fear of potential Logan Act violations, but as a criminal statute the Logan Act has been a dead letter. The act is written very vaguely, failing to define words like "defeat" and "measures" and a number of scholars have argued that it is unconstitutional. Its limited effect has been further eroded by a contemporary concern about free speech rights of Americans.

The law was passed in an intensely partisan atmosphere in the 1790s and for the most part it has been used as a partisan rhetorical tool. When sitting administrations are annoyed by actions of congressmen or individuals allied with the opposing party, they occasionally threaten to invoke the Logan Act. Whenever you hear a politician or a news reporter breathlessly raising the specter of a Logan Act violation, you know you are watching the amateur hour. There is virtually no chance anyone will ever be prosecuted under the Logan Act.

> **Whenever you hear a politician or a news reporter breathlessly raising the specter of a Logan Act violation, you know you are watching the amateur hour. There is virtually no chance anyone will ever be prosecuted under the Logan Act.**

The reason for this is clear. While it is a perfectly reasonable notion that private citizens should not undercut executive branch negotiations, this is a very murky area in practice. Think about it: the Logan Act aims to prevent private citizens from influencing the policies of foreign governments or opposing the policies of the American government. But isn't this exactly what lobbyists registered under FARA do? Don't they intend to advance the interests of foreign governments in the U. S.? Perhaps not directly against the interests of the U. S. government, but how and where is this line to be drawn? If one lobbies to remove a country from the U. S. terrorist list, is this opposing the American government? If one aims to change an American law that injures a foreign client, is this? If one wants to alter the current law to provide more or less foreign assistance to a foreign government, is this? It is very hard to know when an action which is regulated under FARA would become a violation of the Logan Act.

Bringing a charge under FARA is far easier for a prosecutor than bringing a charge under the Logan Act. Indeed, we are seeing some new ground being broken here with charges against former General Mike Flynn. Flynn spoke on various occasions with Russian ambassador Sergei Kislyak during the 2016 presidential transition period. Is it wrong for an incoming administration to speak with foreign government officials, or even to suggest that the incoming administration's policies will differ from those of the current administration? These kinds of questions have been in the air since the beginning of the republic, and increasingly so since the advent of modern communications. A Logan Act violation would be impossible to prosecute successfully; far easier to prosecute a FARA violation.

What we are seeing is not a genuine concern about Flynn's reporting his connections to Turkey under FARA. We are seeing the threat of a FARA prosecution being used to gain testimony about an unrelated matter. Had Flynn never played a role in the transition or the incoming administration, there is no chance his failure to register for an unrelated country under FARA would have become an issue.

Indeed, circumventing FARA has become something of an art form in Washington, especially by former high level government officials. Former officials do not usually register as lobbyists, leave aside as foreign agents. To be a "lobbyist," or worse yet a "foreign agent," would be far beneath the dignity of distinguished individuals such as these. Former high level officials do not sully their reputations. They do not lobby; they "strategize" or better yet, provide "strategic advice." Never mind that being paid to offer strategic advice when the intent is to affect U. S. government policy, is clearly covered under both FARA and the LDA.

Providing counsel or strategic advice offers a high-sounding gloss to contrast one's actions to the grubby, day-to-day world of shoe-leather lobbying. Today there are nearly 1,800 registered foreign agents, representing more than 500 foreign clients, on record with the Justice Department. The number of individuals who should be required to register, according to the plain English words of the statute, is undoubtedly far higher. The likelihood of the small FARA unit of the Justice Department, located at 600 E Street, NW, itself uncovering and choosing to pursue former Congressmen, former executive branch officials and Washington attorneys is very small indeed.

There are foreign clients that an ethical, or even a garden variety patriotic firm would not represent. Would representing a sworn enemy of the United States like North Korea be a good idea? Decisions about who to represent and who not to represent, however, are left to the discretion of lobbyists themselves, as we have already seen in the case of the former State Department official who represented the Sudanese government. The argument usually made by lobbyists in these unpleasant cases is that they are working diligently to bring their clients around to less intractable opposition to America and American values. I have never seen a case where this actually happens.

Sometimes lobbyists who represent domestic or foreign clients will enter into the executive branch. The concern here is that these lobbyists will seek to help their former clients by favoring their policies, providing them with information, or in other ways. The Obama administration, having first said it would ban lobbyists from serving altogether, established a two-year period in which lobbyists could not serve in any area in which their former clients had an interest. This policy has been adopted by the Trump administration. These restrictions, as well as post-employment restrictions, are offered up in the spirit of combating the scourge of "special interests" or "draining the swamp."

I have no particular objection to limits of this sort, though it has always struck me that they are usually proposed by people who have no direct experience in the lobbying world. One would have to suppose that new administration employees would be so venal and so little attached to good government, that they would put their former clients' interests above those of their administration or even of the United States.

This is not beyond the mind of man, though there is a rather poorly thought out psychology at work here. Even while being paid handsomely by their clients, there is often a kind of master/slave or at least employer/employee relationship at work—and the lobbyist is neither the employer nor the master. I recall a conversation with one of my clients while standing on the corner of 1st and C Streets, SE. "You know Senate Finance Committee Chairman Roth, don't you?" my client asked. "Yes, I do." "Can you get a meeting with him about a tax issue?" Without being presumptuous, I said I thought it was likely that I could. "Here," my client said, handing me her cell phone, "Call him."

Does any reader assume that if I went into the executive branch my every instinct would be one of slavish responsiveness to this former client's interests? I am not saying that getting even would be the order of the day, but perhaps a heaping dose of governmental even-handedness.

VI. INNOCENTS ABROAD

Congressional Travel

Dinner Reservations in Rome

Where to eat? We had arrived in Rome several days earlier and had two jam-packed days of meetings with Italian government officials. It was Saturday and our schedule was free. Several knowledgeable people, including one from our embassy in Rome, recommended the most sought after, hot new restaurant in town, especially the outdoor patio. It was a perfect evening for dining outdoors in Rome, as so many evenings seem to be. The only difficulty was how to secure reservations, even for so august a traveling party as ours.

Our delegation was comprised of four United States Senators, including the Chairman of the Senate Foreign Relations Committee, their spouses, several staff, a protocol officer and our military escort officer. The group decided to split up in equal numbers, each to go its own way. I was with the Chairman and his wife, another Senator and his wife, and one of our staff. Our staff member, who claimed deep familiarity with all things Roman, assured us there was no difficulty in securing a table at the desirable new restaurant. This seemed agreeable, so we set off for a mid-afternoon stroll around Rome. Several hours later we came to a fine-looking restaurant with an outdoor patio surrounded by a five-foot hedge which created privacy from the road.

Our staff expert suggested we wait outside while he went to talk with the maître d'. There was an animated discussion, much gesturing and frequent finger pointing. The maître d was shaking his head in a manner universally understood to mean "we have no table for you."

Our staff member re-engaged. Soon they were poring over a reservation book. Further arm waving ensued. Heads were shaken, voices raised and fingers pointed. At last, the maître d' seemed satisfied. Our staff member beckoned us forward. Our Chairman, a man of considerable politeness and deference, said he hoped we had not created a problem. "No problem at all," our staff member reassured us. We were seated at a table for six, me directly across from the Chairman and facing the hedge which surrounded the patio. We ordered drinks and had a look at the extensive menu.

As we did, I noticed out of the corner of my eye the arrival of the other six members of our traveling party. I wondered how they would fare with the maître d'. Again, much arm waving and finger pointing ensued. My curiosity was piqued, though I said nothing to the rest of my table who had not noticed their arrival. At last, the exasperated maître d' pointed directly at our table. Head shaking followed. More pointing at our table.

It gradually dawned on me what was occurring. The other group, under the guidance of our military escort, had apparently made dinner reservations at this restaurant before we had even arrived in Rome. Our staff member knew this and had persuaded the maître d' that we were the party who had made the reservation. We were sitting at their table, along with the only chance in the world to eat at this restaurant this Saturday evening.

Dejected, the other party made its way back out onto the street. None of this had attracted the notice of the Chairman, who would have been distraught to learn of this culinary sleight-of-hand. Nor did the Chairman notice what happened next.

Behind the Chairman's head, the hedge slowly parted. Our military escort appeared. He had a long knife between his teeth and pointed directly at our staff member. This was an image of such striking hilarity it remains lodged in my mind to this day. To complete the story, our military escort was Major Jim Jones, who would later go on to be the Supreme Allied Commander of NATO and Barack Obama's first National Security Advisor. We laughed about this incident afterward, though I am not sure even now he entirely sees the humor in it.

****

Our stay in Rome was part of a longer Congressional delegation trip to Europe. These trips are generally referred to by the acronym CODEL. They are often pilloried by the press as a gross waste of time and taxpayer money. "Gotcha journalism" regularly refers to them as congressional "junkets."

I could not and would not defend each and every trip abroad taken by members of Congress. Some itineraries display an almost uncanny overlap with leading golf courses around the world. But as a general matter, it has always struck me that these foreign trips are extremely beneficial.

For my part, I never learned as much in any other seven days as I did on a week-long CODEL. It is one thing to predicate foreign policy views on opinions puffed up in the corridors of a congressional office building. It is quite another to speak directly with foreign leaders, to inspect forward American military positions, to seek the views of U. S. military leaders on the ground, to discuss trade policy with foreign legislators, or to review a foreign assistance program as it is actually implemented.

As the reader knows from the previous chapter on signaling, I yield no pride of place to critics of wasteful government spending. But these admittedly costly trips are invariably eye-opening, offering both new insights and a tangible context of understanding.

What I have always found particularly annoying is the hypocrisy of the national media, including the esteemed Washington *Post*. One can read in the very same newspaper about the provincialism of Congress and dripping sarcasm about congressional junkets. Indeed, it has become something of an urban myth, repeated all too frequently, that members of Congress are yahoos who simply aren't familiar with anything beyond the borders of America. One reads reports that—fill in the blank—most, or many, or a large number of members of Congress do not have passports. This is simply not true. A recent New York *Times*-sponsored survey found that 93% of members of Congress hold valid passports. My own guess is that the actual percentage is higher than that. Another study found that 417 members of Congress traveled abroad between the years 2000-2014. Many members of Congress have either studied abroad or worked abroad, and as many as 20% can speak a foreign language well enough to conduct business in that language.

None of this seems to deter individuals from making up foolish statistics about the insularity of members of Congress. Russian Foreign Minister Sergei Lavrov asserted several years ago that more than 80% of members of Congress have never left the U. S. This was his dubious explanation for congressional support for sanctions against Russia. More recently, Michael Bloomberg asserted that many members of Congress have never traveled abroad. This was by way of explanation about his concern that Congress might adopt a tougher trade policy toward China. One can reasonably guess that these fictions will appear again and again in the future.

CODELS are valuable in another way as well. We hear much today about how members of Congress no longer socialize across the political aisle. Indeed, the lack of inter-party socializing has been blamed for some of the seemingly unbridgeable differences between our political parties today. Where are the days when President Reagan and Speaker O'Neill could argue vigorously during the day and share a drink in the evening?

In my experience CODELS have played a positive role in bringing together Democrats and Republicans. CODELS frequently include members of both political parties, and these trips deepen personal relationships across the aisle. Meeting together with foreign leaders, discussing their reflections on these meetings afterward, and sharing meals in new and different environments can form the basis of deep bonds of friendship.

> **CODELS have played a positive role in bringing together Democrats and Republicans. CODELS frequently include members of both political parties and these trips deepen personal relationships across the aisle.**

I certainly felt that way as a staff member on numerous CODELS. I mentioned in the previous chapter I was relatively confident I could secure a meeting for my client with Senator Bill Roth, the then-chairman of the Senate Finance Committee. My confidence was rooted in a CODEL on which I had traveled with Senator Roth. Most of the American public is familiar with Senator Roth as the co-architect of the Kemp-Roth tax bill and the namesake of the Roth IRA. I was familiar him from our European CODEL and one evening in Denmark in particular.

One evening after our official meetings were concluded, some of us stole off to a local bar with Senator and Mrs. Roth. Senator Roth became known to me that night as a gentleman to whom a Danish Inuit woman who was no more than 4' 3" in height and devoid of every other tooth, took a surprising liking. She did not know who he was, of course, but she made her feelings very clear by sidling up to him and making other expressive gestures. No one was more amused by this unexpected turn of events than Mrs. Roth, a federal judge and a most gracious woman.

CODELS are an excellent way for members of Congress to get to know one another in deep and lasting ways. There is less good to say about how American diplomats abroad respond to CODELS. At times American diplomats respond warmly and helpfully, especially if the congressional visitors are well-known and can provide entrée to meetings with prime ministers, kings and queens, or popes which ambassadors would have little ability to secure on their own.

But more often one gets a sense that our diplomats abroad regard congressional visitors as an unwelcome intrusion on their turf and a waste of their time. They hint openly they have more important things to do than entertain the great unwashed. One might contrast this behavior with that of the military escorts who accompany CODELS; they are unfailingly pleasant and responsive.

I tried to address this problem when I began work at the State Department. As the State Department's lead outreach to members of Congress, I took it as my responsibility to try to inculcate a new attitude about CODELS. I advanced the notion that CODELS offered an extraordinary opportunity for the State Department to shine.

The State Department does not have the "toys" that the military uses to impress Capitol Hill. The State Department cannot take members of Congress to observe night landings on an aircraft carrier or a mid-air refueling of a B-2 bomber. Ask yourself: would a member of Congress prefer a photo with U. S. troops in Afghanistan from their state or district or a photo with an Agency for International Development officer? Which photo would appear in the next newsletter to constituents? As one of my colleague and I joked, what should the State Department do—invite members of Congress to Foggy Bottom to watch someone send out a cable? The Defense Department has very significant and substantial advantages in this regard.

That is why it seemed to me that CODELS represent such a unique opportunity to advance the State Department's interests. Members of Congress are on our diplomats' "turf," as it were, and a helpful, thoughtful outreach to them would be appreciated. I have to admit, however, I do not think I was very successful during my tenure in changing the culture of the State Department.

Foreign Cultures and American Intelligence Gathering

Running in Morocco

The chairman of our congressional delegation was an avid runner. Knowing this, our embassy in Morocco arranged for a group of Moroccan runners to join the delegation on a morning run around the old city of Fez. I don't know who these runners were, but they must have been part of Morocco's Olympic team. They took off like a shot.

I was not much of a runner myself, and soon fell hopelessly behind the pack. Happily, I was accompanied by our military escort officer, Colonel Tom Lynch. Tom is an extremely capable guy—Roger Staubach's center on Navy's legendary football team, later a Navy admiral, Superintendent of the Naval Academy and today a TV regular selling mortgage products to veterans. Running, however, was not among Tom's best skills and he and I usually settled in well behind the pack.

We did so that day in Fez as well. Soon the group was out of sight. We confronted several choices of direction. Had they gone left or right? Which way now? We were hopelessly lost. Worse yet, we found ourselves in the souk, a labyrinth of narrow streets filled with vendors, known and unknown animals hanging from hooks, and every imaginable food item one might ever—or never—want to buy. Two generously-sized Americans in running shorts added to the spectacle.

We turned this way and that, with little hope of success. Eventually we came to the street on which we had begun our morning's run. As we did, we noticed a security vehicle that had been assigned to watch over the group. We hopped into the vehicle and we raced back in the direction of the pack. We prevailed on the driver to take us several streets ahead of the pack and drop us off on a side street that crossed the main road. A few minutes later the pack appeared and passed our position. As it did, we fell in right behind them. Well rested from our car ride, we kicked our way to the finish line with great bravado. We said in unison "Great run, huh?"

This was not the only running experience that Tom and I shared. On another occasion during a four mile run in Oslo we achieved nothing less than a natural impossibility, a latter day miracle. We ran what seemed straight uphill for four miles and returned to our starting point. Amazing.

****

It is one of the great virtues of CODELs to learn about the lives and customs of foreigners with whom the United States government must deal in its conduct of foreign policy. This kind of direct knowledge is without equal and if policy makers had more of it, we might spare ourselves many foreign policy misadventures great and small.

As natural egalitarians—and this is a great virtue of Americans—we tend to suppose that at bottom all foreigners are just like us. It may well be true in some philosophical sense that we are all equal, or as is said in some religious traditions that we are all valuable in the sight of God. But this certainly does not mean that we are all the same. Our differences run from customs relating to food and dress to very different ways of thinking about the world and our place within it.

One evening we joined our Moroccan hosts for a fancy dinner; they had pulled out all the stops to express their gratitude for the delegation's visit. The main course consisted of an enormous bowl of food of—at least to me—totally unknown provenance. It was accompanied by warm milk, which I can report to a certainty did little to enhance the main course.

This dinner prompted a lively conversation back in the hotel later that evening. Several staff members and I from our CODEL were enjoying a drink with an American embassy official who had attended dinner with us. The topic proposed for discussion—and this is a party tip for the reader—was what is the worst meal you have ever eaten? I ventured that that evening's fare was certainly in the running. Soon enough, however, all entries gave way to the undisputed winner. Our embassy official had previously served as the Deputy Chief of Mission (DCM) at the American embassy in neighboring Mauretania. He and the American ambassador had been invited as honored guests to a dinner at which no expense was to be spared. They began with a round of Johnnie Walker Black Label. So far so good.

As they were escorted to the dinner table a horrible, animal-like screeching arose from the courtyard. In came the main course, a steaming hot, quivering camel's liver, replete with hairs sticking out here and there. It had just been liberated from the poor beast in the courtyard. The host cut it and placed hearty portions on each guest's plate. Our embassy friend said that with the aid of the Johnnie Walker he had brought to the table—and by cutting his liver up and moving it around—he was able to get down a respectable portion of his dinner. All in the service of American foreign policy.

He became the victim, however, of diplomatic rank; when the host was not looking the ambassador took his portion and plopped it squarely on the DCM's plate. It is doubtful that U. S.- Mauretanian relations were deepened that evening, though probably no great harm was done either.

There are far more meaningful distinctions between Americans and foreigners. One example is illustrated by American intelligence reporting about the fall of the Shah of Iran in early 1979. The intelligence community, including State Department analysts and the

American ambassador in Tehran all reported until the very end that the Shah's position was secure. The consensus view: the Shah might be forced to make some accommodations with noisy Islamic opposition leaders, but his rule was not threatened. Shortly afterward he was overthrown and driven from Iran, replaced by the Islamic theocrats who have ruled Iran ever since.

I asked a friend of mine who worked in the intelligence community how they had missed all this. His answer was interesting. He said that intelligence estimates were based on matters with which Americans were familiar. They had made no real inroads into understanding, or even talking with the opposition. Moreover, he said, the intelligence community focused on things it could count: the Shah had so many troops at his disposal; his army had so many tanks; and his secret police had so many SAVAK agents.

What was missing of course was the role of religion in mobilizing discontent with the Shah's rule. Americans are a religious people, at least compared with our West European friends, but we tend to keep our religion separate from the public square. When was the last time a serious religious conversation took place at a Georgetown cocktail party? As such, our intelligence analysts tended to discount the very great power that religion can have in moving people to action. Religion may move the "bitter clingers" in certain backwaters of America, but it certainly does not move our decision-makers when they engage in policy-making. Indeed, this is rather the point of the separation of church and state, a notion which has taken deep root in our society's elites.

Analysts more open to the force of religion in human life might have looked at Iran differently. Even today this strikes me as a blind spot in our interpretation of other parts of the world; the CIA's long-term estimates for 2030, for example, tend to focus on measurable, countable factors: income, poverty levels, GDP growth and the like. Rarely do they credit the importance of ideas as forces which shape human history. Even today our leaders and intelligence analysts often subscribe to a mistaken connection between poverty and revolutionary behavior. Marx called religion an epiphenomenon and no one better exemplifies this view than the intelligence analysts of modern commercial republics.

What is the typical U. S. government response to the root problem of extremism and terrorism? It is to combat it by proposing to spend more money. If only we could address the problem of poverty, it is suggested, we could eliminate religious extremism. But where has the connection between poverty and religious extremism ever been demonstrated? If one considers the 9/11 plotters and bombers, or the leadership of many terrorist cells, they are not comprised of mainly poor people. Bin Laden certainly did not want for money.

The causal chain actually works the other way around. The reliance upon extreme religious views is both what holds down many Middle East economies and what inspires terrorism. Extreme religious views are not a happenstance result of deeper economic problems; the economic problems are all too often the result of the religious views.

All this, of course, makes problems like religious extremism very difficult to address. It is far easier to request a larger foreign assistance budget on the premise that throwing money at the problem will solve it. In this way one can measure one's commitment and success— however little they have to do with the real problem.

> **Our leaders and our intelligence analysts subscribe to a mistaken connection between poverty and revolutionary behavior. Marx called religion an epiphenomenon and no one ever exemplified this view better than the intelligence analysts of modern commercial republics.**

At the risk of political incorrectness, I will advance a theory about the Middle East which has led to serious misunderstandings on our part. The theory concerns the meaning of truth. What do we understand by the word "truth?" Serious philosophers have said, and I believe it to be so, that we in the West operate on what might be called a correspondence theory of truth. What is true for us is when our words match up with, reflect or correspond to something in the external world. True words uncover or reveal what is there. If we say the table over there has four legs and is brown, this is true if the table over there actually has four legs and is brown.

There are places in the Middle East that seem to operate on a different meaning of truth. Here a proposition is advanced. If it is not contradicted and stands in place—displays its power—it is true. Truth consists, in a rough manner of speaking, of what stands without being contradicted by others.

I once knew an individual in which this process was displayed beautifully and clearly. The first time he spoke, his words filled the air. If uncontradicted, the second time he spoke he expected you to believe it. And if uncontradicted by the third time he spoke, he believed it himself.

This has ramifications for how Americans and Middle East natives look at something like pricing. Both might agree in principle that the value of an item is what the seller and buyer agree to. Americans, however, tend to believe that the initial price which a seller asks for an item reflects something of what the seller properly thinks is the value of his time and materials plus a profit. The Mideast seller, however, has a very different notion; the value of an item is whatever he can make someone pay for it. It reflects nothing about the item itself, but about the dynamics of the words used in the sales process. Americans can be taught to haggle—not to accept at face value the first price a seller offers—but it is not our first instinct to do so.

Failing to understand these different views of truth can hobble our diplomacy. We have been told over and over, for example, by the Pakistani government that it is seriously addressing the problem of terrorism along its Afghan border. We do not always believe this, because we have many other ways to determine the truth or falsity of this claim.

If we do not stop the conversation then and there—and insist that this be sorted out in a way agreeable to us—these claims will stand and Pakistani actions will not change. When raising this matter with Pakistani officials, it simply must be haggled out to a conclusion before other items are discussed. If Pakistani claims are allowed to go unchallenged they will stand as true for Pakistanis.

In short, raising our concerns about an issue like this is far from sufficient. We cannot hope to succeed by raising our concerns and then moving on to other issues. Even if we reduce aid to Pakistan by, say, 25% because of its unwillingness to address terrorism, the Pakistani government will believe that its claims are 75% true.

In this context what is necessary to win a policy argument is to secure the agreement of the other side. We Americans are often too polite to contradict our interlocutors to their face. We are even less willing to stop a conversation in midstream in order to force agreement on a disputed point. We move on, and when we return to our own shores we grouse about the duplicity of what we have heard.

In this context truth is not object-ive, but subject-ive. Truth is not what agrees with something "out there" but what is in agreement with what interests the speaker. Lies are not something that clash with objective reality; lies are what do not have the power to prevail. Lies are what are powerless.

Differing notions of truth are not unique to the Mideast but they are perhaps most starkly displayed there. All of this is to say that there is much to be learned from travel abroad, at least if one is willing to learn something about our own working assumptions as well. I would not deny for a moment that humans everywhere share many common traits. But we have certainly figured out how to express them in ways different from one another.

Appreciating foreign Cultures

"Can I Have That Painting?"

Our motorcade sped down the streets of Rome. We were on our way to meet the Prime Minister of Italy and in those days security was very tight. Our vehicles passed under an archway and came to a stop in a broad interior courtyard. We were whisked into the building and directly into the Prime Minister's ornate office. He greeted us warmly.

We did not know too much about the Prime Minister beyond the brief sketch that our embassy had provided. Italian Prime Ministers tend to have a rather brief half-life. Like most Italian Prime Ministers—then and now—he was new to his job, and our delegation aimed to quiz him on the new government's policies. The American ambassador in Rome who accompanied us on this visit was equally interested to learn about the Prime Minister.

The Senators and the Prime Minister exchanged views on a variety of Italian domestic and foreign policies. The Prime Minister was generous with his time and more than responsive to questions from our delegation.

In the course of the conversation it emerged that the Prime Minister was a rather well-known artist. He pointed to the oil paintings hanging on his office walls and mentioned that these were his own work. Though I hasten to add that I am not an art connoisseur, the paintings seemed to me quite good. It must have seemed that way to one of the Senators in our delegation as well (as a still-sitting Senator he shall remain nameless).

He pointed to one of the paintings which he particularly liked. He turned to the Prime Minister and asked "Can I have that picture?" My audible gasp was drowned out by the audible gasps of the other delegation members, the American ambassador and the Prime Minister's staff. These paintings undoubtedly had a market value of thousands of dollars. What could have prompted such an inappropriate question? And what might the Prime Minister say in response?

The Prime Minister was cool and unflappable. He beckoned a staff member and spoke to him in Italian. With extraordinary finesse he told the Senator "I have a gift for you" and returned to the conversation.

Several minutes later his staff aide returned with a handful of small folders. The Prime Minister said that he appreciated very much the Senator's kind words about his paintings and he wished to give each of us a complete set of 8½" by 11" reproductions of his most well-known paintings. He handed one packet to each of us. I marveled less at this modest gift—though I still have it—than I did at his extraordinary skill in defusing an awkward social situation. Italian Prime Ministers may not have much electoral staying power, but they certainly possess an abundance of social skills.

****

We have all heard of "the ugly American," a term popularized in Eugene Burdick and William Lederer's 1958 book of the same name. The book features American diplomats who career about the world failing to understand or appreciate the customs and values of other nations; they possess an ostentatious certainty about the superiority of the American way of life. Foreign clothes, food, architecture, customs—nothing quite measures up to what is American; whatever is different must be inferior. In the Italian Prime Minister's office we were in the presence of a living incarnation of such a person, who assumed that the Prime Minster would be honored to give away his valuable artwork to an American member of Congress.

For every ugly American there is probably an equal or greater number of his exact opposite, especially these days. These are Americans who, bowled over by the novelty of a different way of life, conclude that what is different is somehow better. These are the people of whom it is said that they have "gone native." In over-estimating what is new and different there seems to be a psychological reward no less powerful than the certainty that one's own way of life is best.

> **There are Americans who, bowled over by the novelty of a different way of life, conclude that what is different is somehow better. These are the people of whom it is said that they have "gone native." In over-estimating what is new and different there seems to be a psychological reward no less powerful than the certainty that one's own way of life is best.**

In these cases one hears the pseudo-superiority that comes from lording it over the uninitiated. "What, you haven't enjoyed the scallops in Ibiza?" "You haven't lived until you have seen the sun setting behind Mount Kilimanjaro." "You simply have to try the meditative practices of the Tibetan lamas."

This latter disease is far more common than the former among today's American diplomats, who seem to slide insensibly into overvaluing the views of countries to which they are posted. The Bureau of Near Eastern Affairs at the State Department provides perhaps the best example. It is not infrequent for diplomats to be posted over and over again to Middle East nations. There are 16 Muslim nations in the Middle East with a total population of more than 400 million. There is one Jewish nation with a population of six and one half million Jews. These postings form the basis for a deep familiarity with and sympathy toward Muslim nations. A "clientitis" develops which informs the outlook of many Middle East experts at the State Department. There may no longer be the overt anti-Semitism that once characterized a State Department whose officials were drawn from America's well-established upper class families. But the net effect remains roughly the same in terms of the State Department's orientation, which heavily favors Muslim nations over Israel. Perhaps this is another reason why American embassy officials in the Middle East often regard congressional visitors, who are invariably more sympathetic to Israel, as yahoos.

Herewith a clarifying example. A dispute arose between two of my State Department colleagues. The head of the Near Eastern Bureau favored allowing Saudi Arabia to join the U. S. visa waiver program. Under this program a country's nationals are not required to submit to in-person interviews with U. S. consular officials to obtain a visa; applying for a visa can be done online. Nations whose nationals have an excellent record of returning home after temporary visits are eligible to join the U. S. visa waiver program. For obvious reasons, this is a much sought after status. In supporting Saudi Arabia to receive visa waiver status my colleague was encouraged strongly by the American ambassador in Riyadh. The ambassador saw this status as a "deliverable" with which he could impress his Saudi hosts and assure them of his strong support for the kingdom.

Lined up against my colleague, however, was the head of the Bureau of Consular Affairs, which actually issues visas. She pointed to the fact that 19 of the 20 September 11th hijackers were of Saudi origin. She knew who would get the blame if another incident occurred after Saudi Arabia had been granted the easier status of a visa waiver country. She was dead set against the idea.

Not wanting to take this dispute to the secretary of state, who rightly wished that such disputes be settled (if at all possible) at a lower level, the two opponents hit upon an idea. In as much as I handled relations with Congress, I was to be the tie-breaker. I should make discreet inquiries on Capitol Hill and gauge the sentiment on the Hill about this issue. They agreed to abide by my recommendation.

The reader can imagine the temptation inherent in such a situation. I was personally opposed to allowing Saudi Arabia into the visa waiver program. I could have made up my report out of whole cloth. But I thought that was a bit unfair and so I reached out to key members on the Hill, some Senators and some House members, some Republicans and some Democrats. A week or so later the three of us reconvened and I reported my results: sentiment on the Hill was opposed to granting Saudi Arabia visa waiver status. My colleagues agreed to drop the idea.

I would like to be clear that I did indeed conduct due diligence on this question. I made up no results and I reported straightforwardly what people on the Hill had told me. Now it is always possible that I interviewed more members whom I knew in advance would oppose a Saudi visa waiver, but I will leave it with the reader to judge if that comports with how they see this author.

What I can say for certain is that from that day forward I was a great favorite of the Bureau of Consular Affairs. There would be no standing in line at the post office or mail order delays for my friends who needed new passports. On one occasion I turned around a passport request in less than 20 minutes. Unfortunately, having departed the State Department some years ago, I too now stand in line at the post office.

Judging between American and foreign institutions and ways of life is a deeply subjective matter and it would not be my place to guide the reader in any particular direction. I will say, though, that it has always been my view to favor the American form of government, even in its current sclerotic state. The separation of powers has always struck me as an indispensable feature of any and all good governance.

The value of the separation of powers was illustrated in an amusing way during a CODEL meeting with President Hosni Mubarak of Egypt. We met with President Mubarak in one of his ornate palace offices in Cairo. After some discussion of Middle East issues, President Mubarak asked if our delegation had visited the pyramids. Our delegation chairman said yes, they were very impressive. But had we visited the pyramids in the evening when there was a narrated light show? This was the best way to see the pyramids. No, our chairman said, we had not.

President Mubarak explained that the show's narration rotated between English, French and German each night. Our chairman protested that the delegation really needed to leave Egypt that evening, but President Mubarak insisted. He snapped his fingers and asked a staff member to find out which was the show's language for that evening. After a few minutes the aide returned and whispered something in President Mubarak's ear. He responded in English: "Not any more it's not."

We later learned that that the scheduled language had been changed from French to English with the snap of the president's fingers. Worse yet, we were unable to change our flight schedule and skipped the evening light show. We could only guess the displeasure of hundreds of French tourists who had bought tickets for that evening, only to suffer the indignity of listening to the show in English. If *Schadenfreude* were a French concept, I suppose we would have been experiencing it. I know it betrays my absence of worldly sophistication, but as our aircraft ascended into the night sky over Cairo Mel Brooks' line came to me: "It's good to be king."

While I strongly favor the American form of government, I would like the reader to know that as an aspiring international sophisticate I also favor German beer, Japanese gardens, French food and Italian fashions, to name just a few of my worldwide preferences.

Declining American Influence

Who's In Charge Here?

My lobbying partner and I waited in the vice president's anteroom. We were scheduled to meet with the vice president of the Dominican Republic in his office in Santo Domingo. We had prepared carefully for our meeting, honing our arguments for why a certain tariff was unfair and needed to be repealed. We had entirely persuaded ourselves of the justice of our case and we were hoping to persuade him as well.

The meeting went well, indeed beyond our wildest expectations. The vice president listened carefully to our arguments and much to our surprise, announced immediately that he saw merit in our views and would work to change the tariff promptly. That day, we thought, we had earned our pay.

That evening we attended a dinner at the home of our American client. Uplights lit the swaying palm trees and the ocean lapped gently against the rocks beneath the beautifully set outdoor table. We were eager to share the news of our success with our client. We took him aside before dinner and told him the good news about our meeting with the vice president. He seemed not at all surprised. We were surprised that he was not surprised.

What gradually became clear during the course of the evening was that we had not persuaded the vice president with our carefully crafted arguments at all. He had been persuaded well in advance and our meeting was more of a formal ratification than an exercise in persuasion. How had this happened? Who had persuaded him in advance?

As the reader will probably guess, it was of course our client himself. It turns out that several members of the vice president's staff had once been on the payroll of one or another of our client's extensive business operations in the Dominican Republic. So too had the president's chief of staff—and might be again one day in the future. So too had numerous other government officials in a position of influence on any and every issue relating to our client's interests.

There seemed to be very little that happened in the Dominican Republic that was not carefully scripted in advance by our clients. On only one occasion did I ever note a potential challenge to them and this was fleeting. Our clients and my partner and I were invited to a dinner on the yacht of the international arms dealer Gaith Pharaon, who was visiting the Dominican Republic. His yacht was so large it did not fit in the marina and had to be tied up along the sugar cane loading dock. Here was a *mano a mano* threat: who's yacht was larger? Dinner for 60 on Mr. Pharaon's yacht seemed to be no problem. There was a transparent circular shower in the midst of Pharaon's sprawling stateroom. A bit ominously, he had a number of biographies of Saddam Hussein stacked on his bedside nightstand. It seemed from all we could observe that Pharaon's yacht was larger than our client's, but given the shadowy nature of his business he moved on quickly and quietly to parts unknown. Our clients were happy enough to see him go.

****

There are nations where the United States maintains an outsized influence. In some cases the affairs of other nations are shaped largely by U. S. government officials. To oppose U. S. policy is to run the risk of losing U. S. military support and/or American foreign assistance. In other cases, as described above, American dominance is expressed less through the U. S. government than through a leading corporation or industry.

Both of these kinds of dominance are far rarer today than they once were. Following World War II, the United States was disproportionately dominant in a way the world had never seen. This was not a result of American scheming but rather a simple emerging political, economic and military reality of the post-war years. America's dominance enabled it to do what had never been done before, namely, to help other nations with no short-term benefits expected. The war-ravaged nations of Europe—both the victors and the losers—were not expected to repay American largesse. No reparations were expected from the losers. No new territory was demanded.

American policy aimed to build a world economy which would benefit all nations (including the United States) over time. America could afford to do this because no other country could compete with American manufacturing or American agriculture; no foreign industry threatened significant competition. In short, we could afford to be generous. Although the world order the U. S. aimed to create was self-interested in this broader sense, earlier historical hegemons usually adopted a far different strategy; they transferred resources from the provinces to the center. One need not go back to ancient times for an example of the customary victors' strategy. It was the policy of the other major victor of World War II—the Soviet Union—to uproot industrial plants and equipment from Germany and East Europe and move them lock, stock and barrel to the Soviet Union.

American policy in the post-war years was new and different in another way. America had not pursued a pre-war colonial policy in Asia, the Middle East or Africa. This was far different than France and Britain, our leading wartime allies. Both Britain and France hoped that after the war they could return to the status quo ante. At the cost of considerable friction with our former wartime allies, America favored winding down the former European colonial empires. America had nothing much to lose politically or economically in doing so.

Finally, America established a new and different form of economic assistance for poorer nations. To be sure, America offered military aid to strategic allies to build up a solid front of opposition to the Soviet Union. There was nothing altruistic, or even unusual, about this. But America also created a brand new type of aid founded on more abstract and lofty goals—goals like long-term economic development, the rule of law and democracy promotion. Indeed, one could argue—against the few remaining old-style Marxists—that America comes closer than any other dominant nation in history toward orienting its enormous influence away from transactional power relationships and toward more benign and peaceful long-term goals.

All this was made possible by America's dominant position after World War II. In a way, the history of the last half century has been a long, steady movement away from this unusual dominance to a more normal set of international relationships.

> **The history of the last half century has been a long, steady movement away from nearly complete American dominance to a more normal set of international relationships.**

A decade or so after the war—in part because of American generosity—nations began to get back on their feet. By the early 1960's foreign industries, especially Germany's and Japan's, were providing real competition for American firms. One indication of this was the creation of the Office of the Special Trade Representative in 1962. In creating this new presidential office to facilitate the next rounds of trade negotiations, Congress removed the leadership over trade negotiations from the State Department. Congress created this new presidential office to insure a "better balance between competing domestic and international interests." In plain English, this meant that

Congress did not trust the State Department to look out sufficiently for American interests.

Foreign competition for American businesses has continued to grow during the past decades, which has in turn raised questions about the post-war policies which America advanced. Trade in particular has become an area of deep political contention. The substantial reservoir of support for free trade once taken for granted has eroded considerably, mainly among Democrats but increasingly among Republicans as well. America's altered position in the world has no doubt fueled President Trump's intention to negotiate tougher trade deals to "make America great again."

Support for foreign assistance has never been high among the American people. This has been true from the beginning, and foreign assistance remains today a project of American elites. In recent years there has been an interesting new development in the area of foreign assistance. In a number of nations around the world American influence, including that derived from our foreign assistance program, is being challenged by China. But the manner in which China does this is very different from U. S. development assistance, rule of law and democracy promotion programs.

China engages in straight up, transactional aid to countries, especially those with critical mineral and energy resources. While the U. S. may be operating a micro-enterprise program for women entrepreneurs, China is building lavish palaces for foreign rulers, new soccer stadiums and other projects which are more easily visible than American aid programs. China's mercantilist trade policy is replicated in its growing foreign assistance program.

The jury is still out on how this competition will turn out. Evidence favorable to the American approach is how China fares in international favorability polls. When offered a choice between American or Chinese world leadership, most countries around the world—even regular critics of the U. S.—would prefer America's more principled version than China's transactional approach. With the exception of Pakistan and North Korea, there is no country which would rather see China running the world instead of America.

Can America negotiate better political, economic and trade deals than it has done throughout the post-war period? I do not think the State Department and Trade Representative have always driven the hardest possible deal or secured the most favorable results. But even if they had, they would invariably be accused by some faction on Capitol Hill of selling out American interests. "Of course," members of Congress say, "we want an arms deal with Russia—but just not this deal. Of course we want a civil nuclear deal with India—but just not this deal."

There is nothing much to be done about these kinds of criticism. For constitutional, not to say practical reasons, the executive branch does not want to bring Congress into negotiations with foreign governments. It achieves some "buy in" by keeping key members of Congress briefed on the broad outlines of negotiations as they unfold. This helps avoid major surprises, but it is hardly likely to eliminate Monday morning congressional quarterbacking.

The fact is that negotiating is not always easy. As anyone who has ever negotiated anything knows, there is a fine line between being firm and being obnoxious. On one occasion I was engaged in a running argument with the Deputy Chief of Mission at the Israeli embassy in Washington. I was trying to put together an itinerary for an upcoming congressional delegation trip to the Middle East. When would it be possible to schedule meetings with the leaders of the countries we planned to visit? How could we maximize the value of the trip? If we went first to country A, then B and then C, would this work? Or the other way around?

None of this was made easier by the mutual mistrust between the nations we were planning to visit. For example, every delegation member would require two separate passports, as Jordan would not accept a passport that had been stamped in Israel. The entire experience was maddening.

The particular issue with the Israeli DCM concerned our proposed visit to the Golan Heights overlooking Syria. Our delegation wanted a firsthand look at this territory which had been taken by Israel in 1967. This would require Israeli transport from Jerusalem to the Golan Heights. Given our schedule, unfortunately, the only day this was possible fell on the Sabbath. The DCM informed me that because Israelis could not work on the Sabbath, it would not be possible to fly us there that day.

Now I am as open to religious sensitivities as anyone, but this was simply not the correct answer. I repeated that this was the only day we could make the trip. He said again that Israel could not provide a plane ride on that day.

In a none-too-subtle form of influence peddling I reminded him that our committee had just approved three billion dollars of foreign aid to Israel, an amount which the U. S. provided—and still does—to Israel each year. The DCM expressed his appreciation for the assistance but again refused. It was a matter of principle, he said.

Somewhat exasperated, I played a stronger card. I asked if it were not true that the Israeli air force flew combat air patrols over Israel on Sabbath days. As to this, I knew the answer: of course. Sabbath or no Sabbath, Israel could and did fly whenever it considered it important. And by the way, we still needed transportation.

At last we worked out a compromise. We would have an Israeli pilot fly us to the Golan Heights, but the pilot would wear civilian clothes and we would use a civilian aircraft. All of this suited me just fine. The trip unfolded just as planned and the delegation received an excellent firsthand view of an important security frontier.

For this I was very grateful to the Israeli DCM, Bibi Netanyahu.

Successful negotiations usually require compromise. Sometimes these compromises result in outcomes that make very little sense. For example, some years back Jordan was seeking mobile missiles to defend against a potential Syrian attack from the north. Israel objected to this sale, arguing that mobile missiles in Jordan would complicate its military planning and degrade its qualitative military edge. These missiles could be used against Israeli as well as Syrian aircraft, and their mobility would make them difficult to target. A compromise was reached: the sale would go forward but the missile launchers would be cemented in place. It does not take a rocket scientist to see that this entirely defeats the purpose of having mobile missiles. Sure enough, we later visited one site north of Amman where we observed a missile battery cemented in place, looking for all the world like a sitting duck.

Rare is the occasion when any negotiators, including American negotiators, get everything they want. As George Washington said, "There can be no greater error than to expect or calculate upon real favors from nation to nation." This should not be so hard for Congress to understand, as much the same is often true of legislation. The alternative to negotiated or legislated compromises is not usually total victory but no agreement at all.

> **Rare is the occasion when any negotiators, including American negotiators, get everything they want. As George Washington said, "There can be no greater error than to expect or calculate upon real favors from nation to nation."**

On the other hand, there is no reason to display a zeal for agreements at any cost. No agreement is better than a bad one. In the area of international trade, there is much to be gained by settled expectations and clearly agreed reciprocity. But foreign trade is not the same as foreign trade agreements, and one can imagine much of the former without all of the latter.

VII. SCANDALS AND SPIES

Washington Scandals

"I'm the Only Sane One in the Family"

We sat across the table from President Carter's brother Billy. You could not make up a character like Billy Carter. Like his brother, he possessed a very impressive skill set. Unlike his brother, whose ambition was focused and disciplined, Billy was scattered and not always directed toward the best possible ends. But he possessed in warmth and storytelling all that his brother lacked.

When Jimmy Carter became president, Billy saw no reason why he should not benefit personally from this development. In this he was not unlike a long historical succession of presidential relatives. Billy decided to make his fortune by cashing in on his connections. He saw a market in selling used commercial aircraft to Libya. Unfortunately, at the time Libya was under a strict embargo against selling any "dual use items," that is, commercial goods which might also be put to military use. Needless to say, his efforts became public and prompted predictable outrage. A special bipartisan congressional committee was established to look into this matter.

The scandal was nicknamed Billygate, the first of many gate-named scandals so named in order to trade on the hysteria created by Watergate. We have probably not yet seen the last of the "gates."

The Billygate committee's staff was drawn from—seconded as we say in Washington-speak—existing congressional staff, and I was selected to serve on the staff. We researched, we investigated, we probed, we deposed and we uncovered. Though I am not an attorney, others on our staff were. Following the well-established investigative model familiar to attorneys and TV crime show aficionados alike, we worked our way up from lower level figures until at last we came to Billy Carter himself.

We sat down at a long table to take his deposition. When he entered along with an attorney, he extended his hand and said "Hi, I'm Billy Carter." Who else? I was already warming up to him. We covered all manner of introductory details and established the predicate for our investigation. When questioned, he was very open in his responses. He in no way disguised the fact that he had hoped to make a little money out of his brother's presidency. He explained, however, that he would never try to do so illegally. He thought he had broken no laws, and if he had, it had been wholly inadvertently. He responded to lawyer-like questions with straightforward, common sense answers, which is perhaps not always the best course in a legal proceeding. I was struck by the simple humanity he exuded.

As we completed the deposition, we summarized several points and asked if he had anything further to add. "Not really," he said. He apologized for all the difficulty his actions had caused—to us, to his brother and to no one in particular. Somewhat wistfully, he said that he had never intended to create a problem.

He went on to add a final mitigating thought. "You know," he said, "I come from a family in which my sister Ruth thinks that God is talking to her, and my brother thinks he is the president of the United States. I'm the only sane one in the family."

I was hooked. In June of 1980 the committee duly issued its report. Though recommending no criminal charges, it censured him severely. I must say, however, I could not find much malice in my heart toward him, and certainly not enough to wish him harm.

****

There are lessons to be drawn from this experience, and perhaps some wider implications too. One is that families can be difficult and families in public life more difficult yet. There is no end to the number of ways family members have embarrassed public officials—incompetence, theft, bribery, affairs, and social embarrassment to name but a few.

There is not much good to be said about nepotism either. Recently we have seen the spectacle of French presidential candidate Francois Fillon putting his wife on the public payroll with no work assignment at all. Nor did it turn out to be a very good idea to entrust the future of American health care to President Clinton's wife. As I write, Ivanka Trump and Jared Kushner are busily engaged in the nation's business. We will see how this ends, but past results do not promise a good outcome. As a rule it is a good idea for public officials to draw a bright line between their public and personal lives.

There is a broader point to make concerning scandals. It is rare that any presidential administration can escape at least one major scandal. With the possible exception of G. H. W. Bush—and there were numerous minor tempests during his administration—scandals have touched every administration since Jimmy Carter. We have lived through Billygate in the Carter administration; Iran/contra in the Reagan administration; Monica Lewinsky and impeachment in the Clinton administration; Iraqi WMDs in the George W. Bush administration; the IRS, Benghazi and Hillary Clinton's emails in the Obama administration; and charges of Russian collusion in the Trump administration.

What exactly is a scandal? Why do some Washington investigations result in explosive scandals and others die without a trace? One answer, of course, is that some investigations uncover corruption and others do not. This might be called the "official view," which is advanced by many public officials and especially by the media. This view suggests that Washington investigations are on the up-and-up, driven solely by the merits of the cases they consider. This is also the view that most Americans hope is true.

It will not surprise the reader to learn, however, that this view not only fails to clarify the process by which Washington investigations unfold, but it disguises the real reasons why some investigations mushroom into full-blown scandals and others do not. Let's have a look at one case, the actions of the Internal Revenue Service (IRS) during the Obama administration. I choose this case not to make a partisan point, but simply because it illustrates so much about Washington scandals.

It would be fair to say that although IRS targeting of conservative groups was an issue that occupied Washington for a brief time, it never developed into a full-blown scandal. Perhaps this was because IRS actions represented bad judgment rather than impropriety; after all President Obama said in the middle of the Justice Department investigation that there was not a "smidgen" of evidence of wrong-doing at the IRS.

But is this true? The IRS clearly targeted groups of a specific political orientation. These were actions which one might say put into practice what Richard Nixon had only dreamt about with his notorious "enemies list." The actions of the IRS were clearly documented.

The matter grew well beyond the initial targeting of conservative groups. Evidence pertinent to the follow-on investigation was destroyed in what seems like a *prima facie* case of obstruction of justice. The computer of Lois Lerner, who stood at the center of the investigation, mysteriously erased many emails related to the case. Not only was her computer compromised; six other computers in Cincinnati and Washington which were used in the targeting disappeared. Backup computer records could not be found or accessed.

When subpoenaed to testify about IRS targeting activities, Lois Lerner pled the fifth amendment against self-incrimination. Evidence existed of connections and conversations between Lois Lerner, the chief counsel of the IRS, and Justice Department officials. Senior administration officials helped guide the administration's response along the way. The administration conducted its own internal investigation, about which nothing more was subsequently heard until the matter was dropped.

It is interesting to note that there is considerable concern today about whether and how a foreign government—Russia—interfered in U. S. elections. Here was a case in which an agency of the U. S. government itself interfered with U. S. elections. Yet the issue faded away with little consequence. Lois Lerner retired and John IRS commissioner John Koskinen continued to stonewall Congress until he too finally left office.

> **There is considerable concern today about whether a foreign government—Russia—interfered in U. S. elections. Here was a case in which an agency of the U. S. government itself interfered with U. S. elections. Yet the issue faded away with little consequence.**

What are we to make of this? One must dig a little deeper than the official view—which is the same as the naïve view—to understand Washington scandals. There are three sets of actors who play a role in creating a full-blown Washington scandal. First, executive branch officials are indispensable to the emergence of an executive branch scandal. Without the cooperation of at least some executive branch officials—either willingly and openly or by means of leaks—no inquiry can morph into a scandal. Without assistance from executive branch officials it is impossible to establish an adequate fact base for a scandal.

Executive branch officials are necessary but not sufficient for a Washington scandal. The media is also required. The media can make or break a scandal. If the media ignores or only minimally covers an investigation, it is bound to disappear before long. The media provides the oxygen which fuels a scandal; without ongoing, breathless press coverage no scandal is possible. In the IRS case, for example, the media displayed an extraordinary lack of curiosity. Scores of people in two cities were involved. Are we really to believe a diligent press could not uncover a single shard of evidence beyond what emerged from public IRS statements?

The third set of actors consists of the political parties in Congress. What will be the response of congressional Democrats or Republicans to a potential investigation of a president of their own party? In the case of Billy Carter, Republicans and Democrats cooperated in setting up a joint investigative panel. This was a genuine bipartisan investigation.

In the case of Bill Clinton, Democrats opposed the investigation of Bill Clinton from the beginning. Democrats admitted freely that Bill Clinton's actions were unsavory but argued they did not rise to the level of national concern, much less impeachment. It was only the discovery of Monica Lewinsky's stained dress and the president's obvious bald-faced lies that made it impossible for people well-disposed to the president to dismiss the matter out of hand.

In the case of President Reagan and Iran/contra, both parties participated in the investigation. Republicans were less enthusiastic about it, to be sure, but they did participate in the investigation.

In the case of George W. Bush and Iraqi WMDs Republicans were again reluctant participants. Democrats pursued the matter largely on their own, though were a bit constrained by the fact that many Democrats had voted to support the Iraq war. To argue against the Bush administration's assessment that Iraq possessed WMDs was to accuse the intelligence community of falsifying intelligence for political reasons and to argue for their own naiveté in believing it. This was a fine line to walk.

In the case of Obama and the IRS, Democrats opposed Republican efforts to investigate at every step. This was a purely partisan conflict, in which the media sided with the Democrats. This was why the IRS political targeting scandal never assumed any but the most minimal proportions.

In the case of Donald Trump and the charge of Russian collusion, both parties have been willing participants. This has been a bipartisan investigation, especially in the Senate Intelligence Committee. House Republicans have opposed their Democratic counterparts on various issues along the way, but did agree to authorize committees to undertake this investigation.

What can we conclude about this? First, it is helpful, though not necessary, to have both parties on board for an investigation to turn into a full-blown scandal. Democrats were not on board during the Clinton impeachment process but the graphic nature of the issues involved turned this into a major scandal anyway.

Second, it is difficult—except in the Bill Clinton case—for Republicans to create the optics of a major scandal on their own. Without the cooperation of Democrats—which usually also means the cooperation of the media—Republicans have a difficult time gaining traction. Democrats seem to have realized this, and the Billy Carter inquiry is the last time that Democrats have participated willingly in the investigation of a Democratic administration. Not since 1980 have Democrats been willing participants in investigating any Democratic administration.

Republicans have operated a bit differently. To be sure, they have pressed investigations of Democratic administrations when they see evidence of partisan advantage. Benghazi, Fast and Furious, Solyndra and the IRS investigation are examples of this. But Republicans have been more willing to participate in investigations of Republican administrations, including Iran/contra, Iraqi WMDs and Trump's alleged collusion with Russia.

Third, readers should know that Washington investigations are thus not conducted straight up on the merits, or on the basis of a justice that comes down from on high. They tend to be political projects through and through, with both parties calculating their advantages along the way. This is not to say that all investigations are manufactured out of whole cloth; quite to the contrary, there is often plenty of executive branch wrong-doing, impropriety and flat out illegality. But like everything else in Washington, investigations of potential wrong-doing have assumed a partisan edge these days which seems to override every other consideration.

> **Washington investigations are not conducted straight up on the merits, or on the basis of blind justice that comes down from on high. They tend to be political, and usually partisan, projects from beginning to end.**

Finally, there is one additional interesting consideration. I often suspected during Billygate that congressional Democrats were cooperating in the investigation because they were not much fonder of Jimmy Carter than were the Republicans. The same is true, I think, about Republican cooperation in the investigation of Donald Trump; many congressional Republicans are no fonder of him than are their Democratic counterparts. How else to explain four separate Republican-led congressional committees and a Republican Justice Department-named special counsel, especially on the basis of what appears to be as of this writing rather slim evidence of collusion with Russia?

Foreign Espionage in Washington

"Bring Me a Map of Indiana"

I met a Soviet embassy official at a Washington reception. He introduced himself, we chatted briefly and he gave me his business card. He suggested perhaps we could meet for lunch one day. I said that would be fine, which was my customary response, and thought nothing further about it. His business card was filed in my unwieldy pre-electronic rolodex.

Several weeks later I received a call from the Soviet embassy official, who proposed we meet for lunch. We set up a time the following week. The morning of the scheduled lunch I received a friendly call from him. He said that he was contemplating a lengthy trip to familiarize himself with the United States. This is not at all unusual for foreign diplomats in Washington; many enjoy getting out of Washington to see more of the country to which they are posted. I would hazard a guess that the average West European ambassador has seen more of the United States than have most Americans.

In any event, he said he knew that members of Congress usually keep racks of maps and other useful information about their states or districts in their front offices. Some offices even offer local products— peanuts, orange juice or whatever specialty for which the locality is known. These are free for the taking. This is a kind of congressional version of Costco food samples offered up and down the aisles. He asked if I would be so good as to bring along a map of Indiana for him. This would facilitate his travel planning.

Hmm ... This was simply too transparent. Why not bring along a harmless, publicly available document to give to him? No reason of course—except this was a rather obvious way to get someone in the habit of passing along information to a Soviet embassy official. I conveniently forgot to bring along the map. We had a pleasant lunch, discussing a range of issues that were gripping Washington at the moment. He expressed only mild disappointment that I had forgotten to bring along the map.

Some months later he called again to request lunch. He had enjoyed our conversation and wondered if we could continue it over another lunch. I agreed, more hesitantly this time. In nearly identical fashion, he called the morning of the lunch to request a copy of a publicly available document he had read about in the Washington *Post*. He was eager to read it and to learn more about the issues involved.

Once again I forgot to bring the requested document. I explained to him that the report was publicly available and it would be easy for him to obtain a copy for himself. I went on to add that although our conversations had been pleasant enough, I was not much in the habit of carrying around papers with me. I think we understood one another. I heard no more from him.

Later that year, however, I was surprised to read in the Washington *Post* that he had been recalled to Moscow. He was apparently well-connected in the Soviet government, his father serving as a high level official in the communist party. It turned out, though, that he was a serious wife beater, whose violence was too much for the usual diplomatic immunities. He had been asked by our government to leave and the Soviet government agreed.

****

This occasions a few reflections about spying, or espionage as it is called in official circles. Anyone with even a low-level security clearance (more about this in the next chapter) will know that Russia, nee the Soviet Union, engages regularly in spying on the United States. So does China, as do nations like Israel which are American allies. There are many goals of spying, some of which are the well-known national security targets of spy thrillers. There is also an enormous amount of industrial espionage through which foreign nations seek the trade secrets and business plans of American corporations. China is deeply involved in this.

Much information about the United States is available from public sources like congressional hearings, executive branch studies, newspaper and magazine articles, business journals, seminars, and the internet. Congress regularly holds its debates in public and prints public records of some of its committee hearings and of its floor debates. Annual military appropriations, for example, are publicly available, though funds for other purposes are usually embedded in these accounts. I would guess that one could learn 90% of everything one sought to know about the United States from public sources. It is of course much harder to learn about closed societies, the most notorious of which is North Korea. Publicly available information on places like North Korea is scarce indeed.

For these reasons nations with the technological capacity to do so supplement public information by using technologies like signals intelligence, aerial reconnaissance and electronic eavesdropping. The United States excels at all these types of information gathering, though other nations are catching up quickly. In large measure the equalization of these skill sets is due to the fact that cutting-edge technologies these days are often developed in the private sector rather than in closed American government facilities.

At the end of the day, however, there is no substitute for human intelligence. Technology can inform us of other nations' capabilities, but it cannot always tell us much about their intentions. Electronic eavesdropping on foreign government leaders can provide this information to some extent—one has only to recall the flap over eavesdropping on Chancellor Merkel's cell phone—but there are limits to this as well. This is why nations spend considerable time and money, not to mention the risks to agents, to develop human sources of intelligence. There is good reason for foreign nations to cultivate relationships with U. S. government officials and private individuals with access to classified information. At times, this cultivation can be a long-term project which pays off when individuals with little access to valuable information early in their careers move up to new and more important jobs.

Everyone with a security clearance knows all this and is strongly advised to be careful about it. Holders of security clearances are required to participate in briefings and to sign statements acknowledging they are familiar with the many concerns that can arise from holding this type of information. American officials traveling abroad in nations of concern assume their conversations are monitored by foreign governments, especially when staying in foreign hotels. American embassies abroad are "swept" regularly to detect listening devices or other means of electronic surveillance. Even with these precautions, highly sensitive conversations in American embassies usually occur only in very secure locations. These bubbles or Sensitive Compartmented Information Facilities (SCIFs) are constructed to be impervious to foreign eavesdropping. If the reader has ever had a hearing test, he or she will have some sense what these rooms are like.

What is the value of intelligence gained by foreign governments? In some cases it is very high. Spies like Edward Howard, Aldrich Ames and Robert Hanssen supplied the Soviet Union with names and techniques of American spies operating in East Europe and the Soviet Union. This resulted in severe loss of American human intelligence gathering capabilities, not to mention the execution of American agents.

Can one make any generalizations about American intelligence gathering? Intelligence can provide actionable information without which the U.S. government would be operating more blindly than it does. At the same time intelligence is far from perfect and there have been numerous occasions when American intelligence failed to see events on the horizon, including very important events. I have already mentioned the fall of the Shah in Iran in 1979. One might also point to the 1973 Mideast war during President Nixon's administration, the al-Qaeda attacks on 9/11 and the Arab Spring of 2010. These are not minor, obscure events. There has been much retroactive analysis about our intelligence community's predictions concerning the collapse of the Soviet Union. Intelligence gathering on the Soviet Union was far and away the largest preoccupation—and budget item—of the intelligence community for many decades. Perhaps the fairest thing to say is that the weaknesses of the Soviet Union were well-reported by the intelligence community but the speed with which the Soviet empire collapsed was surprising to everyone.

I sat through one intelligence briefing on the Iranian nuclear program which I would not hesitate to call simply ridiculous. The analysis was designed to reach a specific conclusion regardless of the facts at hand. While the facts were unassailable, the interpretation of these facts was highly skewed. Intelligence agencies are usually able to present rather clearly the current state of affairs in the world—how many missiles a country possesses, where its forces are massed, how large are its bank accounts and so forth. Predictions are of course more difficult, especially if as the philosopher Yogi Berra has said, they are predictions about the future.

One difficulty about intelligence estimates concerning the future is that they are often couched in terms of relative certainty. These are often lowest-common-denominator products, composed of the inputs of numerous agencies. They often read "we judge" that a certain conclusion is true with "high certainty" or "moderate certainty." Such uncertainty is perhaps inevitable, though it always should be offset with a description of the range of other possible conclusions. Policy makers deserve that much.

The development of the internet has created many advantages for Americans, but also poses many new dilemmas. Not all of these are related to the world of intelligence. To speak broadly, there are three emerging problems which we as a nation have not yet fully addressed. The first is whether we are witnessing the creation of new oligopolies which exercise an outsized share of influence over American society. Companies like Google, Amazon and Facebook are beginning to dwarf all other American firms in terms of market value and threaten to drive competitors in their sectors out of business.

Secondly, these new information-oriented firms are raising significant privacy issues. There is an ongoing debate about the privacy of Americans vis-a-vis national security agencies. This is an important debate. But at least there is in place a set of policies which offer some degree of protection for the privacy of Americans. The Foreign Intelligence Surveillance (FISA) courts may not be bastions of civil liberties, but at least they offer some oversight of government investigative agencies. The same cannot be said about large private internet-driven corporations which amass enormous amounts of data about Americans' preferences, habits and locations.

Finally, we face issues relating to the fragility of our information systems. If all banking, commercial, medical and other aspects of our lives are bound to the internet, its collapse is a deeply worrying prospect. We have seen minor hints of the catastrophe which awaits if large segments of our information network go down.

To say the least, we have neither thought through a set of rules to guide our thinking about these issues or a set of solutions for these potential problems.

The internet has also created both opportunities and problems in the area of intelligence gathering. The internet provides a significant source of information about foreign governments and their capabilities. At the same time it provides foreign nations with nearly comparable ability to learn about classified U. S. information. Relying on only secure information systems is a good first line of defense. But not all secure systems are fully secure. Chinese hacking into U. S. personnel files, for example, offers a clear case. Hacking into personnel files may provide no useful information about current U. S. policy-making, but it does provide extensive data about current and former U. S. government employees, of which I am almost certainly one. This detailed personnel information could be useful in a variety of ways down the road.

The internet has also raised difficult questions about issues relating to war and peace. The internet can be used not only to discover information, which after all is only a more modern way of spying; it can also be used to attack other nations. Is attacking the financial system of another nation an act of war? Is attacking Iran's centrifuges an act of war? Is shutting down another nation's power grid, which might lead to thousands of casualties, an act of war? Who in the American government has the authority to engage in these actions? If these are war-like actions, should Congress play a role? These are difficult questions which have not yet been satisfactorily addressed.

> **The internet has also raised difficult questions about issues relating to war and peace. The internet can be used not only to discover information, which after all is only a more modern way of spying; it can also be used to attack other nations.**

Government officials have personal lives as well as government responsibilities. There is every reason for government officials to maintain separate, personal communication systems for personal communications. It is also unwise for officials to remove classified information or computers from government offices to offsite locations at homes or elsewhere. As we have seen in the case of Hillary Clinton, using an offsite server to mingle personal and government business leads at best to a lack of government transparency and at worst to easy accessibility to foreign hackers.

Taking these and other steps will help, but they will not guarantee perfectly secure communications. Given rapidly changing offensive and defensive technologies, one simply does the best one can. It may ultimately be necessary to develop new systems of non-interconnected forms of communication. Everyone, and not just government officials with security clearances, already relies on this approach from time to time. People may prefer to speak on the phone about delicate personal items rather than to exchange emails. In some cases, a personal meeting rather than a phone call is the safest way to ensure security. Officials who speak to the press are thoroughly familiar with this approach. They may speak off the record, which allows for plausible deniability in a way that a written transcript or oral recording does not. Perhaps the typewriter, of which I made light in an earlier chapter, will stage a comeback.

There is a recent, very interesting indication that de-linking from the connectivity of the internet may be the wave of the future. The state of Virginia has decided to move back to paper ballots for elections. Virginia will continue its computer-based vote counting, but paper ballots will be available as the ultimate evidentiary base if there is uncertainty about the fairness of an electoral outcome. Perhaps we will rediscover the importance of disconnecting ourselves from communications systems and returning to human interaction for the most sensitive forms of communication.

Security Clearances and Classified Information

The FBI Again

I was approached one morning by one of my staff members on the Foreign Relations Committee. This staff member had come to us as the result of a "trade" which I had made with Senator Helms. Senator Helms had asked Senator Lugar if he would be willing to take one or two members of the Helms staff on the Foreign Relations Committee staff. Preferring not to deal directly with Senator Helms, Senator Lugar asked me to discuss this with Senator Helms.

Senator Helms was a gentleman as always. He said he had one or two staff members who would be excellent additions to the Foreign Relations Committee staff. Having failed to substitute for me his own choice of staff director, he was still not finished trying to exert his influence. I said I was certain that what Senator Helms said was true. I suggested that the opposite was also true, namely, that Senator Lugar had one or two staff members who would be excellent additions to Senator Helms' Agriculture Committee staff.

A smile spread across Senator Helms' face. We agreed on a one-for-one trade. For our part we inherited a well-spoken and engaging young staffer. I was at first a bit distrustful of him, being uncertain where his loyalties lay. But soon enough he proved himself to be both loyal and highly capable, and he played an important role as a spokesman for the Foreign Relations Committee. I never regretted that trade for a moment.

He came to me to say that he had been approached by an official at the Soviet embassy who asked him to lunch. It appeared that Soviet efforts to gain access were continuing apace. Worse yet, he had the definite impression from his phone call that he had been singled out by the Soviet embassy because he was black. The Soviet embassy official had said that he wanted to discuss race relations with him, because he knew that blacks were not treated very well in the United States.

My staff member wondered whether he should accept the lunch. I suggested that he go ahead with the lunch and in the meantime I would call an acquaintance at the FBI who might put me in touch with someone who worked in counter-intelligence. I had a brief conversation with the counter-intelligence officer who said that he would like to speak with my staff member after his lunch. I mentioned this to him, and he agreed to call the counter-intelligence officer after his lunch.

Following the lunch I asked if he had spoken with the counter-intelligence officer. He said that he had, and that it seemed that the FBI wanted him to schedule a follow-on lunch with the Soviet embassy official. More than that I did not ask, and we never spoke about the subject again.

Some years later I noted happily that my former staff member had been appointed to a high level position in the Bush administration. I was pleased with his success. Several years afterward, however, I noted less happily an article in the *Post* which reported that he had been arrested for shoplifting at a suburban Washington store.

****

United States law carefully divides our intelligence gathering agencies from our domestic criminal agencies—at least as far as this is possible. The FBI has jurisdiction over Americans who engage in espionage against our country and this jurisdiction extends to counter-intelligence activities generally. Without knowing so for sure, I supposed the FBI was interested in seeing what my staff member might learn about the Soviet Union's interests. Perhaps this kind of defensive counter-intelligence would eventually lead to offensive counter-intelligence through which the FBI could penetrate Soviet intelligence gathering itself.

For its part, the United States government produces an enormous amount of material which it seeks to protect from other nations. This means that it is also in the business of keeping secrets from the American people. Perhaps as many as 70 million documents are classified each year by the U. S. government and this does not include the myriad information that is gathered up as a matter of course by intelligence agencies like the National Security Agency. How to protect this information? This is not the place to make more than a few observations about what is a very complex process.

The U. S. government operates on what might be called a two-track system to protect sensitive materials. One relates to the materials themselves and the other relates to who can see them. The ability to classify materials derives from the power of the president under Article II of the Constitution. This power is defined in executive orders in which the president delegates the power to classify information to the heads of relevant agencies, or to their deputies. As a practical matter, information is largely classified by the agency which produces it. The current executive order which defines this process is Executive Order 13526, which was issued by President Obama in 2009. The constitutional power of the president to classify or declassify information is generally understood to be rather complete, and presidents would certainly contest congressional efforts to limit that authority.

This system is very decentralized within the executive branch, and therefore very complex. Sensitive information exists about political matters, military matters, scientific/technological matters, social and demographic trends, energy matters, economic matters and environmental matters. The decentralization of the system—while guaranteeing complexity—is probably unavoidable; it is hard to imagine what single executive branch office could make all these determinations.

Classified information falls mainly into three categories: confidential, secret and top secret. There are broad bureaucratic definitions for each—top secret information, for example, is information whose release would cause "exceptionally grave damage" to the national security of the United States. How agency heads might choose to interpret this standard, and they often do so very loosely, is for them to decide.

At the top secret level there exist sub-categories of information which are referred to as compartmented information or code word information, as each compartment is given an identifying code word label. These are known as either Special Access Programs (SAP) or Sensitive Compartmented Information (SCI). While these compartments are not technically beyond the top secret level, as a practical matter they are. Some compartments are very narrowly drawn, allowing only a small number of individuals with an unambiguous "need to know" about this information.

It has always been my opinion that far too much information is classified. This is not a novel view; it has been advanced for decades going back to Senator Daniel Moynihan who in this matter, as in many others, was prescient. As staff we used to joke that secret information meant that it would appear in the New York *Times* the next day, whereas top secret information would not appear until the second day.

I recall a Senate Foreign Relations Committee hearing with representatives of the CIA who were conducting a top secret briefing on Nicaragua. It seemed that whenever the CIA advanced a highly sensitive notion, Senator Dick Stone of Florida would know more than the briefers. I asked him afterward how he knew so much. He laughed and said that his wife's hairdresser was a Nicaraguan émigré and she "heard lots of things."

Provisions of Executive Order 13526 prohibit agencies from classifying information to hide unlawful activities, to disguise incompetence or to prevent embarrassment to their agency. These standards too, however, are largely subject to the interpretation of the classifying agencies themselves.

There are several reasons why government agencies classify too much information. The first is that the incentive system is skewed heavily in favor of over-classification. There is no bureaucratic loss in classifying too much information. On the other hand, if a sensitive matter which is not classified becomes public, embarrassing consequences could backfire on the agency.

> **The incentive system is skewed heavily in favor of over-classification. There is no bureaucratic loss to classifying too much information. On the other hand, if a sensitive matter which is not classified becomes public embarrassing consequences could backfire on the agency.**

This is not unlike other government agency incentives. The Food and Drug Administration (FDA), for example, has every bureaucratic reason to be too cautious in approving new drugs. Only occasionally do individuals learn about, much less experience the glacial pace of new drug approvals. On the other hand, an approved drug which turns out to have serious unexpected side effects is a public relations disaster for the FDA. Bureaucratic incentives always incline agencies toward the least risky result, and in the case of sensitive information that means more rather than less classification.

There are other understandable human motivations at work as well. Classifying information makes that information seem more important and more critical to the work of an agency, not to mention to the importance of those who classify the information.

Assuming that virtually all information held by certain agencies requires classification also spares an agency from the time-consuming process of sorting through information to decide what should and should not be classified. In fairness, it is not always easy to know in advance what might create issues for government officials. We have learned a bit about this from the Wikileaks and Edward Snowden releases of information. It may not create exceptionally grave damage to the national security of the United States if it becomes public that the secretary of state thinks his or her foreign counterpart is an idiot. But it does complicate diplomacy going forward. One could, I suppose, make a *prima facie* case that nearly every word uttered by senior national security figures should be classified.

Classifying agencies are also in a position to determine how long information will remain classified. There is a default date of ten years before items must be de-classified. However, it is easy for classifying agencies to stamp a 25 year date, or even in some cases 50 or 75 years before documents can be de-classified. After 25 years there is a mandatory declassification review. However, as we have seen in the case of information surrounding the Kennedy assassination—which as of this writing is 55 years in the past—agencies still come forward to redact information and prevent it from being made public. Agency incentives regarding declassification are no different than they are for classification.

The second aspect of protecting classified information concerns who can see this information. Individuals are granted security clearances which match the levels of classified information— confidential, secret, top secret and top secret with various code word clearances. Theoretically, anyone who holds a clearance at a given level can access all information at that level. As a practical matter, however, information that is outside the scope of an individual's "need to know" is not necessarily available to such individuals. Anyone seeking this kind of information, even though technically cleared to see it, is likely to arouse suspicion. This standard has become much more difficult to enforce since the advent of computers. Someone like Edward Snowden had access to all manner of information which he had no good reason to know about.

Individuals who gain a security clearance must undergo a background check, sign a non-disclosure agreement and receive a briefing about the penalties for releasing classified information. As a rough rule, the higher the clearance the more complete the background check. Background checks are useful but, as we have seen, not altogether foolproof. Individuals who are deeply in debt, who have close family or friends in adversary nations, or who have other aspects of their lives that could incline them to compromise classified information are important considerations about whether to grant a security clearance. These fact-based considerations are often supplemented at higher levels of security clearance with psychological profiling. Whether these psychological tools are all that helpful is not clear.

Large numbers of people hold security classifications. Roughly 4.3 million Americans hold some level of security clearance, of which about 1.5 million hold top secret clearances. Roughly 2/3s of top secret clearance holders work in the government and 1/3 work for private sector contractors. The process of securing a security clearance is very slow, especially in light of the results which it produces. A recent problem with one of the organizations which conducts background investigations has slowed the process significantly. There is a backlog of perhaps 700,000 individuals at the present moment. Top secret clearances take 8-10 months to obtain, which creates a variety of problems for the requesting agencies.

Hiring more background investigators is part of the solution. But just as with the determination of how much information should be classified, bureaucratic incentives are at work here. The general public neither knows nor cares how long it takes to get a security clearance. On the other hand, if someone who has been granted a security clearance shares classified information with an adversary, this often becomes a public scandal. Why, it is then asked—and usually by outraged members of Congress— was more care not taken in granting a clearance? In short, there is no incentive for background checks to move more quickly and every incentive to move more slowly. Better safe than sorry.

Some creative thinking is required to realign incentives to solve this problem, but since it is a problem endemic to all Washington bureaucracies, one should not expect a quick solution. One simple fix that has always made sense to me is to shorten the scope of review for individuals seeking to re-obtain clearances. Why not simply investigate the background of individuals from the date his or her last clearance was issued? What sense does it make to have to re-trace an applicant's entire life? This and more rapid ways to conduct "continuous evaluations" rather than spending endless time with mandated five year reviews would make sense. Beyond these reforms, modern technology—whose massive accumulation of personal information can have harmful effects—could certainly play a positive role in providing both faster and more reliable background checks.

EPILOGUE

Having now concluded 31 tales of politics in Washington, we have pretty much traversed the length and breadth of the federal government. Apart from whatever morals the reader might draw from these individual tales, what larger conclusions might we reach? How does it stand with our government today? Here are four sets of questions and four potential conclusions.

A Government of Men

It must by now be apparent that our leaders—our ruling class, so to speak— are far from perfect. They are subject to all the limitations of ignorance, self-interest, pride and pomposity as are the rest of us. Though the framers of our Constitution thought we would elect people better than ourselves, they were under no illusion about their perfection. After all, as Madison described artfully in *Federalist* #51, the central problem of all human governance is to create a "government which is to be administered by men over men." Neither we the people nor our leaders are angels.

The framers rejected the idea of a government whose leaders claim authority based upon theology, ancestry, titles or social connections. But neither did they construct a government in which leaders derive their authority based on claims of superior merit. They hoped for leaders of superior merit, but the legitimacy of American leaders derives not from any claim (much less any self-asserted claim) of merit but from their having been freely chosen by the people.

Our leaders may be somewhat more well-spoken, wealthier and better informed on political matters than the average American. This should not be surprising; running for office is difficult work. Running for office requires a degree of self-confidence and perseverance which is not possessed by everyone. It also requires a degree of intellectual agility, not to mention either money or the ability to attract money in order to become known to the electorate. Given the numerous demands of campaigning for office or surviving the sometimes stormy Senate confirmation process, it should not be surprising that our leaders possess more than an average share of these qualities. But neither should it be surprising that our leaders are characterized by the foibles and limitations revealed in these tales.

Are we governed by worse leaders today than at any time in our history? Is our government in worse shape today than ever before? Is the sharp ideological divide that marks our politics today something new and uniquely threatening to our country's future?

We do indeed live in an age of deep partisanship and political contention. But compared with what? Consider the bitter partisanship which overtook the new republic scarcely three years after it was formed. By 1792 Jefferson and Hamilton had become rival poles around which deep and lasting divisions emerged. Party newspapers engaged in vicious attacks that make our political rivalries today look tame by comparison. Would anyone trade our divisions today for those that emerged in the 1790s?

Or consider the decades of the 1820s through the 1850s. After the young nation survived Britain's final attempt to subjugate it— including burning the Capitol and the hasty flight of the president—the nation was fully preoccupied with the one fundamental issue the framers could not solve. Would anyone trade today's partisan differences for the decades-long agonizing political turmoil over slavery? Everything, and especially America's unstoppable westward migration, was suffused with the issue of slavery. Lincoln's Secretary of State William Seward traced every single political, economic and ecclesiastical issue of the time to the issue of slavery.

Would anyone trade the slow growth rate of the last decade's economy—or even the economy Barack Obama inherited in 2009—for the depression years beginning in 1929? Or for the additional specter of rising German and Japanese ambitions in the mid-1930s? Would anyone trade today's threats from ISIS and Kim Jong Un for Hitler and Tojo?

When critics despair over today's partisan bitterness they are usually comparing our time with post-World War II America. Using this period as a baseline is historical cherry-picking of the worst sort. As we have noted, America emerged from World War II with unparalleled world power and a heady, well-earned sense of optimism about the future. This is not a reasonable baseline against which to judge our current partisan rivalries.

But a closer reading of even the post-World War II period displays a somewhat darker, more complex picture. A war-weary nation was confronted immediately with two major foreign policy problems. One was the unraveling of the pre-war colonial system. We faced immediate difficulties with our wartime allies England and France, who presumed—wrongly— that they could recreate their pre-war colonial empires. They looked to America for support in this endeavor, support which was not forthcoming. But despite America's relatively limited colonial past and despite our unwillingness to help re-establish French and British colonial empires, our relations with newly independent nations were also fraught with ongoing difficulties.

The second problem was worse than the first. Beginning even before the war ended, the Soviet Union embarked on a policy of aggressive expansion and subversion. The world was full of hot spots which it had become our (unsought) role to disentangle.

At home, the nation confronted long-simmering issues related to race. Efforts undertaken to eliminate the final vestiges of Jim Crow laws in the south turned upside down the politics of an entire region of America. Many urban centers in America's north were aflame in the 1960s.

One has only to read back into the political campaigns of 1952 and 1956 to see clear fault lines in American politics. American intellectuals solidly supported Stevenson over Eisenhower and cultural critics saw the nation descending into a period of mass conformity. The elections of 1960, 1964 and 1968 were more contentious yet.

Throughout these years, however—with all of their difficulties—it is fair to say there was more political consensus than there is today. Although the center of gravity of the Democratic and Republican parties was center left and center right, respectively, there was considerable overlap between the parties. Many southern Democrats were more conservative than Republicans and many northeastern Republicans were more liberal than Democrats. The national media leaned center left, though nowhere near so far left as it does today. It was the tendency of Republicans—who after the mid-1950s were relegated to congressional minority status for decades—to frequently support Democratic initiatives, though to call for implementing them less fully and less quickly. The country was moving leftward, but at a very gradual pace.

This consensus is gone today. We are now once again in a period of deep partisan division. The resultant political warfare has spilled over into many social and cultural realms. So what? This too will give way to something new, which will produce brand new problems. Maybe it already has.

While we have been fortunate to find exceptional leaders like Lincoln at difficult moments, the general rule has often been to the contrary. Our leaders' imperfections have often and widely been on full display. This remains true today.

Here, I think, is a lesson we might learn with profit from the often foolish behavior recounted in these tales. Our goal should not be to make government loved. This is not just too high a bar; it is the wrong bar altogether. In her campaign memoir, Hillary Clinton suggested that we should not sow mistrust toward the kind of people we need to rely upon: "our leaders, the press, experts who seek to guide public policy based on evidence, ourselves." I suppose the last word in that statement betrays its true intent. But this statement is a far cry from the American tradition described by de Tocqueville: "The inhabitant of the United States learns from birth that he must rely on himself to combat the ills and trials of life; he is restless and defiant in his outlook toward the authority of society and appeals to its power only when he cannot do without it."

> **We should not trust too much in the wisdom of our leaders. We should retain a healthy skepticism about their ability to comprehend the problems we face—both seen and unseen—and their ability to solve them. We should not expect more of our government than it is likely to give us.**

We should not trust too much in the wisdom of our leaders. We should retain a healthy skepticism about their ability to comprehend the problems we face—both seen and unseen—and their ability to solve them. We should not expect more of our government than it is likely to give us. To invest too much hope, much less power, in these officials would be folly. To add ever further responsibilities to the federal government at a time of deep political division is a recipe for failure. To the degree that individuals or associations or communities can solve their own problems, it would be best for them to do so. This is far more likely to succeed than trusting implicitly in the wisdom, the merit or the expressed good intentions of those who govern us.

One-Party Dominance

Our government today, and especially the Congress, suffers from deep sclerosis. How might this be overcome? One way to resolve political divisiveness of course is for one or the other political party to become dominant. There is no doubt that one-party dominance can produce impressive political results. We have experienced periods like this in our nation's history. Following the civil war, the country grew rapidly for half a century. The United States transformed itself into the most powerful economy in the world. It adopted many of the national practices and institutions with which we are familiar today, including the abolition of slavery, the first welfare program (the Freedmen's Bureau), a national tax system, a continental rail transportation system and a national immigration policy.

But this was also a period of near total domination by the Republican Party. It was a time in which Democrats in the south and elsewhere were largely shut out of national political institutions. They aimed to restore themselves to a governing role in the south by returning to many of the practices of the antebellum period. This was a period of great national accomplishment, but hardly a period of happy bipartisan cooperation.

So too was the period of the 1930's and 1940's. This was a time of obvious accomplishment in which the nation slowly recovered from a devastating economic crash, constructed lasting federal programs like Social Security, defeated the two most militarized nations on earth and emerged as the leading power in the world. But it was also a period of largely one-party domination by the Democratic Party.

One-party dominance creates political results by reflecting and imprinting on society the values of the dominant party over a long period, bringing about relatively durable results. But one-party dominance depends upon reliable and continuing support for the dominant party. While it is of course the goal of each party to achieve that support, today's electorate is split, unwilling to provide either party with the reliable, ongoing electoral support necessary for one-party dominance.

The electorate has favored different political parties for the House, Senate and presidency in seven of the last nine election cycles, each time producing legislative and regulatory efforts to undo what has gone before. In speaking to the repeated failures of government in his time, Madison offered in *Federalist* #62 an apt description of our own:

> … no small share of the present embarrassments of America is to be charged on the blunders of our governments; and that these have proceeded from the heads rather than the hearts of most of the authors of them. What indeed are all the repealing, explaining, and amending laws, which fill and disgrace our voluminous codes, but so many monuments of deficient wisdom; so many impeachments exhibited by each succeeding against each preceding session; so many admonitions to the people of the value of those aids which may be expected from a well-constituted Senate?

If we are to have effective government today it will not come as a result of one-party dominance. We are in a period of rough political balance. What we have seen— and are likely to continue to see for some time—is a divided electorate which veers back and forth from party to party, providing only temporary and narrow margins of victory.

Each time a political party wins an election today it breathlessly announces the advent of a new permanent majority which will replace the aberration which has gone before. But there is absolutely no reason to think these claims are true. If we are to have effective government today it will not come as a result of one-party dominance. We are in a period of rough partisan balance. What we have seen—and are likely to continue to see for some time—is a divided electorate which veers back and forth from party to party, providing only temporary and narrow margins of victory.

In part, today's divisions are fueled by the media which has more or less given up its responsibility of reporting the news. The media of the post-World War II decades leaned politically left, but aimed to cover the news with a vestige of objectivity and fairness. The advent of conservative radio and television has pulled back the veil of objectivity from the so-called mainstream media, which today have become undisguised partisans of the political left. Today's media have become every bit as partisan, if not more partisan, than the political parties which they support. We seem to have reverted to a time akin to the early years of the republic in which newspapers were party organs closely aligned with their respective partisans.

Bipartisanship

If one-party dominance is unlikely in the near term, how can we achieve government which is effective and responsive rather than reactive and ideological? Is bipartisanship the solution? Is bipartisanship possible in a period of rough partisan balance?

The major political parties today are moving further apart, not closer together. Over the past two or three decades the trend has been almost uniformly away from bipartisanship. Both political parties have consolidated around their respective political bases. Conservative Democrats and liberal Republicans are relics of the past.

Partisanship has always been a feature of congressional debates, but partisanship today has intruded into nooks and crannies where it never before existed. Consider just several of many possible examples. Senator Mitch McConnell first ran for the Senate in 1984 against incumbent Kentucky Senator Dee Huddleston. McConnell was not favored, but as it turned out he was the only Republican challenger to win election to the Senate in 1984.

In some measure this was the result of a highly effective campaign advertisement. Huddleston had skipped a large number of Senate roll call votes. Given the minor nature of most of these votes, this was probably not a significant dereliction of duty. McConnell's campaign ad featured a bloodhound searching for, but unable to find Dee Huddleston. For most Americans skipping work is not an option, and the ad was extremely powerful. Though the ad was both clever and effective, it had the consequence of politicizing and in turn encouraging meaningless politicized floor votes. Meaningless floor votes today are more often the rule than the exception.

Not long afterward partisanship took hold in a new way at the committee level. Members of Congress come and go from committee hearings, often being double or triple booked. Party campaign operatives noted that when a Senator or House member left a committee meeting, his or her nameplate was still prominently displayed. Here was a visual too good to be true—an empty chair suggesting that a member had not shown up for work. Soon afterward, committees were forced to adopt the practice of turning down nameplates when members of Congress departed.

Presidential nominees which come before the Senate for confirmation today are also judged on a far more partisan, ideological basis than ever before. This process began in earnest with the litmus test on the abortion issue for judicial nominees. Today Senators feel free to quiz nominees about their ideological leanings and even their religious beliefs, masking this intrusiveness as a quest to determine "fitness." Nothing seems off-limits for today's partisan Senators who oppose presidential nominees.

These small examples illustrate some of the many ways in which partisanship has intruded into virtually every aspect of congressional business. Is bipartisanship possible under these circumstances? What would it take for Congress to pass bipartisan legislation? We have noted Jonathan Swift's proposal to cut legislators' heads in half and join them with those of opposition party members. This may strike the reader as delicious, but perhaps a bit extreme. Is there another way?

The answer in theory is yes, of course. Despite the many tools which Congress has created to evade its responsibilities, it remains possible for Congress to act in a timely, bipartisan manner. But this would require both political parties to take steps which are not at all palatable in today's political climate. Consider this tale as an illustration:

In the 1980s Maryland Senator Paul Sarbanes approached me in the well of the Senate. A dour, aloof and somewhat partisan figure, he was not my favorite Senator. I wondered what was coming. "You know," he said, "I had very grave doubts about you and Chairman Lugar. I thought you were headed down the wrong course. But in shepherding this foreign assistance bill through the Committee and on the Senate floor, you have done a good job. I disagree with you on many issues, but you have put the Committee back on the map. It's good to be here legislating on the Senate floor." I am not sure I have ever valued a compliment more highly.

How did this happen? To recap what has been said earlier, the legislative process began at the committee level. The chairman conducted a two day, open markup in which members of both parties were free to offer amendments. Some amendments were rejected, others were modified and accepted, and others which were opposed by the chairman were included over his objection. Is Congress ready for this today?

When the bill was taken up on the Senate floor, committee members felt a sense of ownership. It may not have suited them in every particular, but the bill was a product into which they had input. A similar process occurred on the Senate floor. During two days of open debate many amendments were rejected, others were modified and accepted, and still others were included that were opposed by the majority leader and the chairman who managed the bill on the floor. Is Congress ready for this today?

A parallel bill advanced in the House. Given House rules, amendments which were considered on the floor were far more closely controlled by the Speaker-run Rules Committee. Nevertheless, there was sufficient support for the legislation to garner a decent bipartisan vote.

House and Senate conferees met to reconcile their bills. At that time the House and Senate were controlled by different political parties. Members of the House and Senate had to compromise and accept provisions not just from their fellow partisans in the other chamber but from the other political party. Is Congress ready for this today?

The House-Senate conference provided a chance to clean up some of what had occurred in the House and Senate committees and on their respective chambers' floors. This was a convenient opportunity to drop many provisions in each bill. Each chamber swallowed some new provisions from the other, but along the way fixed many of its own self-created problems. Congress also worked with the administration, taking seriously its concerns about various provisions. Is Congress ready for this today?

I would estimate that when the Senate bill emerged from committee it contained 90% of what its committee chairman wanted. When it passed on the Senate floor, it contained perhaps 80% of what the chairman wanted. But after it was modified in conference with the House, it again contained close to 90% of what the chairman wanted. This has always seemed to me quite good enough for government work. But is either political party ready to compromise even this much today?

The openness outlined above is easy enough to describe. But it would require a sea change in the attitudes of House and Senate party leaders. House and Senate leaders could no longer write legislation in the privacy of their own offices, excluding committees from the process altogether. Nor could leaders propose legislation—especially on the Senate floor—which cannot be amended. To use parliamentary trickery to "fill the amendment tree" is not a way to produce bipartisan legislation. Why would a party which has been shut out of the legislative process support legislation which emerges from it? If one wonders why House and Senate Republicans were nearly manic in scheduling seven years of repeated votes against Obamacare, this might offer a clue.

> **Passing bipartisan legislation is not impossible, but given today's uncompromising attitudes it is vanishingly difficult to imagine.**

Passing bipartisan legislation is not impossible, but given today's uncompromising attitudes it is vanishingly difficult to imagine. It might not require cutting legislators' heads in half, but it would certainly require turning them around.

Reforms

Despite the self-serving illusions which both political parties cherish about their attractiveness to the electorate, neither one-party dominance nor bipartisanship is likely for the foreseeable future. At such a moment creative minds advance numerous political reforms which they believe might bring a measure of efficiency and responsiveness to a federal government—and especially a divided Congress—which urgently requires it. A virtual cottage industry of reformers has grown up to advance favored notions as a cure for our government's shortcomings.

Consider the many reforms that have been proposed in recent years: public funding for political campaigns, additional disclosure of political fundraising sources, eliminating congressional gerry-mandering, same-day voter registration, weighted voting systems, abolition of the electoral college, stronger Federal Election Commission enforcement, lobbying bans for public officials and term limits, to name a few of the favorites.

Each of these proposals may have some merit on its own terms, but none directly addresses the underlying problems which cripple our institutions. Some, like public funding for political campaigns, are purely self-seeking partisan initiatives dressed in the guise of good government. The ostensible purpose of public funding would be to benefit the vast majority of poorer Americans—and presumably the political party who would represent them—who do not currently contribute to political campaigns. It would aim to eliminate a bias toward the rich in congressional decision-making.

Further, it has been claimed—though never demonstrated ---that big donors skew the system toward the political fringes. George Soros and the Koch brothers are cited anecdotally to prove this point. To the contrary, it seems that big political donors are far more attracted toward candidates closer to the political middle—to Jeb Bush rather than Donald Trump, to Hillary Clinton rather than Bernie Sanders.

The likely result of matching public funding would be an ever deeper entrenchment of incumbents. And it is difficult to see what incentive members of Congress elected under a public financing system would have to change the procedures of Congress.

Other reforms like additional financial disclosure may indeed be good government. But how would greater disclosure of indirect financial contributions change the realities of Washington? How would it alter the self-serving system into which new members arrive in Washington? Are we really to believe that greater disclosure would result in an entirely new and improved class of members of Congress, who would somehow transcend the limitations imposed by current congressional practices?

Other reforms like congressional term limits are rooted in concern about the long-term entrenchment of members of Congress. Given the relatively longer tenure of members of Congress these days, this is an understandable concern. But are we to believe that newly elected term-limited members of Congress will somehow miraculously change congressional procedures? It is far more likely that term limits would end up further empowering congressional staff, who already wield too much power. And congressional term limits would require a constitutional amendment to put in place, an effort which would far outweigh the value of any purported benefit it might offer.

The underlying problem with all such proposed reforms is that they do not address the core problems which inhibit effective government. Elected officials who come to Washington as a result of these and countless other proposed reforms would still enter into a system of congressional procedures which are themselves the problem. To what end do we tinker with the system by which we choose new leaders if they enter into the same broken institutions when they arrive in Washington?

There are, however, reforms which would make our government—and especially the Congress—more efficient. These reforms would not require any changes to the Constitution. They would require changes in how Congress functions, changes which would in fact bring it closer to the framers' original intent. Our legislators have taken the formal outlines of our government and made them more complex and self-serving at every turn. Rolling back these complexities might threaten our legislators' current prerogatives, but they would in no way undermine the separation of powers created by the framers. I believe they would also make our legislators more responsible.

What follows are four reforms drawn from the tales above. Two would affect both the House and Senate and the other two would affect the Senate alone. One which would affect both the House and Senate is a fundamental change to the budget process. The current process was put in place in the 1970s to bring coherence to congressional budgeting. It has done no such thing. To the contrary, it has produced a long and almost unbroken record of deficit spending, for which there is no good justification at all. Why the government should spend $800 billion more than it raises in the seventh year of an economic expansion—with no major war underway—is impossible to justify. Worse yet, Congress cannot produce even these sadly unbalanced budgets without the repeated threat of government shutdowns and short-term continuing resolutions.

A good place to start would be to admit that none of the ostensible benefits of the budget process has come to pass. The current budget process addresses less than one-third of total federal spending each year, and it is not this portion of the budget which is driving our massive budget deficits in any event. The so-called entitlement programs hum along each year with almost no congressional oversight at all. Roll all the entitlement programs, including Social Security, into the annual federal budget and then see whether either political party would threaten to shut down the federal government for unrelated policy reasons.

The budget committees have been largely an exercise in toothless futility, with no power to enforce their caps. The only advantage of the budget committees is to produce reconciliation packages which are useful to overcome the supermajority requirement of today's filibuster-laden Senate. If one does away with the Senate filibuster—as I will advocate below—the budget committees would not have even that advantage. The budget committees should either be eliminated or replaced with small leadership-driven committees which have real teeth to enforce their spending decisions.

Moreover, there is no good reason to retain the complex and redundant system of authorizing and appropriating committees. Today's authorizing committees fail to authorize much of anything at all and rules against authorizing on appropriation bills have fallen by the wayside out of sheer necessity. It would make sense to roll the authorizing and appropriating functions together into one combined authorizing/appropriating committee for each substantive area. Combined authorization/appropriation committees would give a great deal of power to each committee in its substantive area. This would be the point. If there were no appropriation bills following along behind authorization bills, we would likely see a heightened level of responsibility from authorizing committee members. They would know they must pass a bill each year which will serve as the basis for their chamber's funding legislation. In order to become law, legislation which emerges from combined authorization/appropriation committees would still have to be passed on the floor of each chamber, reconciled with a bill from the other chamber and presented to the president. Is this not sufficient?

What is the reason for the current extra layers of redundancy? It is to protect imaginary "rights" or "courtesies" to allow as many members as possible to have input into as many issues as possible. None of this can be found in the Constitution. None of this was thought necessary by the framers of the Constitution in order to separate and balance powers to prevent unwise and over-hasty actions.

A second reform would be a substantial reduction in the number of House and Senate staff, an issue we have discussed above. Suffice to say that the more than 12,000 bills introduced in the 114th Congress were largely the work product of congressional staff. Are we really to believe there are more than 12,000 worthy legislative changes that the republic requires?

The sheer size of congressional staff has driven the work of the Congress ever further into the weeds. Each of the 12,000 introduced bills was no doubt accompanied by lengthy explanations of its virtues and heralded with self-congratulatory press releases. Much time was no doubt expended hunting for co-sponsors to demonstrate at least some measure of support for the proposal, not to mention endless pleading with committee and subcommittee chairmen to schedule a hearing on the legislation. Nor to mention the time that opposing staff spent organizing a legislative defense against such legislation.

I have not the slightest doubt that a Congress with 20% less staff would be 20% more effective. Such a reduction would compel members of Congress to address larger, more important issues. I note with interest that a similar point has been made about the evolution of today's Supreme Court: four times as many law clerks, half as many cases decided, and longer, less intelligible opinions.

The framers of the Constitution probably could not imagine a Congress with 10,000 personal staff members. Reducing the number of congressional staff would not be a step away from the empowerment of Congress, but a step closer to the original vision of what Congress should look like.

Other useful reforms would address Senate-specific procedures. What is the rationale for requiring a supermajority in the Senate to pass legislation? It is entirely to protect the "rights" of the minority. Where in the Constitution is there any expressed connection between those rights and a supermajority requirement to pass legislation? If either house passes a bill it must reconcile that bill with the other chamber and that bill must be presented to the president for his signature to become law. Here are two additional levels of negotiation and review which have all the needed effect of tempering and slowing the legislative process.

It is my contention that eliminating the operative 60-vote requirement to pass legislation would make Senators more, not less, responsible for their actions. A straightforward system in which members cast votes on a simple majority basis makes voting more transparent. It eliminates the game of Senators voting to support a motion to end a filibuster and then opposing a bill, or vice versa—thus eating their cake and having it too. Who exactly would this reform injure? Name for me some bills that would have been harmful to the nation if they had required only a simple majority to pass in the Senate.

And by the way, eliminating a supermajority requirement to pass legislation would end the need for the complexities of the current budget reconciliation process.

If this seems too radical, there is a more modest change that at least moves in the proper direction. In order to pass a bill Senate rules require essentially two votes (though not always roll call votes): the motion to proceed to a bill and final passage of a bill. There is certainly no valid reason for a minority—even if it can stop final passage with 41 votes—to block the Senate from even considering a bill. What conceivable justification could there be for this? Without a supermajority the Senate can't even debate a bill? Once again, the principal—indeed the only—rationale for current rules is to protect the mythical "rights" of Senators who are already the most entitled group in our society.

The same is true of nominations. The Senate should continue on the course which Harry Reid and Mitch McConnell have set out with regard to nominees. There is no good reason to require more than 50 votes for any nominee, including those to the Supreme Court.

Requiring a supermajority seems on the surface as if it should bolster bipartisanship. But how has that worked out? This requirement has put a high premium on securing the last votes of the majority party, giving leverage far beyond reason to a handful of outliers. Second, it causes the leadership of the minority party in the Senate to dig in and try to round up a blocking minority from its own party.

A simple majority threshold for nominees guarantees a smoother path for nominees of the majority party in the Senate. But it also makes it easier for nominees to secure Senate confirmation if the opposing party controls the Senate. Since most of these nominees are eventually confirmed anyway, there is little to be lost here except delay. Both parties have argued—when it suits them to do so—that a supermajority threshold produces nominees closer to the political center. What it seems to have done in practice is to put a premium on finding ever new reasons to vote against nominees—not for reasons of fitness, but for reasons of politics.

Several years ago the Senate eliminated some executive branch positions which required Senate confirmation. This is a matter up to the Senate, and there is no reason it could not go further yet. There are numerous additional positions which needn't require Senate confirmation.

Finally, there is an array of ways which Senators can currently stall a vote on nominees which go well beyond the only legitimate reason to do so, namely, a genuine requirement for additional time to investigate a nominee's background. Holds on nominees are 99 of 100 times unjustified and frequently unrelated to the nominee in question. Rules (still including Rule 22) and traditions allowing procedural delays in committee and on the floor should be substantially revised.

Nothing in any of this would change the incentive which Hamilton describes for a president to pick qualified people. That a nominee who can secure 60 votes makes him or her more qualified than one who can secure only 50 votes is a persuasive argument I have yet to hear. In moving to simple majorities, we are not talking about a decline in the quality of a president's nominees; we are talking about reining in some of the myriad "rights" to which Senators now feel they are entitled.

More could be said about a Congress freed up from its many self-created constraints. Such a body might actually be in a position to exercise more care about the powers which it delegates to the executive branch. And perhaps it might exercise more serious oversight over how the executive branch implements the laws Congress passes.

Some or all of these proposals may strike the reader as counter-intuitive. For conservatives especially, shouldn't the goal be to tie up Congress as much as possible, to prevent it from passing new laws? There is implicit in this view a defeatist sense that any and all new laws will be laws which work against conservative interests. Perhaps the current moment of complete Republican control of the Congress and the presidency is a good time to revisit this assumption.

But there is a far larger point. The result of Congress tying itself ever further into procedural knots has served to neuter Congress and to strengthen the presidency, the executive branch, the independent agencies and the courts at Congress' expense. And it is congressional abdication to the executive branch which has ultimately fueled the deepest impulse toward expansive government, a process created by an unchecked administrative state.

There are surely moments when either or both of the major political parties might wish for a weak Congress. Fair enough. But the effect of the reforms I have proposed would be salutary for the nation overall. Simplifying the budget process, cutting congressional staff, ending the Senate filibuster and streamlining the Senate's consideration of nominees might appear on the surface to weaken the institution of Congress. To the contrary, these steps would strengthen the institution of Congress.

> **Simplifying the budget process, cutting congressional staff, ending the Senate filibuster and streamlining the Senate's consideration of nominees might appear on the surface to weaken the institution of Congress. To the contrary, these steps would strengthen the institution of Congress.**

Hamilton's assessment in *Federalist* #22 speaks to this point: "This is one of those refinements which, in practice, has an effect the reverse of what is expected from it in theory."

Each of these proposals, and others which could be added, partake of one common feature: they simplify and demystify congressional procedures. They aim to recreate the well-constituted Senate of which Madison spoke, whose procedures have been corrupted mostly during the past four or five decades. Imagine a world without budget "cross walks," reconciliation, filibusters, 302b's, and the like. Who would lose here except the hordes of self-promoters and specialists who have created a language which only they understand?

It is uncertain Congress could be brought to reform its current self-serving practices. But these practices are the true obstacles to an efficient and responsive Congress, albeit a Congress still operating within the strict confines of the Constitution. With these changes the American public might actually begin to understand what happens in Washington. Imagine this: making good on Jonathan Swift's observation that "Providence never intended to make the management of public affairs a mystery, to be comprehended only by a few persons of sublime genius." Amen.

The Propriety of Humor

Is it appropriate to poke a bit of fun at our betters? Isn't this all too serious? Should we really sow doubt and mistrust about the capabilities of our government? Is it proper to undermine our leaders, the people we have elected to lead us? I might point out that nothing that has been said here compares with the outright attacks today's political opponents launch against one another.

Two types of people seem to find little humor in the human condition. Religious fundamentalists see a world corrupted and set against God's will. Only the most disciplined and tireless efforts can prevail against this world. One can never let down one's guard. In particular, one cannot and should not criticize governments which are carrying out the purported will of God.

If they ever were, these people are no longer much in evidence in contemporary America. Today one finds them mostly among the zealots of ISIS, the Iranian mullahs or other Islamic fundamentalists who see themselves as warriors of God in a wayward world. Their behavior can cause considerable pain and suffering, but is often ultimately self-defeating; they tend to become ever stricter until normal human beings simply cannot abide the purity of their commands and overthrow them altogether. There is far more misery than humor to be found here.

The other type is a more recent historical phenomenon, found far more frequently in contemporary America. These are the ideologues, often but not exclusively on the political left. They do not aim to make the world perfect in the eyes of God, but in the eyes of man—namely, themselves. These are people who worship humanity and whose aim is to perfect it. These are people who invariably see government as the principal instrument for the achievement of human betterment.

For these people man is born free and is everywhere in chains; it is the task of committed ideologues to break these chains and establish a heavenly state on earth Their aim is to break every tie to the past, which is the source of imperfection and evil. There is not much humor to be found among these people either. They seem perpetually unhappy that they cannot fully bend the world to their will.

Although these types aim at different goals, their tactics have much in common. Not least is their willingness, even eagerness, to use government as the instrument of choice to compel the world to adopt their version of perfection. At the end of the day their practical effect is the same; their received visions of perfection express themselves in immoderation and an intense desire to impose their will on the world—or at least on those poor souls who are in their vicinity.

The world, however, is an imperfect place as are we humans, and it is likely to remain ever so. This is no argument against efforts to improve the lot of humanity, much less to say that all government systems are equally imperfect. Our form of limited government is surely better than all others, if for no other reason than that it limits and moderates the reach of those who seek to use it to perfect humanity. That is why we should try to ensure that it is limited in scope but also competent and effective in achieving its limited ends.

> **Our form of limited government is surely better than all others, if for no other reason than that it limits the reach of those who seek to use it to perfect humanity. That is why we should try to ensure that it is limited in scope but competent and effective in achieving its limited ends.**

There is much that is amusing in our imperfect world and the source of that amusement is usually our imperfections themselves. A sense of humor derives from our genuinely curious human predicament, namely, that we can think and see and know beyond ourselves, as it were, all the while sensing our own and others' limits and foibles. Yes, we should always work toward what is better. But we should do so with a bit of humility about whether we always know in great and specific detail what is better. And we should do so with a special and abiding humility about the means we use. In particular, we should never lose sight of the imperfections of that preferred instrument to compel human behavior, namely, government power.

A sense of humor is a good and useful tool to preserve a proper balance between what we can and cannot reasonably expect from government. I would go further: the surest indicator of a decent, limited and reasonable government is whether, and to what degree, making fun of that government is permitted. Try joking about Vladimir Putin on Russian television; or Nicolas Maduro through what remains of the Venezuelan media; or Kim Jong Un in any nook or cranny of North Korea; or ISIS in a village square which it controls.

So yes, let's aim to improve the lot of human beings. But let's do so with a sense of moderation about what the imperfect governments of men can achieve. Let's not criminalize our political differences. Let's leaven our criticism of opponents with a bit of humor. And for the rest, it would be wise to temper our demands for ever more rights and entitlements to be provided by so imperfect a vehicle as government. Better perhaps to leaven these demands with a measure of gratitude for what we have.

Acknowledgments

The assistance of many people is required for a project like this. I would like to thank all those who helped—wittingly or unwittingly—in drawing this picture of the current state of American governance.

I am indebted to Senator Richard Lugar and his talented staff for introducing me to the realities and rhythms of practical politics. I have criticized many members of Congress—hopefully not unfairly—in these pages. To all this Senator Lugar stands as an exception, and as one who comes as close to the framers' ideal of an enlightened legislator as anyone I know.

I am grateful to the staff which we assembled at the Senate Foreign Relations Committee. As mentioned in the text, we aimed to create the best foreign policy team in Washington, and the talented members of our staff helped to make this intention a reality.

I am also grateful to Secretary of State Condoleezza Rice and to my own staff at the State Department for providing an opportunity to understand the Congress from the other end of Pennsylvania Avenue. I would like to thank especially Bruce Brown for his unparalleled expertise on the Senate confirmation process and for his careful reading of this book in manuscript form. I appreciate his professionalism and that of our entire State Department band known familiarly as "H."

And I am grateful for the many academic colleagues with whom I have debated the issues raised in this book. I have had the privilege of teaching undergraduate and graduate students at Penn, Michigan, Georgetown, Christopher Newport and the University of Virginia. I am especially grateful to Professor Gerry Warburg of the University of Virginia for the stimulation of his often dissenting views, for the civility with which he expresses them and for the many opportunities we have had to collaborate.

Finally, I am grateful to my family, especially my wife Susan. Having heard many of the stories with which this book's chapters open, she provided the initial encouragement to write this book as well as many helpful additions along the way. I also thank our children Amanda, Jason, Jessica and Jonathan for their help in many tangible and intangible ways.

Authors frequently observe that all errors contained within are of their own making. No one has ever said so with more sincerity than I do here. I take full responsibility for all errors of fact, inartful descriptions and overly provocative interpretations of the current state of our politics.

CPSIA information can be obtained
at www.ICGtesting.com
Printed in the USA
BVHW031757150519
548354BV00002B/60/P